MIDSUMMER DREAMS
AT MILL GRANGE

CW00953298

COMING SOON BY JENNY KANE

Autumn Leaves at Mill Grange
Spring Blossoms at Mill Grange

MIDSUMMER DREAMS AT MILL GRANGE

Jenny Kane

An Aria Book

This edition first published in the United Kingdom in 2020 by Aria,
an imprint of Head of Zeus Ltd

A CIP catalogue record for this book is available from the
British Library.

ISBN 9781035903726

Typeset by Siliconchips Services Ltd UK

Cover design © Cherie Chapman

Aria
c/o Head of Zeus
First Floor East
5–8 Hardwick Street
London EC1R 4RG

www.ariafiction.com

Dedicated to Tammy and Evie, without whom visits to Northmoor House (the 'real' Mill Grange) would not be the same.

Prologue

March 8th

The Thomas checked her mobile. EMERGENCY CALLS ONLY was written in bold type across the top of the screen.

She tried connecting to her Wi-Fi.

Nothing happened.

Relief made her shoulders sag, as a wide smile knocked away some of the nervousness she felt about starting a new job in an unfamiliar part of England.

Here, she could avoid the constant barrage of social media alerts and unwanted texts, calls and emails. Here, she could start over.

Positioned at the top of a high rise of land, not far from the southern border of Exmoor, the Victorian manor house called Mill Grange rose from the centre of a gravelled drive, taking command of the surrounding scenery. Three tiers of a once-loved terraced garden fell away from the house in tatty overgrown rows. At the foot of these gardens ran a semi-encircling band of encroaching woodland, which the Ordnance Survey map Thea was clutching declared to stretch down to the River Barle on one side and the meandering River Exe on the other.

Huddled beneath her thick jumper against the sharp March wind, Thea was enfolded in a sensation of freedom and peace. The very stillness of the air, the lack of any visible overhead wires or street lighting, made her feel as if she'd driven into a Victorian time capsule. A Roman historian and archaeologist to the bone, she felt daunted by the prospect of taking on the restoration of a manor centuries removed from her field of expertise. With its fourteen bedrooms, seven bathrooms, numerous associated rooms, outhouses, and the mill after which it was named, a quarter of a mile away on the edge of Upwich village, it was not a task for the faint-hearted. However, the early spring sunshine, which caused the house's granite walls to glitter with welcoming promise, seemed to be telling her it was going to be alright.

Alongside her Roman studies at university, Thea had trained in industrial archaeology and museum management, and was well-qualified for the job in hand. But this challenge, to turn Mill Grange into a heritage centre, was vastly different from her last posting at the Roman Baths in Bath. She could feel herself prodding the outer edges of her comfort zone.

At least she wouldn't have to face the unknown alone. Her best friend, Tina, had been associated with the project for some time. Then there was the team of volunteers who'd been working on restoring Mill Grange, on a casual basis, for the last five years. A tingle of anxiety dotted Thea's palms as she wondered how they'd take to being guided in their endeavours after pleasing themselves for so long.

Flicking an unruly stray brown hair from her eyes, she circuited the outside of the manor house. Thea's boots made satisfying crunching sounds against the gravel as she attempted to banish her nerves, peering through each window as she went. The eclectic mix of original Victorian and reproduction furniture and artwork she saw within took her breath away. Squinting and pushing her eyes as close to the glass as she could, she studied the wallpaper. It was original. She was sure of it. With every new step and glimpse of the treasures within, she felt more exhilarated.

She could do this.

Thea checked her watch. The courier arranged to deliver the keys to the double doors that would take her inside Mill Grange would not arrive for another hour.

She stood still and listened. Birds called overhead. The breeze rustled the newly budding leaves. Otherwise there was nothing. In that moment Thea felt as if she might be the only human being left in the world.

Rather than being overwhelmed by the isolation of the place, as she walked from the house, down the sloping dew dampened grass towards the long-abandoned kitchen garden, Thea felt more relaxed than she had in weeks.

John would never find her here. It was for his own good. She couldn't face another excruciating conversation like the one they'd had in February.

One

It wasn't him.

It couldn't be. He'd moved away.

At least, he'd told her he had.

If Thea had any doubts about her vision, the sinking feeling in her stomach confirmed her fears. Her body had sensed her ex-boyfriend's presence before her brain had finished joining the dots.

A coach-worth of Japanese tourists was following a stressed tour guide around the outside of Bath's Pump Room. Assessing the amount of lemon cake and espresso she had left, Thea wondered if she should abandon her café lunch and trust to the crush of tourists to shield her from the man she'd hoped never to see again.

Telling herself that the chances of John Sommers spotting her were slim, Thea blew ripples into the top of her coffee. *So what if he does see me? We've been apart for three months now. He won't want to talk to me.*

Returning to the novel she'd been reading as she sat

outside the Abbey Café, Thea was unable to prevent her eyes lifting from the page every few seconds to see if he was still there. On the third surreptitious raise of her eyelids, she finally convinced herself that John had disappeared from view – or that maybe she'd imagined his presence in the first place.

She hadn't finished exhaling with relief, when a voice from behind made her jump.

'If it isn't the gorgeous Miss Thomas! What a coincidence.'

'What do you want, John?' Placing her cup onto its saucer, Thea gave an internal groan of resignation.

'I thought it was you. A pointlessly tiny cup of coffee, a slice of lemon cake and a novel. Such a giveaway! Although I had to do a double-take because your hair is wrong.'

Thea's hand automatically went to her chocolate brown ponytail. 'What do you mean it's wrong?'

'You've grown it.' It was clear from his tone that the change of style did not meet his approval.

Self-consciously, Thea muttered, 'Well, I like it,' into her coffee.

Oblivious to his lack of tact, John smiled in a way that made his emerald eyes shine with the promise of mischief. 'I wasn't one hundred per cent sure it was you, but I had to check. It felt like the right thing to do.'

'The right thing to do?' Wary, and unsure she wanted the answer to her next question, Thea asked, 'How did you know I was here?'

Ignoring the enquiry, John pinched a few cake crumbs from her plate. 'I wanted to ask you to come out to dinner with me tonight.'

Thea almost choked on her coffee.

'I want to talk to you. It's been ages. We have a lot to catch up on.'

'It's only been three months, John. We have *nothing* to catch up on.'

John Sommers was the only boyfriend Thea had ever dumped, and he'd made it as difficult as he could. And even then he'd refused to fully let her go.

'We only dated for a year. It was nice for a while, but then I discovered we wanted different things from life. It took all my courage to tell you it was over.' Hooking her bag onto her shoulder, Thea stood up. 'I'm sorry I hurt you, John, but I couldn't make myself love you. Nor could I mould myself into the woman you wanted me to be.'

'You couldn't then. I can see that.' John's expression became serious. 'However, things are different now.' He centred his attention on the bowl of sugar cubes in the middle of the table. 'I'm extremely successful. I've taken a promotion which has brought me back, to Bath.'

'Back to Bath?' Thea held her jacket across her chest. 'But you only moved to Newcastle two months ago.'

'You remember the company I worked for here, Sure Digital?'

'Of course I do! It's all you ever talked about.' Thea found herself reaching for the dregs of her coffee. 'You only left them a couple of months ago.'

'For a better post in Newcastle, yes...' John's eyebrows knitted together as he rubbed his chin. He looked like a caricature of someone trying to think. 'With hindsight, I was unreasonable to expect you to come with me.'

'You didn't *ask* me to come with you!' Thea regretted

her reaction as soon as she saw the glimmer of hope flash in John's eyes.

'I should have said as soon as we got to the restaurant. I see that now. Just think of all the archaeology in the Northumberland and Tyneside area you could have explored up there.'

Trying her best to follow John's disjointed logic, Thea sat back down with a resigned sigh. 'It would have made no difference. I have a life here. Anyway, I left you before you told me you were leaving.'

John flapped the point away with a flick of his wrist. 'It's immaterial now, because Safe Hands Digital up north, and Sure Digital here, are merging. And guess whose old school friend needs someone to head up the merger and run the newly combined IT department?'

Thea sighed into her cup. 'I wonder.'

'Exactly! Yours truly. So here I am, back where I belong, plus with a prestigious position within Sure Digital.'

'You got a promotion because of who you knew from school?' Disbelief robbed Thea of a more dynamic response.

'I'm exactly the sort of man you need in your life if you're going to continue pursuing a low-paid career path and pay rent in such an expensive area. With me, you'd never have to worry about money again. Sure Digital is going places, and I'm the man at the helm.'

'I love my job and…' Thea's stuttered words faltered as she clutched her bag in front of her like a shield. 'John, did you listen to a single word I said when we split up?'

He gave her an encouraging smile. 'I've thought very

carefully about where I went wrong, and I've fixed it, so we'll be alright now.'

'Alright now?' Thea shook her head. 'How did you come to that conclusion? I'm sorry, John, but I meant what I said. I just don't love you. It *is* over. We *have* split up, for all the reasons I gave in the restaurant—'

'When you walked out in the middle of our first anniversary dinner.'

Guilt made Thea's freckled cheeks flush. She'd felt sick at the prospect of dumping him at the time, but as she'd sat, listening to him talk about their future, the house they'd have, the 'jollies' she'd go on when she accompanied him on business trips, and how in time they would need an au pair for their children – it had all felt too much.

'I know my timing was terrible, John, but you freaked the hell out of me.' Thea absent-mindedly played with the crumbs on her plate. 'I'd been having an occasional night out with you, when you were in town – that's all! I had no idea you were planning how we were going to spend the rest of our lives! It was like listening to you input my life onto a spreadsheet.'

John brushed off her summary of their breakup. 'Like I said, I realised I was being rather old-fashioned. Blame my parents. Mum always followed Dad everywhere. I assumed you'd do the same for me.'

Thea opened her mouth to speak, but John held up his hand so he could finish. 'I realise now I was being selfish. I should have listened when you said you need your career, so of course you can have it. When our children come along, we can always get some kind of childcare.'

'Childcare?'

'I know you want children one day, you told me.'

'One day.' Aware she was beginning to sound like a stunned parrot, Thea lifted her eyes from her plate and regarded John properly for the first time since he'd gate-crashed her lunch. 'How did you know I'd be here?'

'Oh, that's easy. Your social media pages have pictures of you, and occasionally some other woman, sat here. There were comments about lunching near the abbey. It wasn't hard.' John looked pleased with himself as he added, 'You'd be surprised what people give away about themselves on Facebook. You should be more careful, you know. This time it's only me, but what if it was some kind of stalker?'

Thea's words came out slowly, as if they were battling through fog. 'You've been watching me?'

'Of course.' He spoke as if it was the most natural thing in the world. 'We didn't have time for a proper goodbye before I moved to Newcastle. I wanted to make sure you were alright.'

'But I *left* you. *I* hurt *you*, not the other way around. I'm the last person you should care about. Why are you here?'

'Because I miss you, silly.' John beamed. Thea had the strangest idea he'd ruffle a hand through her hair if they hadn't been in a public place. 'I'm prepared to forgive you for making such a scene on our anniversary. So, let's draw a line under that and start again. Where would you like to go for dinner tonight?'

9

Two

Thea stared out of the attic bedroom's small sash window, struggling to calm the apprehension which was making her stomach act as if it was a washing machine stuck on the spin cycle. Spotting a flash of blue among the tangle of overgrown hedges and leftover autumn leaves, she picked up her binoculars and focused on five azure petalled flowers, complete with hairy stems and oval leaves. A clutch of woodland forget-me-nots was winning the fight against the mass of undergrowth that connected the garden and the woods. It was the glimmer of hope Thea badly needed.

Scanning the full sweep of the manor's terrain, she hunted for more signs of life. Buds on assorted tree branches and rain-drooped Campanula soon filled the lenses and made her smile away some of her apprehension.

The over-loud tick of the carriage clock, perched on the room's unusable fireplace, broke into Thea's moment of escapism. Turning to the rickety single bed, under which she'd stuffed the few belongings that had accompanied her from Bath, Thea wiped her perspiring palms down her jeans.

What was wrong with her?

She was used to having constant battles with her inner shyness and lack of confidence at work, but usually she won the fight. Since she'd taken the job at Mill Grange, however, her ability to hide her insecurities and self-doubt had deserted her in the face of the project's established volunteers. Tonight, Thea was determined to change that. She had to, or there'd be no hope of finishing renovating the manor in the timeframe the Trust had given her.

Jogging down the two sets of narrow Victorian backstairs to the kitchen, Thea resolved to pull herself together. 'You're a professional woman. You know what you're talking about. You *can* do this.'

Pushing open the narrow double doors towards the kitchen's Aga hugging warmth, Thea sank into an oversized wingback armchair. Cocooning herself beneath a pile of throws, she critically examined the site of that day's restorative activity.

Two nearby seats, companions to the chair upon which she sat, gave off a satisfying aroma of buffed leather. Three kitchen shelves, which had been in danger of collapsing under the twin strains of damp and wear, had been replaced, and every cupboard was empty, ready to be washed out the following day. For now, Thea allowed her mind to skirt over the mountain of cupboard contents and ornaments which sat in random heaps on the dining room table.

Every one of the kitchen's vast external surfaces had been scrubbed to within an inch of its life with the aid of willpower, elbow grease and Radio Two. Mabel had made it clear she'd rather have listened to Radio Four. They'd always listened to Radio Four *before*.

Before, meant before Thea. *Before* her.

Thea winced. Something had to be done about the steely-haired seventy-five-year-old, with permanently rolled up sleeves, a different apron for everyday of the week and coordinating rubber gloves. But what should that something be? Mabel Hastings had been at the tiller of the restoration of Mill Grange for so long that, even though Thea had been employed by the house's trustees as overseer of the project, she couldn't, or wouldn't, let go.

Mabel was a dynamo of activity. Set her in the direction of a task and she was off; unstoppable until every cobweb had been vanquished and every spider had packed its suitcase ready to emigrate to the safety of one of Mill Grange's many outbuildings. And goodness knows there wasn't a grease stain or blocked toilet that could go the distance with her. The problem was that in Mabel's eyes, there were two ways of doing things: her way, or the wrong way. Thea's way definitely fell into the latter category.

There was no doubting Mabel's methods were effective, even if they generally involved some magical cleaning compound that had vinegar at its heart and left the lingering aroma of acetic acid hanging around for hours afterwards. But although Mabel was thorough, she was not fast. Nor was she an easy woman to talk to, or persuade into doing something she didn't wish to do.

Taking comfort in the bouquet of polished leather and fresh cut wood (minus vinegar for once) infusing the air, Thea closed her eyes. At least John would never find her here. There was no chance of tracking her on social media (which she'd stopped using after his unwanted arrival in Bath). She'd changed her mobile number and email address anyway though. Just in case.

Taking a deep breath, Thea levered herself from the cushioned safety of the armchair. Dwelling on the past wouldn't help. Not if she wanted the immediate future to be the success it deserved to be. She owed it to Mill Grange itself, if nothing else.

Heading to the huge oak table that dominated in the centre of the oblong room, Thea stroked its smooth sides. Local legend claimed that Mill Grange had only been built because Lady Upwich had fallen in love with that very table, but couldn't get it into her current home. So, in 1856, Mill Grange mark two had been constructed, extending the original house to surround the table.

Thea wasn't sure how much of that was true.

Mabel was convinced of every word.

Thea would have liked to check for historical proof, but the trip she'd promised herself to the archivist's office in either Taunton or Exeter hadn't yet happened. There was just so much else to do if the house and mill were going to be ready to open in August.

As she pushed her shoulders back, Thea's private determination to make the manor perfect urged her on. She'd wanted a fresh challenge as well as a fresh start away from her past, so when Tina, who worked for the Exmoor Heritage Trust, had mentioned that they were advertising for a project manager and eventual curator for Mill Grange, the timing had felt like a gift from the Goddess of Wisdom – Minerva herself. Thea had applied straight away.

An involuntary shudder tripped down Thea's spine as

the memory of the last time she'd seen John nudged itself, uninvited, to the forefront of her mind.

It had been four days before she'd started her new job. Once he'd finally accepted that she didn't want to go out to dinner with him after his unexpected arrival at the Abbey Café, and following a dozen subsequent failed attempts to engage her interest, John had turned up in her local pub in Bath. Looming over her seat and blocking Thea's view of the scattering of early evening locals, John had spoken quietly. There had been a smile on his face, but she'd noted the strain in his eyes, and she'd had to battle with her conscience not to invite him to join her for a drink just to be kind.

His tone had been serene, but she'd had a horrible feeling he was close to bursting into tears, when, as if caught in some eighteenth-century time warp, John had spelt out why it was unacceptable for Thea to be in a pub on her own. It sounded laughable; it *was* laughable. But it wasn't funny.

Feeling hemmed in and increasingly responsible for John's desperate behaviour, Thea had tried one last time.

'I'm asking you to leave here for your own good. Sort yourself out, John. You deserve better than this. I've told you I don't love you. I'm sorry – I wish I did, for your sake – but I just don't.'

Doing her best to shake off the spectre of her ex, who, thankfully, she hadn't seen since, Thea addressed the empty kitchen. 'If I can cope with John and his warped approach to romance, then I can cope with Mabel's overzealous good intentions.' She danced a finger along the grain of the polished oak table. *Time I stuck to the reliable things in life, like coffee, cake and history.*

★

April 4th Evening
The kitchen clock struck a quarter to seven. The meeting wasn't due to start for another half an hour. At least four of them would be early. Not one of them would be late.

None of the seven volunteers working to restore Mill Grange would want to miss what had been building up as a 'Thea versus us' showdown for the past fortnight.

She wasn't sure how it had happened. In her naïvety, Thea had assumed the volunteers would be glad to have someone take the worry of time and expenses from their shoulders. Surely the job was easier for them, unpaid as they were, if they could get on with the tasks she saw as the most urgent. The main thing was to have the house ready to open in time for the approaching summer holiday period.

In reality, every suggestion or instruction she'd made had been listened to politely, before the volunteer in question reported to Mabel, as they'd always done. Sometimes the tasks Mabel had in mind coincided with Thea's. Often they didn't, and the allotted job would be substituted for another.

Thea had been polite and considerate, constantly making allowances for the fact that she was the newcomer. But no amount of explaining and cajoling made any difference. After fourteen exhausting days of making a concerted attempt to be accepted as manager, she had become tired of fighting against the way things had been done prior to her arrival.

Annoyed at her failure to manage the group, and resisting the urge to grab the emergency bottle of wine she'd hidden in the fridge, Thea put on the kettle. If she was going to get through this with her soul intact, it was going to take more than the heavily sugared lemon cake Tina had made her. It was going to take coffee. Strong coffee.

Heaping rather too many beans into the grinder, Thea wondered how her workforce would react if they discovered she'd been living in the attic since her arrival.

It hadn't been her intention to use what had once been a maid's bedroom as anything other than a temporary holding point for the few belongings she hadn't put into storage and a place to sleep for two or three nights. Her new working routine however, had become so busy so fast, that Thea hadn't got round to searching for anywhere to live. She needed to be on site during every hour of daylight if there was any hope of opening on the day the trustees had demanded. Anyway, all the available, affordable rental accommodation was over twenty miles away, along remote moorland roads. Finding a home simply hadn't happened. The guilt of living in secret, rent-free, was offset by the knowledge that the only time Thea stopped working was when she slept.

The sound of boots crossing the stone chipped courtyard outside the kitchen door tied her stomach into a dozen knots.

'Get a grip, woman. You co-ran an entire museum in Bath, for goodness' sake. You managed a team so big that you never did find the time to meet them all. Surely you can sort out eight people and get them all to play nicely!'

As a voice at the back of her head unhelpfully pointed out that it was much easier to tell people what to do if you'd never set eyes on them, the back door opened and Tina bounced in.

Thea smiled. The word 'bounced' summed Tina up perfectly. Ever since they'd met as archaeology students at Durham University fourteen years ago, Tina had faced life with an endless ability to shrug off a crisis. Thea had learnt early on that much of this was an act. Tina's way of coping with the ups and downs of existence was to grab everything with both hands and tackle the consequences later – whether good or bad. It was a technique Thea admired and envied, but could not replicate however much she wished otherwise.

'Am I the first?' Tina wiped her walking boots on the mat, flicking a blonde pigtail over her shoulder as she waved a bottle of prosecco in her friend's direction.

'You are.' Thea nodded towards the alcohol. 'You're not optimistic then?'

Laughing, Tina tucked the bottle into the fridge next to the Pinot Thea had already put there. 'And neither are you by the looks of things.'

'That's either to help smooth over the widening cracks between me and the volunteers or to drink in a pathetic bout of self-pity afterwards.'

Tina headed to the nearest cupboard. 'I'll get out some glasses.'

Wishing she could borrow some of Tina's confidence, even if only for half an hour, Thea sighed. 'All I want is for them to see I haven't come here to overrule or undermine them. I'm just an extra pair of hands and an onsite pair of eyes to make sure we stay to schedule. I didn't expect my employment at Mill Grange to be considered as a hostile coup.'

'I know, but they've been here for five years. Until now, there hasn't been a schedule. The only person they've had keeping an occasional eye on things is me, and I only come in once a week for a progress report. Otherwise, it's been…'

'Mabel.'

Tina pulled a face. 'Ever since Mabel was entrusted with a set of manor house keys, she took on the unofficial role of group leader with all the solemnity of someone receiving an OBE from the Queen, which she'll probably get one day because she is a community whizz and deserves one. But she's such a dominant person and so good at organising things, that no one's stopped her.'

'Or has been brave enough to try?'

'Quite.' Tina wrinkled her nose. 'Right now, she feels her territory has been stamped on.'

'By me.' Thea ruffled a hand through her straggly hair. 'How on earth can I convince Mabel I'm not anti what she's done or what she's doing? Honestly, every time I walk into a room with volunteers in, the conversation stops. I feel like I'm trespassing in my own workplace. It's like one of those Westerns where a cowboy comes into a new town and the whole bar freezes.'

'It has gone a bit them and us.' Tina grabbed some paper plates from her bag ready to dish out the cake. 'It's because they've gone their own way for so long. And, to be fair, done a brilliant job.'

'More than brilliant. What they've achieved is incredible. I keep trying to tell them that, but all I get is polite but sceptical "you are just saying that" smiles.' Thea shook her head as she considered her pensioner crew of unstoppable scrubbing brushes and beeswax polish. 'In five years of popping in and out for the odd hour here and there, they've cleared the overgrowth from a quarter of the garden, uncovered the dried leat course down to the river, cleaned the original wallpaper and got every bathroom and kitchen fixture working. I think they're amazing. And I've told them so.'

'But?'

'But it is going to take a lot more to have the place open to the public on time. I'm hoping that when I tell them the trustees have settled on 4ᵗʰ August as launch day, then they'll finally understand that we still have a mountain left to climb.'

'I'm glad the trustees have confirmed a date at last. I was beginning to think my persuasive skills were failing me.' Tina checked her phone. 'It's 4ᵗʰ April today, so that's four months exactly.'

'There's a danger Mabel will think that's ages away. But it isn't.'

Tina hugged her friend. 'Together we'll convince them, and by the time it's nine o'clock everyone will understand exactly why you're here.'

'Hopefully.' Thea was less convinced. 'Or they could walk away. They are volunteers after all.'

'Tell them the truth. Lay everything the trustees want out in the open. I think you've been too nice. Too polite and keen to be friends with them. You're their boss. It's time to kick butt and demand respect!'

'Hence the alcohol and the cake?'

'Well, it can't make it any worse, can it?'

Three

The meeting hadn't started, yet no companionable chatter criss-crossed the table. The lemon cake remained untouched. Mugs of tea and coffee mugs cooled, un-drunk. The alcohol sat unopened. Thea struggled not to squirm as eight sets of eyes rested on her. Only Tina was smiling.

The faces of the volunteers – five women and two men – held an air of awkward patience which declared they'd listen politely, but then they'd carry on as they had before.

With an encouraging nod from Tina, Thea cradled her coffee cup. Taking comfort from its warmth, she broke the uneasy silence.

'First of all, I'd like to thank you all, not just for coming out this evening, but for everything you've achieved at Mill Grange over the past five years.'

Not allowing anyone the chance to comment, Thea ploughed on with a speech she'd been semi-rehearsing on and off since she'd arranged the meeting two days ago. 'It's incredible what you've done, and—' seeing a flicker of objection in Mabel's eyes, Thea hurriedly raised her palm '—I don't mean incredible in a patronising way. You've had few resources, a limited budget and no training. Everything you've achieved has been for the pure love of it. I have tried to tell you how much I admire your work ethic and how much I can see you all care for Mill Grange…'

'But?' Mabel put down the tea mug she'd just lifted up with an exaggerated thump.

'There is no but.' Hoping her rising anxiety didn't show, Thea continued to address the stony faces around the table. 'Whatever I've done to offend you, I'm truly sorry, but we need to work together. We owe it to Mill Grange.'

'We?' Mabel's eyes narrowed. 'You turn up one day out of the blue, without a word of warning, and take over. How do you think that made us feel?'

'What?' Puzzled, Thea turned to Tina, who appeared equally baffled. 'You didn't know I was coming to work here?'

Mabel tilted her head to one side, clearly unconvinced that Thea hadn't been aware she'd been a surprise to them. 'We did not.'

Tina lowered her coffee cup from her lips. 'You were sent an email, Mabel. I was copied in on it, so I know it was both sent and received. The chief trustee, Malcolm, fired it off to you personally as he sees you as the volunteers' spokesperson.'

'An email.' Mabel spoke flatly as she looked down at her clenched hands, and Thea guessed that checking her email was something that rarely crossed the old lady's mind.

Taking the diplomatic path, Thea said, 'Obviously it can't have reached you, Mabel. The Internet is hardly reliable here. So, it appears I was thrust upon you without warning. But I promise you, I didn't know you were unaware of my appointment.' She looked across to Tina for confirmation. 'To be honest, I was surprised a representative from the volunteers wasn't at the interview.'

'In normal circumstances they might have been. Perhaps because you came so highly recommended, they didn't see the need this time.'

Thankful that most of the volunteers were beginning to look less hostile, Thea took a sustaining sip of coffee. 'Maybe we can start again?'

There was a general murmuring of agreement from everyone but Mabel as Thea ploughed on. 'I can only apologise for the trustees' lack of consideration. It makes me appreciate how easy you've made my job, even more than I did already. Much of what I was led to believe needed doing has been done.'

There was a further sense of the air thawing around the table as Diane, a wiry former schoolteacher sat next to Mabel, confirmed, 'You honestly didn't know we hadn't been told about your forthcoming appointment or arrival?'

'Not a clue.' Thea took a further sustaining gulp of coffee. 'Frankly, if I'd been in your shoes I'd feel severely put out, but the reason for my appointment – or at least the appointment of a manager – is a good one.'

'Why?' Mabel's voice cut across the room, its natural authority grabbing back any wavering allegiance from the group.

'Why me, or why a manager after all this time?'

'Both.'

Thea licked her lips. 'Why me, I can't answer...'

'I can.' Tina leant forward, her slim fingers playing with the stem of a wine glass. 'Thea got the job because she is well-qualified, has a wide knowledge of history, archaeology and architecture, and most importantly, she knows how to run a heritage site.' Tina picked up a slice of cake and took a healthy bite, adding through crumby lips, 'Plus, she's a fabulous human being who is great with the public.'

Flushing pink and not wanting to leave anyone the chance to comment on this, Thea cut in. 'As to why now, well, at last the trustees have decided on a date for the opening of Mill Grange. A day on which you can show off all your hard work and the restoration will be declared complete.'

This announcement caused instant muttering of surprise among the volunteers.

'We will be opening to the public on Sunday 4th August. That gives us a meagre four months to carry on pulling off miracles and do anything and everything we can to get the house ready on time.'

As Thea had feared, Mabel immediately waved away the time issue. 'That's an age, child. When you're as old as I am, you'll understand how much can be accomplished in a short period *if* you work as hard as we do.'

Feeling her hackles rising at the implication that she might not pull her weight, but not wanting the meeting to disintegrate just as she was beginning to hope they were making progress, Thea said, 'Something you have proved already, Mabel. But, at thirty-two, I'm hardly a child. Having co-run a large museum for the past five years, plus various archaeological sites before that, I do have a fair idea of what needs to be done.

'With that in mind I've made a list of the practical things

that absolutely *have* to be sorted by August. That's aside from things that it would also be nice to do, if possible.' Thea rested her palms on the table and found herself leaning forward as if addressing delegates at a conference. 'If we work like stink we have a good chance of not letting the Exmoor Heritage Trust down and more importantly, not letting the people of Upwich down. This is to the advantage of the village after all. That's where the majority of the woollen mill workers would have lived in the past, and where the local café and pub will be welcoming more custom if we can get visitors flooding in here.'

The suggestion that this was all for the village clamped whatever Mabel was about to say behind pursed lips, as Derek, one of two male volunteers, broke his silence. 'What you're saying is that we require more manpower – and womanpower naturally.'

'Exactly. We could do with at least a dozen more hands on deck.' Thea gave him a grateful smile. 'It's not just the practicalities of getting the manor in shape. It's the administration, the social media management, the posters, the advertising, the...'

'Social media?' Mabel made the phrase sound as if Thea had suggested they started gun-running.

'It's not everyone's cup of tea, I grant you, but it's an effective, cheap way to spread the word about Mill Grange. You want people to come and appreciate this beautiful place, don't you?'

There was a murmuring of agreement as Mabel muttered, 'Well, yes, but I really don't want to...'

Thea seized her chance. 'You don't have to, Mabel.

None of you do unless you want to. That's why I've been employed: to do all the tedious jobs that go with running a heritage centre.'

There was a second of silence before Diane said, 'We ought to make a communal list.'

Thea produced an A4 pad from her bag. It already sported a list so long it made her stomach turn over whenever she saw it. 'An excellent idea, Diane.' She pushed the pad into the middle of the table. 'You're all welcome to add to this so we can create a mutually agreed plan of what has to be done. However…' She paused, forcing herself to catch the eye of everyone at the table. 'It has to be stressed that you are volunteers. Please don't feel you have to do more than you want to. I'd love everyone here to be part of this, especially as the finishing line is in sight. But *no one* is obligated to stay the distance apart from myself and Tina.'

Sensing her friend was running out of steam, and that everyone in the room was waiting for Mabel to offer guidance, Tina got to her feet, picked up the prosecco and, without asking if anyone wanted a drink or not, proceeded to dispense the bubbles. 'I think this calls for a celebration.'

Thea's eyebrows rose. 'You do?'

'Absolutely! We have a dream team here. The best group of volunteers under the sun, including an incredible organiser in the shape of Mabel here; and Derek and Bill can dig, hammer, saw, paint and chop with such skill that they put Titchmarsh and Walsh to shame.' Tina winked at the two retired craftsmen, as she poured a larger quantity of fizz into their glasses before gesturing to the three women sitting opposite. 'The dynamic Biggleswaite sisters, Edna,

Ethel and Alice, can stitch and clean their way out of any given situation. Not to forget Diane, who has a fantastic eye for what is needed where and when.'

'Do I?' Diane blushed as she risked a glance at Mabel, who'd gone uncharacteristically quiet.

'You most certainly do.' Tina retrieved another bottle from her bag, and filled Thea's glass before approaching her own. 'Everyone here has a skillset which, when combined with everyone else's, makes the Mill Grange gang a force to be reckoned with.'

Derek laughed. 'You make us sound like a load of kids instead of a pile of pensioners.'

'You have the energy of kids and the determination of adults.' Tina gave him a flirty raise of her perfectly plucked eyebrows. 'Can you think of a better mix?'

Whether it was Tina's rousing speech, the alcohol, or a combination of the two, Thea felt the frost lift as everyone but Mabel chatted excitedly about the work ahead over their cake.

Thea, vowing to buy Tina a large G&T and accompanying pub lunch at the Stag and Hound the following day, took a gulp of prosecco. Then, flourishing her pad in the air, she drew all eyes back to her.

'As you can see, this list is very long, but not impossibly so if we divide up what has to be done. As Derek said, we require more volunteers, but for now, can you give me an idea as to who is currently doing what?'

Mabel sounded wary as she asked, 'What do you mean?'

'I mean, if I said cleaning out the inside of the kitchen cupboards was tomorrow's priority, which of you would want to do that rather than the other jobs which are also in the to-do queue?'

'Umm…' Ethel pushed a strand of curly, badly applied blue rinsed hair from her forehead. 'Well, we get told what to do, and we do it.'

'Get told?' Thea frowned. 'But you're volunteers, aren't you?'

An uneasy shuffling around the table confirmed what Thea had already started to suspect. Mabel had been allocating jobs as orders rather than requests.

As no one else had spoken, Thea glossed over the situation. 'How about I put a list of the most urgent tasks on the notice board in the scullery? If you put your name against what you'd like to do, I'll do the jobs that are left over.'

Thea glimpsed Mabel out of the corner of her eye. She looked a bit lost and Thea felt a stab of sympathy for the woman. However bossy she was, none of it was ill-intentioned. 'Mabel, could I take advantage of your knowledge and pick your brains?'

The old lady was openly surprised. 'You want my help?'

'Of course. You've been doing my job, unpaid and un-thanked for years. Who better to consult with?'

Mabel sat up straight, immediately rallying. 'Are we agreed that more volunteers are needed if Mill Grange is to be finished on time?'

'That is a top priority.' Thea made sure she addressed the whole room, but knew it would be Mabel who replied as she asked, 'Do you know anyone else who'd like to help?'

'I do, but it's a case of knowing people who have the time to help.'

'Would it be worth spreading the word around the local groups? I understand you're a leading light in the local WI and a few other societies, Mabel?'

Thea saw Derek holding back a snigger. They all knew Mabel Hastings ran every committee within a ten-mile radius of Upwich.

'I've done that, but I will ask again if you think it'll help.' Mabel spoke with the tone of someone who was sure it wouldn't.

'How about local radio?' Tina dabbed at some lemon cake crumbs with her fingertips. 'If we did an appeal for more help on radio it would reach a wider audience than the usual locals.'

Further murmurs of approval filled the kitchen as a sense of disquiet marched into Thea's stomach. 'Who would like to do the appeal? Any volunteers?'

Tina shook her head. 'You'd have to do it. Makes it sound more official.'

'Quite right.' Mabel spoke in unexpected support. 'Although, wouldn't television be better? I could get us a slot on the local BBC news show.'

'How could you do that?' Thea's stomach accelerated to full spin cycle.

'My nephew is a researcher for BBC South West. It'd be no problem. They're always after local interest stories.'

'Oh.'

Diane was nodding profusely, keen to make up for her previous defection from Mabel's party line. 'That's a fabulous idea.'

An air of excitement filled the earlier battleground as panic rose in Thea's gut. The last thing she needed was to be on television. She'd worked so hard to leave no trace of where she'd gone after leaving Bath. If John saw her on the news, all of that effort and sacrifice would have been for nothing.

'Fabulous idea, Mabel. I think you should do it. You're the face of our volunteer force after all. You'd be great.'

'Well, that's very sweet of you, my dear, but no. As Tina said, you're the official flag bearer of the Mill Grange project now. And anyway, a job like that requires a younger, prettier face.'

'Oh. Thank you, Mabel.'

Four

April 4th

'Why the long face? That went really well.' Tina leapt around the kitchen, piling paper plates into the cardboard box that doubled as their recycling bin.

'They enjoyed your cake.' Thea dabbed at some sugar-crusted crumbs.

'Lemon cake has always been my signature dish.' Plucking a handful of antiseptic wipes from their dispenser, Tina ran them over the table. 'Can you actually have cake as a signature dish?'

'I don't see why not.' Thea's hands plunged into the washing up. 'It was delicious.'

'Thanks. I learnt to make it before I went to university. Mum swore it would guarantee me friends for life.'

'Which it did!' Thea smiled as she remembered Sunday afternoons in Tina's shared house with fresh cake, coffee and a pile-up of students watching a movie they'd rented from Blockbuster.

Lounging next to the sink, Tina fixed Thea with a searching look. 'So, why the defeatist expression when you should be celebrating your victory?'

Staring into the water, Thea played an excess of foam between her fingers. 'I can't do the television thing. Radio would have been risky enough, but television shows your face.'

'I believe that is the whole idea of television.'

Sighing, Thea let her hands rest beneath the bubbly surface. 'Do you remember me telling you about John Sommers?'

Tina frowned. 'The last bloke you dated? The one who was so upset when you ended it that he moved away?'

'The very same. Although it turns out he was going away anyway.'

'What about him?'

'He moved back to Bath again.'

Tina laid down her drying cloth. 'You've been holding out on me.'

'It's more not wanting to bore you with a ridiculous problem.'

'Go ahead – bore me.' Tina threw a towel into Thea's hands and steered her back to the table. 'John was the one who suddenly landed you with an ideal home/corporate wife life plan, yes?'

'That's him.'

'Why's he back in Bath?'

'An old school friend offered him a better job. John turned up out of the blue in February to tell me he'd had a rethink, and that he still thought we should be together, and that he didn't mind if I kept my job once we were married

– although he didn't say married, but that was the general impression I got.'

'Turned up?'

'He found out where I spent my lunchtimes by tracking me on Facebook.'

'That's creepy.' Tina wrinkled her nose. 'Isn't it?'

Thea sighed. 'I know I hurt him, but I honestly had no idea he'd fallen for me good and proper.'

'Maybe he hasn't. Maybe he's just fallen for the idea of you being his wife? No offence meant.'

'None taken. You could be right.' Thea picked up her empty wine glass and twirled the stem through her fingers. 'Either way, for reasons I can't fathom, John announced he wants us to try again.'

'Oh hell.'

'Quite. As far as I was concerned our time together was nothing beyond a fling and a few meals out. John was hardly ever around. He was always off career-building. Then, on what he called our first anniversary – which it sort of was, I suppose – he suddenly told me which schools our children would be going to.'

'That's enough to freak anyone out, though I suppose he meant well from his point of view.'

Thea nodded. 'It was horrible and I hated doing it. I spent ages in the toilet summoning up the courage to tell him, but it would have been cruel to leave him thinking I wanted the same as him. Wouldn't it?'

'Of course it would!' Tina gave a sympathetic smile. 'But I can't blame him for falling in love with you.'

'You know, now I think about it, I reckon you were right before. I doubt John's ever *really* loved me, although he might believe he does. I just fitted his image of the perfect "businessman's wife". I remember him saying he pictured me "looking great in family photos with two children on my knee." That was the point at which I made a hasty exit for the bathroom with an excuse of desperately needing to pee, and tried to think how to get the hell out of there in the kindest way possible.'

'Bloody hell, I thought *we* were the ones supposed to be stuck in the Victorian past, not him.' Tina gestured around the antiquated kitchen. 'No wonder you left him!'

Thea ran her eyes around the kitchen. 'I hoped I'd be out of reach here.'

Getting up to bolt the kitchen door, Tina said, 'John found you in Bath, and now you're worried he'll come here if he sees you on TV?'

'It sounds insane, doesn't it? I'm no one special, and I felt awful for crushing his plans, however unrealistic they were. If he comes here, he might try to win me back again. It's tiring saying no all the time.'

'You're worried you'll cave in and go out with him again because it's easier?'

'No, yes… I don't know. He's so good at hitting my guilt-chip.' Thea shrugged. 'I don't understand why he wants me. The man has pride and he's intelligent. He's not bad-looking either. He could have anyone he wanted.'

'But the one thing he wants is resisting him.' Tina tapped her fingernails against the oak table. 'Is John used to getting what he wants?'

'Hell, yes.' Thea nodded. 'He *always* gets what he wants.'

'Apart from you.'

Thea was horrified. 'Do you think that's it? That, for the

first time in his life someone has said no, and he's stamping his feet like a spoilt toddler?'

'Could be.' Tina pulled thoughtfully at her blonde pigtails. 'How old is he?'

'Thirty-seven.'

'Perhaps John feels the clock is ticking, and his chances of having the perfect family are ebbing away. As you already know each other, the groundwork is done – and you're so much younger than him.'

'Only five years, but I take your point.'

'What the hell did you see in him in the first place?'

'I need more wine before I answer that.'

Tina was on her feet, plonking two glasses and the emergency bottle of Pinot on the table. 'So, what was it about John in those heady days of a year ago that made you go out with him in the first place? It must have been something special. I don't remember you dating anyone else for ages before that.'

'That's because I didn't. And, with hindsight, that was the thing.'

'The thing?'

'Apart from a brief three-day disaster in my first year at university, and another brief encounter a year after I moved to Bath, there hasn't been anyone beyond a few dinner dates. I was the only one out of all my friends who had no proper boyfriend or girlfriend during my entire university education. When John asked me out while attending a work pre-Christmas do at the Roman Baths that I helped organise, I was so surprised I said yes. He can be very charming. He's interesting and intelligent, but...'

'But he rarely stops talking about himself?'

'Exactly.' Thea examined her grubby jeans, jumper and worn trainers. 'It was my fault. I was so flattered someone found me attractive that I let him talk; I laughed in all the right places and was basically a pathetic excuse for a female. Until I woke up in a Chinese restaurant a year later.'

'We've all made that sort of mistake.'

'But usually when we're sixteen, not thirty-two!' Thea shook her head. 'Perhaps I'd have had better luck with blokes if I took a bit more trouble with my appearance, but I never saw the point as a student, when I spent so much of my time scrabbling in the dirt on archaeological sites, and then I just sat in an office in Bath on my own, so there was no real need to be anything other than clean and smart-ish there. Now, I'm back to the comfy scruffs.'

Tina examined her own beautifully manicured fingernails and then Thea's unvarnished chipped nails and dry hands. 'That's the difference between what we do for a living, nothing more. I gave up the mud and sand for shuffling paper, walking around various houses and offices holding nice clean clipboards and talking to people. You roll up your sleeves and get on with real work.'

Thea gave her friend a fond smile. 'It's all real work, but one kills your hands quicker than the other.' Noticing the assessing expression on Tina's face, Thea found herself shifting her chair backwards. 'Why are you looking at me like that?'

'Now don't bite my head off, but when was the last time you had a haircut?'

'How did we get from me not wanting to go on television

in case my ex spots me, to wondering about the state of my hair?'

'No need to sound so terrified. Viewing the hairdresser's as a place of torture is supposed to end once you reach ten.'

'We have already established that I'm an emotional late developer.' Thea pushed her fringe from her eyes. It was rather longer than she usually allowed it to get. Now Tina mentioned it, she couldn't remember the last time she'd had a trim. She found herself curling her fingers into her palms to hide her nails. How had she got so tatty?

Tina cut through Thea's spiralling thoughts. 'I'm not saying you should have a makeover or anything. You're one of those annoying women who are attractive without makeup, but it would do you good to have a haircut. It's relaxing and good for the confidence.'

'What do you mean I don't need a makeover? Look at me!' Thea ran her hands over her face. 'I'm a mess, and yet John still—'

'Ahhh...' Tina suddenly understood, or thought she did. 'You haven't been bothering in the hope that John would be put off, and you've got into the habit of not bothering. That makes sense.'

'I haven't bothered because it never crosses my mind to bother. Of course, now I'm wondering if I should put a bag over my face and invest in some cotton gloves.'

'Don't be daft. You know I didn't mean anything like that. I'm saying you'd feel more confident if you made an effort sometimes.'

Thea groaned. 'And I'd look better in front of the television cameras. I really don't think I can do it, Tina.

Are you sure I can't persuade you to step in? You're used to talking to strangers. These days I'm more comfortable talking to broken pots, bits of brick and the spiders whose cobwebs I dust away.'

Tina pushed Thea's wine glass closer to her friend's hand. 'John might not watch the local news. Chances are slim if you think about it.'

'He'll see it.'

'Why so sure?'

'John thinks it's everyone's duty to keep abreast of the news. Local and national, and sadly, as Somerset encompasses Bath these days, he'll get the same news as us.'

'Oh.' Tina's forehead creased into furrows. 'I'm beginning to feel grateful I never met him. Hang on, why didn't I meet him?'

'Largely because you were busy here, and then you had that two-month sabbatical in Tuscany.'

'So I did.' Tina beamed. 'Tuscany, land of Roman remains, excellent red wine and a very attractive waiter called Ethan.'

'Ethan? Hardly Italian?'

'Scottish, darling... very much so. Son of some Lord or other in the Highlands.'

Thea laughed. 'If you say so.'

Reluctantly dragging her mind from her Scottish-Italian encounter, Tina returned to the matter in hand. 'John finding you via Facebook bothers me a bit.'

'Yeah. I know what you mean. Me too.' Thea stared at her glass. 'After that first time, he kept popping up in Bath to ask me out. Each time I said no, I felt sorrier for him.'

'Maybe he was trying to wear you down until your patience snapped, and you took him back.' Tina dabbed some cake crumbs up with her finger. 'I wondered why you wanted this job so badly. It is several centuries away from your historical period of passion.'

'To be honest, he was merely the catalyst. I fancied a fresh challenge. Although I loved my job at the Baths, I wasn't meeting new people.'

'Men, you mean?'

'People in general; but I wouldn't say no to the chance to meet a decent bloke. Wouldn't you like someone to come home to sometimes?'

'Of course.'

'Remembering the queue of chaps interested in you in Durham, I wouldn't have said you'd have problems finding one.'

'Finding one isn't a problem; finding the *right* one, on the other hand...'

'And your version of "the one" is still someone with a castle and a unicorn?'

Tina laughed. 'If you mean someone older and more experienced than me, with a bit of money in the bank, then yes.'

Thea's eyebrows rose. 'That matters to you? The money I mean?'

'Too right. My last two boyfriends were nice enough, but we hardly did anything or went anywhere as we never had enough cash. I'm tired of making do.'

'Your job's not that badly paid, is it?'

'It's not a disaster, but my rent is high and it costs forty quid in petrol to get from home to here – or wherever else I'm sent – each week. Even with the Trust's token gesture towards mileage allowance it costs a fortune to run my car. Then there's food and clothes and…'

'I get it. You're expensive and high-maintenance!'

Tina stuck her tongue out. 'Pretty much.'

'All this makes no difference though. I came here to restore this house and meet new people. So far, all I've met is a load of pensioners and a wall of silence. After making a breakthrough tonight, it would be churlish to refuse Mabel's offer of a television interview. Especially as it's an excellent idea.' Thea could feel the alcohol soothing her insides. 'Maybe I can sweet-talk Mabel into doing the broadcast, or perhaps I could bribe you into doing it after all? I'll buy you all the wine and chocolate you could ever want.'

'Stop right there! You're doing it. You're the face of Mill Grange now. Anyway, I'd go to pieces.'

'You wouldn't.'

'I hate large-scale public speaking and stuff. It's very different to having a conversation with a landlord about an abandoned cottage or whatever. You've done it loads, at meetings and conferences and stuff.'

'True, but not for ages and I don't like doing it. I'm much better off chatting to the spiders. I'm a ball of nervous tension the whole time I'm addressing more than two people at once. It's terrifying.'

'You're still good at it though.'

'Maybe.' Thea pushed a stray hair from her cheek. 'Anyway, I haven't got much choice if we want to keep things smoothed over with Mabel, have I?'

'Don't worry, these things take ages to arrange. It may never even happen.'

Thea pushed herself to her feet. 'Come on, let's clear up or you'll never get home tonight.'

'Talking of home, where did you find lodgings in the end? Did they have room at the pub in the village?'

Thea had almost told Tina on a few occasions that she was sleeping on the job, but they'd never been out of earshot of other people for long enough. 'Well, actually I'm staying—'

The high-pitched bell of Thea's mobile phone echoed through the kitchen.

'Oh my God!' Tina jumped off her chair in surprise at the shrill sound in the otherwise silent house. 'How come you have a signal? This is a dead zone for most phones.'

'I only get a phone signal in here, nowhere else.' Thea looked at the number. 'It's Mabel. You don't think...'

'Answer it!'

Thea managed to contain her nerves until Tina had gone. Promising her friend she'd be leaving to find her bed very soon, which wasn't exactly a lie, Thea locked all the doors.

Adopting her nightly routine of telling herself the house absolutely was not haunted, as she walked up the ill-lit servants' stairways and along the deadly quiet corridors to the attic, Thea dropped onto her bed. Thanks to Mabel's vast supply of useful connections, Thea was to expect a small television crew to arrive at the manor in two days' time. She felt her palms start to sweat. The only saving grace was that it was to be a pre-recorded interview and not a live one.

'John won't see it,' Thea told the crack in the ceiling

plaster. 'It will be a tiny feature at the end of the news. He will have got all the depressing information of the day he desires and have switched the TV off before the "and finally" bit. And, even if he does see it, he's only just started a new job, so won't be able to take time off.

I hope.'

Five

Turning over, Thea punched her pillow and checked the time. It was five o'clock in the morning. She couldn't have had more than an hour's sleep for worrying about being seen on television by John. The spectre of that one person witnessing her first ever broadcast far outweighed any natural nerves she may have had about appearing on screen in the first place.

Giving up on sleep, Thea hauled herself out of bed and pulled on yesterday's clothes. She needed a plan, a way to persuade Tina that she couldn't appear before the cameras – one that was more convincing than her fear of John seeing her. And that meant she needed coffee and fresh air.

The dew-soaked grass seeped moisture across her trainers' toes at record speed, but Thea ignored the sensation as she surveyed the scene before her. The vista across the gardens and down into the woodland beyond deserved to appear on television. 'But not with me stood next to it!'

Sitting on a bench, making a mental note to add 'sand and paint benches' to her to-do list, Thea sighed. It all came down to persuading Tina that, as the Exmoor Trust's representative, she'd be much better off representing Mill Grange.

'The Trust!' Thea felt the stirrings of an idea nudge at her brain, but it would involve a little underhand persuading.

Thea addressed a pheasant that was having an early morning stroll across the lawn. 'Tina will forgive me – eventually. And she knows how worried I am about John seeing me on the local news. After all, I'd do it for her if our places were reversed.'

Thea swallowed back an attack of guilt and got to her feet. If she got started now on writing out how her conversation with Malcolm at the trust office might go, then by the time he got to work, she'd be ready to turn on the charm – or at least try to.

'Me and Mabel?'

'That's what Malcolm Ware said, and as he's the head trustee I didn't like to argue.' Thea was struggling to disguise her relief at not having to risk the discovery of her newfound hidey-hole. 'He was thrilled with Mabel's idea for getting Mill Grange on the television. But rather than me take the helm, he wants to flag up the Trust's role in the proceedings by having you front the interview. Then he suggested that Mabel should be on hand in case they want her to chat about what future volunteers could expect to do.'

Tina looked as sceptical as she sounded. 'Are you sure you didn't persuade Malcolm that's what he wanted?'

'All I said was that Mabel had got us a slot on the local news, and how it was an excellent opportunity to put the work the Trust is doing in the local area on the map.'

'So you did steer him into choosing me to do it!'

Thea blushed. 'Well, maybe a little bit, but you know I can't do it Tina. I've worked so hard to go off-grid, if John sees it he might come here to help, and it'd all have been for nothing.' She passed a consoling cup of coffee in her friend's direction. 'I swear I didn't have to say anything to Malcolm about how I thought you'd be the perfect face of Mill Grange.'

'But you would have if he hadn't got in first.' Tina anxiously twirled her pigtails.

'Maybe.' Thea confessed. 'Look, I'm sorry I landed you in it, but as Malcolm never even hinted at me doing it, he clearly expected you to be the one to front the report anyway.'

'Possibly.' Tina took a sip of her extra strong coffee. 'Have you told Mabel yet?'

'I have. She repeated her claim that someone younger and prettier should be there with you, before accepting the situation without a fight and booking a haircut.'

Tina laughed despite herself. 'Alright, you win on this one, but if they ask Mabel who is in charge of the restoration and she gives out your name, you'll be no better off, will you?'

'Oh God, I hadn't thought of that. She wouldn't, would she?'

'Not unless she's asked to, but there's a good chance the question will come up. I don't mind saying that I'm in charge on behalf of the trust, but Mabel's a law unto herself. If you want to make sure your name isn't mentioned, then you're either going to have to tell her about John, or you'll have to come up with a damn good reason why not.'

April 6th

'They just called. They'll be here in an hour.' Mabel patted her new coiffure as she arrived in front of Thea's desk.

'An hour?' Thea checked the clock at the corner of her laptop screen as her stomach did a backflip. 'Right, so that'll be about two o'clock. Have you told Tina?'

'I came straight here. I'll go and track her down now.'

'I'll come with you. She said something about wanting to check if a safety rail would be needed between the garden and the steeper parts of the drop into the wood.'

Having spent the last twenty-four hours trying to think of ways to ask Mabel not to mention her name on air, and having come up with nothing that didn't sound false, Thea was about to ask Mabel to only give out trust details and not her name, when she saw Tina dashing towards them.

'I have to go!'

'What? Why?' Thea felt her stomach turn to jelly as Tina came to an abrupt halt.

'A text just came through from my housemate. God knows when she actually sent it. The house could be ankle deep in water by now what with the crap signal round here.'

'What are you talking about?'

'A burst pipe. Apparently our kitchen resembles a pond. I'm really sorry, I must go.'

'But...'

Tina kept marching towards her car with Thea and Mabel hot on her heels. 'But what?'

'The television people are on their way. They'll be here in under an hour.'

Tina's hand came to her mouth, 'Oh my God, in my panic about the house, I totally forgot. I'm really sorry Thea, but you'll have to do it. I have to go home.'

'Of course you must!' Mabel cut in before Thea could suggest she went to dry out her friend's kitchen instead. 'Thea and I will be just fine. Now off you pop.'

Having virtually shooed Tina away, Mabel turned to Thea and gave her a critical stare. 'If you hurry you'll have time to go grab a shower and change into something presentable. Off you go! This is for Mill Grange, remember!'

Cursing fate and dodgy plumbing with every step she took, Thea ran up the manor's back staircase. With Tina's words about her less-than-well-kempt appearance echoing in her ears, Thea risked a glance in the ancient bathroom mirror. It had been just over two weeks since she'd started working at Mill Grange. Eighteen days of using mirrors which were spotted with age and clouded with years of neglect. Hardly reliable indicators of one's appearance. Thea rather liked them.

Now she was being forced to peer beyond the clouded parts of the glass, she saw just how much of a bird's nest her hair had become, and how huge the bags under her eyes were. Neglect felt like a word she could apply to herself, along with the manor's mirrors.

The lack of an iron at Mill Grange also meant she'd had to (semi) un-crease her only shirt and smart black trousers by hand. Although her outfit had served her well for years, now that she examined it properly, Thea saw how the black suit material had taken on a washed-out grey tinge, and the white blouse was thinning in places.

Crossing her fingers and hoping that the crew would bring a makeup artist with them – and that they wouldn't take one look at her inexpertly applied foundation and despair – Thea left the bathroom with a resigned groan.

All the time she'd been washing and changing, Thea had fought to keep the spectre of John at the back of her mind. If that was going to remain the case, she needed to keep busy right up until the television people arrived. After wasting ten minutes guessing what sort of questions they'd ask her, Thea had reached the point where she feared she'd forget her name and the reason she was at Mill Grange as soon as the camera rolled, when a knock on her bedroom door broke through her nerves.

A buoyant Mabel was virtually hopping from one foot to the other in excitement. 'They're early! Come on, Miss Thomas, it's time to show off Mill Grange.'

Mabel picked up the television remote control and pressed the off button. Pulling the notebook she used exclusively for her WI committee work towards her, she switched her attention from the local news to the allocation of seats in the coach she'd hired for an outing to Buckingham Palace.

'What you up to, love?' Bert lay down his newspaper and watched as his wife attacked her latest project.

'Making a seating plan for the trip to London.'

Bert chuckled. 'You can't tell people where they're allowed to sit on a bus.'

'I can and I will.' Mabel wrote a few more names on her seating plan. 'Anything to stop a repeat of Mrs Paxton's wind ripping from the front of the coach to the back, and gassing us all in the process. If I sit her on the wheel at the back, the noise will be disguised and the air conditioning will limit the damage.'

'Won't she fart more due to the juddering of the wheel beneath her butt?'

'Oh, go and play one of your silly games!' Mabel gave her husband a stern look, before switching her attention back to her plan.

Chuckling, Bert picked up his tablet. 'I wish the grandkids hadn't introduced me to Tetris. Bloody addictive!'

'Bert! Language!'

Rolling his eyes, Bert Hastings eased himself from his chair and joined Mabel at the tiny table that was squashed against the living room's far wall. 'Come on, love, enough work for one day.'

'Maybe.' Mabel picked up the remote control and aimed it at the television. 'I just want to watch the news again in case...'

Bert gently prised the remote from his wife's fingers. 'It won't be on again tonight. Thea did a good job. You know she did. You should be pleased; it was your idea after all.'

'She did Mill Grange proud.'

'But?'

'She comes in without so much as a by-your-leave and…'

'And you feel sidelined because they didn't have time to interview you as well, and after all your years of hard work someone else has arrived at the last minute to steal your glory.'

'Bert! It's not about glory, it's about—'

'Mabel, my girl, I've loved you since the moment I laid eyes on you fifty-six years ago. As a result I know when you're disappointed and put out. In this case I can see why. It's a real shame you didn't get a go in front of the cameras, but I've met Thea; she's a good kid with a job to do. Why don't you let her take the strain? It isn't as if you haven't got your plate full.' Bert gestured to the pile of labelled box files on the table. One for each of the seven committees his wife ran.

Mabel was quiet for a while, before repeating, 'Thea was good on the television, wasn't she?'

'Excellent. A natural, I'd say.' Bert put a frail hand over his wife's. 'Has she done TV in the past?'

'She didn't say so. But then she didn't tell us she was coming to Mill Grange either.'

'Which wasn't her fault. An overlooked email is no one's fault.' Bert spoke with the infinite patience needed for his wife when her avalanche-style good intentions had been disturbed or gone unappreciated. 'And she's going to be stuck with all the jobs you don't want to do. Four months to get the place open to the paying public is nothing, you know that.'

Mabel gave a single brisk nod. 'Hot chocolate before bed?'

'Please.'

'I'll make it, if you can work out how to allocate coach seats in such a way as people won't ignore my instructions and sit where they want anyway.'

'What do you mean you didn't watch it?' Tina passed Thea her drink and crashed onto the cushion covered pew near the pub's open fire. 'I watched even though I was squeezing water out of the living room carpet at the same time.'

'I went straight back to work at the manor. No television, remember. How's your house anyway?'

'Oh, it's fine. Landlord's promised new carpets downstairs and luckily the emergency plumber stopped the flow of water before it reached above carpet level.' Tina flapped away talk of her domestic emergency. 'I could find the news on catch-up TV and record it for you if you want to see yourself in action.'

'Thanks, but no thanks. I doubt I would have watched even if I'd had something to view the news on. I dread to think what I sounded like.' Thea took a mouthful of wine. 'At least I didn't look too much of a disaster after the makeup woman attacked me with her range of brushes. I have no idea what she did, but it seemed to work.'

'You looked great. You still do, despite the blob of whatever the hell that is on the leg of your jeans.'

Thea absentmindedly rubbed at the stain. 'I had a quick investigation of the stables when I got back. Probably a bit of paint from one of the old tins stacked in there.'

Brushing non-existent dust off her miniskirt and tights, Tina said, 'At least you won't need to worry about clearing the stables alone. After that appeal, you'll be inundated with helpers.'

'You think so?'

'Bound to be. You've probably got a heap of emails awaiting your attention from willing volunteers. Hopefully they'll be a nice chap or two among them. One each if we're lucky.'

'I doubt it. I know you like older men, but we need workers all day, which will mean retired folk. I can't picture you dating an octogenarian.'

'We could get students wanting work experience over the end of the Easter and early part of the summer holidays, and people on a work break or unemployed folk or...'

'Or John.' Thea felt queasy as she put down her wine glass. 'Do you know why I drink Pinot?'

'No.' Tina frowned, thrown by the abrupt change in conversation.

'Because I know sod all about wine, but I know I like it.'

Tina was confused. 'And that's a problem because?'

'I never try new things. I'm so stuck in what's safe.'

'And yet you gave up a job you loved and took this one. A job that's not even secure.'

'Not secure?' Thea sat up a little straighter. 'What do you mean?'

'Nothing.' Tina hid her face in her glass. 'I just meant that the restoration won't last forever.'

'No, you didn't. The truth, Miss Martin, if you please.'

'It's probably nothing.' Tina crossed and re-crossed her legs before leaning closer to her friend so no one could overhear them. 'I was in the office at the trustees' headquarters today.

I caught wind of a rumour that the Trust is running out of money. I don't know what that means for us, or if it's even true.'

'I see.' Thea sighed. 'Well, if John did see the TV thing and has a mad idea about volunteering, then perhaps I won't be around for him to hassle me. I think I need another drink.'

'I shouldn't have mentioned it. It could be nothing.'

'Let's hope it was a case of catching the wrong part of an unrelated discussion, or we could both be out of a job.'

'I *really* don't want to think about that. I love my job so much.' Tina drained her glass and stood up to get some refills. 'And it seems unlikely they'd hire you and then fire you before the house was restored.'

'Let's assume you misheard or heard something that doesn't apply to either us or Mill Grange. Some things in life, we aren't meant to know.'

'True.' Tina gave a half-smile. 'Talking of things we aren't meant to know – I popped into Mill Grange early this morning prior to my inspection of the garden fence. Thought I'd find out how far you'd got with cleaning the bedrooms while you were hitting the paperwork. I went into the attic.'

'Ahh.' Thea chewed her bottom lip. 'I was going to tell you the other day, and then the interview thing came up and...'

'You're living on site?'

'Yes.'

'And eating stuff out of the box in your room that needs very little cooking, hence leaving no trace in the kitchen?'

'Yes.'

Tina was quiet for a moment, before asking, 'Jacket potato with your Pinot?'

John scribbled down the contact details written across the bottom of the television screen as if they were the answer to his prayers.

There'd be a few creases to iron out at the office if he were to take time off, but he'd worked very hard to ensure the merger was a success. He deserved a holiday.

John's gaze fell to the invitation on his designer glass coffee table.

It was time to win Thea Thomas' heart.

Six

Taking refuge in the technological dead zone of the walled garden to the left of the house, Thea stared at the disintegrating greenhouse which rested against the southern wall, pointlessly catching the best of Exmoor's morning sun. She was supposed to be deciding if it could be saved, or if it would be more cost-effective to have it pulled down. In reality, she was staring blankly into space while an internal battle between her anxieties and common sense took place.

It had been three days since the television appeal had gone out. There had been a follow-up piece by the local newspaper, and ever since, they'd been inundated with enquiries. So far six students were expected over the imminent Easter holidays to help with general cleaning, clearing and tidying, and the seven strong volunteer force of retired personnel had doubled. There had also been dozens of calls and messages asking when Mill Grange would be opening, if school trips could be booked in advance and, in one instance, if the manor could be booked to host a Christmas craft fair that December.

With each new email and fresh ring of the manor's landline however, Thea's stomach cramped with apprehension. She should be thrilled by how successful the appeal had been, but with every enquiry the same question shot into her mind; what if it's John?

'He'd already have been in touch if he was coming. It's over. You can relax now.' Doing her best to believe what she was saying, Thea started to count how many of the Victorian greenhouses' tiny panes of glass were cracked or smashed. It would be such a shame to have it pulled down, but at the same time, extremely expensive to repair. No wonder the volunteers had left this part of the grounds untouched bar the occasional culling of undergrowth.

Making a few notes so she could talk the matter over with Tina later, Thea faced the garden as a whole. Kicking aside fallen leaves and branches left from autumn, she made out the outline of forgotten vegetable plots and neat square beds which would, she assumed, have been the source of much of the manor's fresh produce.

An economic crisis thirty years ago had sent the last of the Upwich family to Australia, and the house into the hands of the Exmoor Heritage Trust. At first they'd only had the funds and time to make sure Mill Grange didn't completely disintegrate, but then, five years ago, a grant from the Arts Council had come to its rescue. That money – if what Tina had overheard related to them – must be running out. If Mill Grange was going to survive, it needed to start earning money for itself.

Thea checked the time on her mobile: just gone eleven. The members of the board of trustees should have had time to drink their morning coffee, empty their inboxes and be ready to be disturbed by a phone call. Heading to the scullery, Thea felt a sheen of perspiration dot her palms at the prospect of the call she had to make.

Pushing away a childish wish that Tina hadn't let slip that there might be a funding issue, Thea wondered how to phrase her enquiry. She could hardly ask outright if her job was already in jeopardy. Deciding to start her conversation with the good news that the appeal for more unpaid help had worked well, and that she believed, should all the promised goodwill be forthcoming, they would be ready for the Open Day on 4th August (something she intended to say while keeping her fingers crossed behind her back), she would wing the rest of the conversation.

'Isn't it fantastic?'

Tina danced through the narrow kitchen door just as Thea was reaching for the kettle.

'What is?'

'The response to the appeal for helpers of course! The trustees are chuffed to bits. And good on you for calling them to tell them the news. They're nice people, but sometimes they forget to say obvious things like thank you and well done!'

Thea gave a weak grin.

'You okay? You don't have the air of triumph I expected to see this morning.'

'Tired, that's all.'

'Liar.' Tina slid two mugs towards Thea, suddenly serious. 'John hasn't been in touch, has he?'

'No. To be honest, I think I overreacted on that.'

'You mean making you uncomfortable enough to be the catalyst that made you leave your job and your home so you could squat here?'

'Shhh…' Thea looked round in case one of the volunteers was within earshot.

'Don't worry, only Mabel and Diane are here, and judging from the direction the stench of vinegar is coming from, I'd say they were in the dining room.'

'Oh hell! I think I'm becoming immune to the smell; I hadn't even noticed.' Thea groaned. 'The aroma of acetic acid hanging around each moveable item in the place for months is all we need! Why the hell does Mabel add vinegar to every cleaning solution going?'

'It's that book she's got.'

'Book?' Thea added a second spoonful of coffee beans to the grinder.

'One of her grandchildren bought her a book about cleaning and conservation for her birthday a few years back. It expounds the virtues of using vinegar as an effective, non-corrosive and environmentally friendly cleaning agent. Mabel has sworn by it ever since, and I've always opened a lot of windows in her wake.'

'I'm not sure about the non-corrosive bit, especially considering the quantities she uses.' Thea shook her head. 'What's wrong with using warm water and bicarbonate of soda? It does the job and doesn't make the house smell.'

'Do you really want to tackle that issue now, when you've got her playing nice?'

Thea felt her shoulders sag. 'It might not matter anyway.'

'What do you mean?'

'I'll tell you in the garden. I want your opinion on the greenhouse.'

Tina stood next to Thea, her ankle boots sinking beneath the undergrowth, uncaring that her tights were slowly soaking her from the ankle up as she regarded the dilapidated greenhouse.

'Common sense tells me to have it pulled down, but the historian in me wants to restore it. I need you to give me the businesswoman's eye.'

Laughing at the notion of being considered a businesswoman, Tina waded closer to the accumulation of metal and glass. 'Sometimes I hate the money side of this job. Can't you imagine it in all its former glory? Rows of small lead-lined glass panels running the length of the wall, with tomatoes and cucumbers and suchlike protected beneath. Grape vines climbing the supporting wall and the sun reflecting off the entire building. It would have been stunning.'

'You old romantic, you,' Thea teased. 'But I know what you mean. Even now, with its rather ghostly Miss Havisham edge of decay and neglect, it has a majestic beauty about it.'

Tina dug her phone from one of the many pockets that covered the oversized parker she wore. 'I'll make some notes and we'll get a quote. Restoring it might be unrealistic, but if we find out how much it would cost to replace the glass and any remaining leadwork with a safer, but authentic looking alternative, then we'll know we at least tried to save it.'

'Before it's pulled down anyway.'

'Probably.' Tina held up a measuring tape she kept in another coat pocket. 'Do you have the measurements for the greenhouse anywhere, or do we need to play with my ever-present tape measure?'

'I have them in the office.' Thoughtful, Thea added, 'Seems everyone in the area wants Mill Grange to work out and open to the public.'

'Of course they do. This is a hugely important place to the locals. Many of them have lived in Upwich their whole lives; they have family who worked in the mill or ancestors that worked in the manor or on its grounds.'

Thea nodded. 'That's why it's going to be hell telling them.'

'Telling them?'

'After you told me about overhearing that discussion about the Trust being short of money, I couldn't sleep. I decided I'd better fish for information.'

Tina's happy glow dimmed, 'Oh hell…'

'They haven't said anything to you?'

'I've been on the road between sites. I haven't been back to head office today. They don't do bad news by email or phone unless they are certain the signal won't give out halfway through the conversation or the email won't get lost in the weird Internet ether we have around here.'

'Makes sense. Anyway, I called the trustees to tell them the work is on track for 4th August. I told them how much future interest there is in the manor being hired for event hosting and school trips and stuff.'

'And?'

'I spoke to Grant Davies, the guy who interviewed me. He passed me onto Malcolm Ware.'

'The head trustee.' Tina groaned. 'That can't be good.'

'He was very nice about it, but the bottom line is, if we can't turn the manor around so it can open to the public on time, without any additional expenditure, then the house will have to go to private sale.'

'What!' Tina's smile disappeared in a puff of indignation. 'Did he say someone was interested?'

'He claimed not. He seemed rather embarrassed by the situation. Said they'd made a mistake with the figures and had rather overreached themselves.'

Tina blanched, 'God, I hope it wasn't my figures that were wrong!'

'If you presented them with the same figures you showed me after I took the job, then it wasn't you. I checked your estimates in case we could shave some money off here and there. You were spot on across the board. That means we can kiss this greenhouse goodbye, as well as anything extra we could have done.'

'Such as?'

'I was considering opening the mill up to have workshops in there on Open Day. People spinning wool, felt making, and so on.'

'That would have been good. You could have made money for the house from classes as well.'

'Exactly.' Thea turned to Mill Grange and admired its granite stonework. 'This would make a fabulous home. I can imagine the Christmas parties... but it's so big.'

Tina started to pace. 'Hang on, did Malcolm say it *might* be sold if you couldn't do this in budget, or that it was definitely going to be sold?'

'Just that we needed to do the job within budget and on

time. But you know how slim the chances of that are.' Thea kicked at a ball of weeds. 'I feel so guilty. Part of that budget must be going on my wages, yet now I'm here nothing has changed. I'm supposed to assist with the renovation and speed it up. In fact, because of me being a drain on resources, it may never open to the public at all.'

'This is not your doing. Come on.' Tina started to walk towards the kitchen. 'I need to take these soggy boots off and make a call to find out precisely what the situation is. In the meantime, you go and find Mabel. Why don't you see if you can rescue a few ornaments from a lifetime of smelling of salt and vinegar crisps?'

Seven

Thea followed the scent of vinegar along the main corridor from the scullery, past the kitchen and into the dining room.

The eighteen-place mahogany table had been covered with three thick protective cloths. Across its surface, lined up in precise regimented rows, were Toby Jugs, Hummel figurines, an assortment of vases and umpteen snuff boxes of different shapes, sizes and provenance.

No allowance had been made for their fragile state or, in the case of some of the vases, their extreme age and value. Each piece had been treated to a robust dip in one of Mabel's vinegar and washing up liquid bath concoctions. As Tina had told her the ladies had arrived only two hours ago, and had now left the room; they'd obviously worked at a speed which focused on finishing the task quickly rather than safely. It was enough to make a member of the National Trust cry.

Wondering if this uncharacteristically careless zeal was

in direct response, perhaps even a childishly deliberate one, to her declaration that time was short, Thea shoved open a couple of the stiff sash windows. Adding 'wax the window runners' to her ever-growing to-do list, she wrenched back her shoulders. It was time to stop dancing around like a nervous schoolgirl. She'd been given this position because she was good at her job. Her hatred of confrontation was going to have to be dumped fast if she didn't want Mill Grange and its contents to dissolve beneath Mabel's rubber gloved hands.

'I have to carry on as if nothing has changed,' Thea muttered under her breath as she examined the drying ornaments. There was no obvious damage, but she knew she'd have to waste time she didn't have giving each piece a thorough inspection later. Inhaling deeply, she hoped Tina was having a productive and helpful phone call to the trustees.

Reaching the main door, she flung it open to let in some fresh, if rather cool, spring air in time to see Derek's battered old Jaguar pull onto the drive.

Leaping from the car with his usual energy, Derek waved. 'If you're after Mabel, she's in the stable. I saw her and Diane as I drove up.'

'How did you know I was looking for Mabel?'

Derek grinned. 'You wear a very particular expression when you're searching for Mabel.'

'Do I?' Thea, suddenly very aware of all her facial muscles, put a hand to her cheek.

'Sort of determined, but afraid.' Derek shrugged. 'Lots of people adopt the same posture with Mabel.'

'I'm not the only coward in the village then?'

Laughing, Derek leant against his car, swapping his driving shoes for walking boots. 'Far from it. Why else do you think she runs every club and society in Upwich? Her heart is pure gold, but everyone's terrified of her.'

Unsure if she should feel better or worse about how she approached Mabel, Thea asked, 'Any tips on how to get what I want from her, in the interests of saving the manor from a lifetime of smiling like a discarded crisp packet?'

Derek raised both his hands to the sky and winked. 'Some secrets are destined never to be known.'

Thea couldn't help smile. Derek, at a spritely seventy-two, had as much oomph as Tina. He reminded her of her much-missed grandfather. Thea found herself fighting an urge to give him a hug. 'What's your plan of attack for today?'

'Taking a scythe to the patch of land that connects the scullery path to the old kitchen garden, boss. Then I'll get a bonfire going. Sound okay?'

'Sounds utterly perfect.' Thea beamed. 'Thanks, Derek. Actually, I don't suppose you'd mind some help?'

'Of course not. The more the merrier. Did you fancy a bit of fire setting then?'

'Tempting, but I was thinking of the students who are coming to help. Three of them will be here this afternoon. I wasn't sure where they should start, but helping you clear the pathway would be fantastic.'

'I'd be delighted.' Derek rubbed his hands together. 'Better not let them near a scythe or a fire until they've signed some health and safety forms, though.'

'Fear not.' Thea gestured an arm in the vague direction of her office. 'I have a pile of documentation all ready for them to sign their safety away.'

As Derek headed towards the old butler's quarters, which was being used as a temporary garden equipment store, Thea thought she heard him whisper, 'Good luck slaying the old dragon, my girl.'

The stable block was formed of three interconnected loose boxes which, once upon a time, had accommodated six horses. Two for pulling the family carriage, one for the servants' cart, a palfrey for the lady of the manor and two hunting stallions. Now they held a mountain of broken furniture, empty-ish paint pots, trestle tables and fold-up chairs last used over thirty years ago when the village fete had annually pitched in the gardens, along with a mound of dried-out autumn leaves, cobwebs and evidence of mice.

In the midst of all this, Mabel and Diane gossiped, while sweeping as much of the blown- in foliage as they could reach with stiff brooms. Thea called out a welcome to announce her arrival, partly so she didn't make them jump if they hadn't heard her approach and partly because, if they'd been talking about her, she didn't want to hear it.

'Looks like you're winning the battle over the spiders!'

Diane pulled a face. 'I hope so.'

Taking her chance, Thea, hoping to appear approachable and not in any way cross, said, 'I wanted to thank you for doing such a thorough job in the dining room. All the ornaments are drying nicely.'

Mabel's shoulders visibly unclenched. But the sensation was short-lived as Thea added, 'I just wondered if you'd mind not using so much vinegar in the solution next time. It isn't very good for the ornaments and—'

'I'll have you know that I have it on good authority that is exactly how such things should be cleaned and...'

Mabel was getting into full flow when, against all the laws of nature, Thea's mobile phone burst into life.

As Thea fumbled for her phone, Mabel growled, 'You said your mobile didn't work anywhere but the kitchen?'

'I didn't think it did.' Thea snapped with rather more force than she'd meant to, as she connected the call. 'Hello?'

The line crackled uncertainly, as if it had heard Mabel's indignation and wasn't sure whether it was allowed to connect properly or not. Thea was aware of a male voice speaking to her from the other end of the call, but she couldn't make it out. 'Hello, I'm terribly sorry, this is rather a bad line. Would you mind repeating that please?'

After a hiss and crackle the line cleared and a rich caramel voice that sounded vaguely familiar said, 'Is that better? Signal is shocking here. Is that Thea Thomas?'

'It is. I'm sorry, I missed your name. Are you calling about volunteering at Mill Grange?'

'I am. It sounds fantastic. The way you brought the place to life on television was wonderful. Tell me, have you done much television work?'

Surprised by the question, Thea said, 'None at all.'

'Well you should do more, you're a natural.'

A blush started to form across Thea's cheeks. 'That's very kind of you, Mr...'

'Cowlson. Shaun Cowlson.'

'Shaun Cowlson?'

Thea regretted saying his name aloud as soon as she heard Mabel's voice behind her gasping out, '*The* Shaun Cowlson? Off the television?'

Closing her eyes, Thea found herself temporarily speechless as her mind raced back to a conference she'd attended a year after finishing university. She'd been there giving a talk on behalf of Bath Museum Services on Romano-British fort construction and location. Shaun Cowlson had been the keynote speaker on the same day. He'd asked a colleague of hers out on a date.

Aware that Shaun was still talking, Thea drew her attention back to the conversation, trying to ignore Mabel, who'd stepped nearer, presumably in the hope of eavesdropping.

'We met a few years ago, but I don't expect you to remember.'

Thea's free hand dug into the warmth of her coat pocket. 'I remember. We both spoke at the same conference.' Not wanting to go off down memory lane with a man who'd broken her friend's heart, Thea got to the point. 'So, how can I help you?'

'I'm in the area for a while and I'd like to help at Mill Grange. I'm pretty sure I'm qualified.'

Ignoring the teasing tone in his voice, and dropping to a whisper in the hope that Mabel and Diane wouldn't hear, Thea muttered, 'But why? Surely we're a bit out of your time range. Isn't there an archaeological excavation you're supposed to be recording your show from?'

Shaun's declaration that he was between projects was overshadowed by Mabel's cry. 'If that man is offering to help us, then snap his hand off, girl! A TV celebrity on the volunteer list would really put Mill Grange on the map.'

Walking away from the stables to leave Diane and Mabel cooing over how much they loved Shaun's television show, *Landscape Treasures*, and how if they were thirty years younger they'd be setting their caps at him, Thea gave a mental groan. She hated to admit that they were right. Frankly, if they were going to pull off a miracle and get Mill Grange open to the public, they needed all the help they could get.

While Shaun was explaining that the latest episode of his show, based in nearby Devon, had been subject to a scheduling change, hence his freedom for the next few weeks, Mabel tapped on Thea's shoulder.

Swinging round, she was confronted with a disconcertingly excited Mabel holding up her ever-present clipboard. On it she had scribbled in capital letters, 'ASK HIM TO OPEN THE MANOR IN AUGUST.'

Mabel and Diane trailed Thea back to the kitchen. They didn't stop asking questions the whole way.

'Was that really Shaun Cowlson?'

'Is he coming here?'

'When's he arriving? I ought to get a haircut before then?'

Thea's eyebrows rose up her forehead as Diane added, 'So should you, Thea dear. He's single, you know, and quite a catch.'

She was spared from responding when Mabel spoke up. 'Don't be ridiculous Diane, the man could have anyone he liked.' Thea bit her tongue at this implied slight. A slight that Mabel instantly trumped with an accusation of job negligence.

'Did I hear you say you'd spoken at the same conference as him? You didn't let on you knew famous people. You should have roped him in the minute you got here if he's a friend. Anything and everything to get the house reopened – isn't that what you said?'

Reaching the kitchen, Thea waved at Tina to leave the pile of paperwork she was doing at the end of the table, to come and join them. 'Sorry to disturb your account checking. We have just had an interesting call.'

'Interesting! Is that all you can say?' Mabel was incredulous. 'It's a gift from God. I don't understand why you didn't bite his hand off and have him here within the hour!'

No, you wouldn't, you stupid old bat. That man hurt my friend, Becky, badly. His history with women alone is enough for me to want to keep him away from me, and more specifically Tina. My friend is vulnerable when it comes to wealthy older men – not that I expect you'd ever understand that!

As these thoughts swam around Thea's head, she turned to Tina. 'Do you remember the first conference I attended as a speaker, not long after I joined the team in Bath?'

'I do. You were excellent.'

'Thank you.' Thea brushed the compliment away. 'And you remember that Shaun Cowlson was the keynote guest?'

'Ah, yes.'

Grateful for Tina not elaborating on the memory, but picking up from her tone that she too recalled Becky Gibson's post-relationship reports about her time with Shaun, Thea explained the situation.

Once the contents of the phone call had been relayed, Tina poured everyone coffee. 'He would bring in interest. Extra volunteers would come here just so they could meet

Shaun and get an autograph. *Landscape Treasures* is very popular.'

This statement met with fervent agreement from Diane and Mabel, who simultaneously straightened their aprons, as if expecting their archaeological hero to walk in there and then.

Thea doodled a flower against the corner of her notebook. 'You agree then, Tina, that he would be an asset and we should ask him to cut the ribbon for us on Open Day?'

'I do. Although, I'm less sure he should work here before then. If he did, it would have less impact to have him here to launch Mill Grange as a heritage centre. Better maybe, if he helps while keeping out of the public eye if he wants to. Then he can appear during Open Day as a fresh face. What do you think?'

Rather than protest as Thea had expected, Mabel seemed to like this idea even more. 'You mean us original volunteers would get him here, all to ourselves?'

For one mad second Thea thought she could see the old woman's mouth watering. 'I'm not sure we could pull that off. It is a good idea, but he's six foot four. That's a big man to hide, and word is bound to leak out. And, let's not overlook the fact that Shaun might not like that idea. Remember, I haven't even mentioned Open Day to him yet.'

Two shrill female voices rang across the room. 'Then ask him!'

Eight

It had been a relief to turn her attention to the group of students from Exeter University, who'd arrived for a tour of the house and grounds before their health and safety checks.

For a moment Thea had been worried that they wouldn't want to wade around in the damp chill of the garden with Derek, but her fears were unfounded. The chance to engage in some physical, messy and non-academic industry was welcomed by three lads eagerly pulling on wellington boots.

As she'd hoped, Derek was fantastic with them. Within minutes they were pulling up brambles and weeds while sharing risqué jokes and life histories.

'That man's a godsend.' Thea sank onto her rickety desk chair and pulled her laptop closer.

'Derek?' Tina smiled. 'He's one of the good guys. Used to be a master craftsman. I imagine he's always been good with his hands.'

'Tina!' Thea couldn't help but laugh as her friend winked at her. 'He's old enough to be your granddad.'

'I was merely appreciating our luck at having such a skilled man on site.'

'Yeah. Right.' Logging onto her emails with her habitual sense of trepidation stirring in her gut, Thea said, 'What sort of craftsman?'

'A thatcher.'

'Wow. That is a craftsman. No wonder he's so good with people.'

'What do you mean? Thatching must be a lonely job.'

'Possibly, but you would never employ a thatcher you didn't trust. And it's a long job – you'd have to get on with the residents of whichever property you were re-roofing for weeks, if not months, at a time.'

'That would explain his patience.' Tina picked up a piece of paper and waved it across the desk. 'There was a call while you were out. A Sam Philips. Said you were expecting him for his volunteer induction at two o'clock. His train has been delayed, so it'll be nearer three.'

'No problem.' Thea scanned her email inbox through narrowed eyes, as if not looking properly would ensure she didn't see the name she dreaded seeing. It wasn't there. Perhaps John had missed the broadcast after all.

'I got hold of the trustees.'

'Ah.' Thea looked up. 'I was putting off asking you about that.'

'Basically, I don't think we need to worry. Money is going to be tight and the timing is going to be tighter, but as you and I thrive on impossible situations we will win this. Mill Grange will open on time and it will be amazing.'

'Since when did we like impossible situations?'

Tina laughed. 'We're British, darling. "Spirit of the Blitz", "Never Say Die" and all that.'

Not feeling full of the derring-do Tina was expounding, Thea regarded her friend shrewdly. 'But will it be sold anyway?'

Tina tipped up her chin. 'Not while I live and breathe!'

Thea was standing in the doorway to the butler's pantry, wondering if they had enough garden equipment to supply the growing taskforce, when a taxi pulled up.

She hadn't asked people to declare their age when they applied to be volunteers, so she'd assumed Sam Philips would be over sixty-five. As he climbed from the cab she found herself staring. He clearly wasn't a retired gentleman. Far from it.

Suspecting she was gawping like a goldfish, Thea snapped her lips closed and headed towards the taxi. 'Mr Philips?'

'Sam.'

'I'm Thea. Pleased to meet you.'

As he turned around, Thea realised he was probably older than she'd initially guessed. Her assumption on seeing his short but decidedly muscular frame in garden-worn jeans and a fisherman's jumper with a ponytail tucked safely between that and his back, had been that this was a man in his early twenties. Now she saw his life-worn face, Thea added another ten years.

Sam hooked a large backpack onto his shoulder and looked at the manor. 'It's as beautiful as it looked on the television.'

'Thank you.' Thea felt the heat of the newcomer's eyes flick from her, to the house, and back again. 'Would you like to look around?'

There was the briefest hesitation, before Sam replied, 'Just outside, if that's okay with you.'

'I'm happy for all help, inside or outside, but don't you want to leave your things indoors? You can lock them in the old scullery. It's doubling as my office for now.'

'You are very kind, but I'll stick my bag in there, if that's alright.' He gestured to the pile of forks and spades lying on the floor outside the pantry. 'I'm guessing that's acting as a shed?'

'It is.' Wrong-footed, but sensing she shouldn't ask too many personal questions, Thea said, 'Let's explore the grounds. They are even more stunning than the house, in a way.'

Tina hung up the phone with a sense of satisfaction. While she hadn't managed to magic any additional time or money, she had persuaded her employers that, if they were going to have any chance of getting Mill Grange open on time, then she would be better off forgoing her usual circuit of their properties for a few weeks and mucking in at Mill Grange full time. She'd also, to her personal relief, been told her job was funded separately to Thea's, and was secure.

Feeling a little guilty that her livelihood was safe when Thea's wasn't, Tina glanced out of the little office in the kitchen garden. She was about to call out to Thea, when the latest volunteer came into view.

'Whoa!' Tina watched as Sam Philips smiled at Thea as

he bent down and pointed something out to her. Her friend looked radiant in the company of the newcomer.

'Not a pensioner then.' Tina caught herself preening her hair from her eyes, and then sharply told herself off. 'Don't be arrogant, woman! Just because a man who isn't old enough to be your grandfather has arrived on the premises, it doesn't mean he'd be interested in you. Anyway...' She took in his tatty clothes and slightly lopsided walk. 'He has a ponytail and is way too scruffy.'

Realising she was still staring at the newcomer, a contrary voice at the back of her told Tina that, while she hated long hair on men, his face sported the perfect amount of stubble. He was probably scruffy because he'd come to dig the garden. Forcing her eyes to her desk, Tina was surprised to find her pulse racing.

'If you'd like to come up to the house, we'll get the legal paperwork bit done. Then you can either crack on today, or let me know when you'd like to come, and we'll go from there.'

Sam peered up at the sky, 'You know, it's such a lovely day, would you mind bringing the forms outside? It seems a shame to miss a second of fresh air sometimes, doesn't it?'

'Absolutely.' Thea, hoping her incomprehension didn't show, added, 'No problem. If you perch on a bench in the garden, I'll fetch what we need.'

Pushing open the scullery door, Thea called to Tina, 'Could you pass me a clipboard, pen and a set of the health and safety forms, hun? My boots are filthy.'

'Sure.' Tina gathered up a set of papers. 'He looks nice.'

'Sam Philips. He's lovely. Gently spoken.' Thea lowered her voice. 'He won't come inside though. Doesn't even want the usual tour around the house.'

'That's odd.'

'Maybe he's claustrophobic.' Thea took the form. 'I'll have to adjust this so it has him cleared to work outside only, as I haven't done the "don't slip on the polished wooden stairs and trip over the rug corners because I don't have the funds for an insurance claim" speech.'

Tina stole another glimpse out of the window. 'Shame. He's the closest man to our age I've seen in months.'

'And he's lovely. He just likes fresh air. Probably been stuck in a desk job for years and is making the most of his temporary freedom.'

'You realise you've said he is lovely twice?'

'Have I? Oh, well he is.'

'How long is he volunteering for?'

Thea signalled with her forms. 'I won't know until he's filled these in, will I?'

'Right.' Tina wiped her hands down her skirt in an unusually self-conscious manner. 'Oh, I almost forget. I spoke to Malcolm again. He has agreed that I can work from here for a while. That way I can help with jobs you need an extra pair of hands for, and I can make sure we're squeezing everything we can out of our allotted budget.'

Thea beamed as a fraction of the anxiety that had been building in her shoulders melted in the face of Tina's smile. 'That's brilliant. You're a star. Thank you.' She tilted her head in Sam's direction. 'You should go and talk to him.'

'But it's a bit weird that he won't come indoors. Anyway, I absolutely don't do ponytails on men.'

'Tina! You can't just judge someone like that without even speaking to them first.'

'I know, but he isn't going to fit in with my plan, is he?' Watching through the window that looked across the garden towards Sam, Tina saw him take a penknife from his pocket and use it to prune the plant next to him while he waited. 'Anyway, why on earth would he like me? I'm a superficial nightmare.'

Thea poked her friend in the ribs. 'Well, there is that!'

'Oh!'

'I'm only joking, although I've a good mind to send you outside with the forms just so you have to talk to him. He's a bit shy, but very capable. He knows shed loads about gardening. Sam's already pointed out where the ground will work best for vegetables and where for flowers.'

'And you believed him.'

'Because I've seen the old plans. I know he's right.'

'Oh.'

'You've got to get past this older rich bloke thing, you...'

The ring of the landline stopped Thea's delving into Tina's love life. 'Now you're going to have to take the forms out to Sam for me. That's Shaun Cowlson's number. If I don't answer, Mabel and Diane will lynch me.'

'Thea?'

Shaun yelled down the line, forcing Thea to lift the receiver from her ear. 'You don't have to shout. I can hear you.'

'Oh, sorry. The line was so crackly last time I thought I'd shout louder.'

Thea leant against the scullery sink so she could watch Tina and Sam through the window. 'How can I help?'

'I wanted to accept your offer to formally open Mill Grange to the public.'

Thinking she must have misheard him, Thea said, 'Sorry, the line must be playing up after all, could you repeat that?'

'My agent received a lovely message from you accepting my offer to volunteer for the next few weeks and asking me to open the manor on the 4th August.'

As she watched Sam read the forms, and Tina trying hard not to make it obvious she was looking at him with open curiosity, Thea's mind filled with murderous thoughts towards Mabel. It had to have been her. No one else would have the nerve to ring Shaun's agent just to get what she wanted.

'The thing is,' Shaun went on, 'my agent says I can't do the 4th August. The lady she spoke to said 21st July would be fine instead, so I'll open the manor then. Until then I'm….'

Thea was aware Shaun was still talking, but she was no longer listening.

21st July… that's two weeks earlier than planned. That's ridiculous. No, it's impossible…

'Is five o'clock okay?'

'Five o'clock?' Realising she was sounding unprofessional and as if she didn't know what was going on – which she didn't – Thea fell back on a familiar lie. 'Forgive me, the line cut out. Five o'clock for what on which day?'

'Today. To have my volunteer safety induction with you.'

Nine

April 8th

'How dare Mabel put me in this position?'

Crashing onto her desk seat, Thea glared at the list that confronted her. Every time she crossed something off it, she added at least two more tasks to the bottom.

'And this is so typical of him,' Thea muttered under her breath. 'Mr Shaun "I'm a celebrity so the world has to adjust to suit me" Cowlson. As if I didn't have enough to do. Now I've got to have another battle of wills with Mabel. Wasting time I don't have explaining why we can't possibly take two weeks less on the restoration and…'

'Hi there, I just wondered if you knew when…' As Diane pushed open the office door, she caught sight of the project leader's face and stopped dead. 'You okay, Thea? You look cross.'

'Cross? Cross doesn't even come close I'm…' Realising she was in danger of shouting, Thea hastily calmed her voice. 'But not with you, Diane. Forgive me. How can I help?'

'I wondered if Shaun had called to confirm what time he was coming? We'd hate to miss his arrival.'

Thea stared at Diane. She couldn't believe this. A few days ago she'd dared to think she was making headway with the volunteers at Mill Grange. Now nothing seemed further from the truth.

'*You* knew he was coming today?'

'Yes.' Diane looked uneasy.

'Well, I didn't. Not until he called me a few minutes ago. No one saw fit to tell me. Just as no one saw fit to inform me they'd phoned Mr Cowlson's agent, on my behalf, in the first place.'

'You didn't know?' Diane's expression creased into a crosshatch of worry lines.

'I did not.' Thea took a deep breath. There was no point in shooting the messenger, or whatever the correct metaphor was for this situation. 'Perhaps you could do me a favour, Diane?'

'I'll try.'

'Can you round up the volunteers that are here? Derek is in the garden with the students. I'm not sure where Mabel is. I think the Biggleswaite sisters were planning to come in, although I haven't checked the sign-in sheet for an hour or two, so they might not have arrived. Then there's Tina and the new guy, Sam.'

Unsettled by a quietly seething Thea, Diane didn't argue. 'Where would you like everyone to gather?'

Remembering Sam's request to stay outside, Thea said, 'On the drive, by the butler's pantry in ten minutes. Please.'

★

'Diane said you'd called an emergency meeting. What's going on?' Tina stuck her head around the office door in time to see Thea throw a heap of paper into the recycle bin with the force of an erupting volcano.

'I may or may not be about to kill Mabel. The more people around to prevent that happening, the better.' Thea dragged on her boots. 'What time is it?'

'Just gone four.'

'Less than an hour! Typical, bloody Shaun Cowlson.'

'Shaun? Did you decide to accept his offer of help then?'

'No, I didn't. As helpful as his level of experience would be, the number of people who'd pitch up here that don't want to volunteer, but do want to hang around so they can grab an autograph would be counterproductive.'

'So, how come he's…?'

'Mabel.' Stamping out of the scullery, hoping her anger wouldn't dissolve into a heap of apologetic embarrassment until after she'd said what needed saying, Thea continued to fume.

Jogging to keep up as Thea stomped along, Tina laid a placating hand on her friend's shoulder. 'Presumably Shaun doesn't know he's inconveniencing us if you didn't speak to him yourself?'

Her insides fizzed with indignation. 'That's no excuse. He's in the business, he knows exactly how long restoration takes!'

Tina held back from pointing out that Shaun had no idea how long this project had been ongoing, so couldn't possibly know when their end date was supposed to have been.

Derek was waiting in the driveway with Diane. Mabel

was walking from the direction of the stables and a wary-looking Sam stood at the very back of the group. Clearing her throat nervously, Diane said, 'Umm… none of the others are on site at the moment, Thea.'

Reminding herself that her job and the future boost to the village economy could depend on this, Thea gripped her latest list so hard it crinkled.

'First, my apologies to Sam. I had intended to introduce you to everyone over a cup of tea and some of Tina's most excellent lemon cake tomorrow. However, my hand has been forced into holding this impromptu meeting.' She turned to address the remainder of the small gathering. 'Sam will be helping us in the gardens and woodland. Sam, this is Derek, Diane and Mabel. Tina you've met. Ethel, Edna, Alice and Bill will be here later today or tomorrow.'

As Sam raised a hand in silent greeting to the group, Thea kept talking. She didn't dare stop, because if she did, she knew her inbuilt desire to avoid altercations at all costs would take over.

'Someone has seen fit to ring the agent of the TV archaeologist, Shaun Cowlson, and invite him to start volunteering here from today and to open the manor for us.'

Derek and Tina's eyes fell on Mabel. Diane kept her gaze fixed on the gravel, while Sam observed the unfolding tableau with inquisitive silence.

'While every extra pair of hands is required to get Mill Grange up and running, what we don't have time for is the number of *Landscape Treasure* fans that a celebrity's presence would bring here – people who wish to loiter rather than help. Also – and this is the crucial point here – that same person has taken it upon themselves to agree to

Mr Cowlson opening the manor, not on 4th August as the trustees requested, but on 21st July!'

'What?!' Tina was aghast. 'That's insane, there's just no way—'

'It gets worse.' Thea felt her cheeks start to colour crimson as her instinct to sidestep confrontation tried to stop her talking; but now she'd started her mouth had taken on a life of its own. 'I've spoken to one of the junior trustees. Apparently they're delighted that we are ahead of schedule, despite what Tina and I told them. Can you imagine how untrustworthy we're going to appear when I call them to explain that this is not the case? At best, it looks as if I have been making out Mill Grange needs longer to work on than quoted, at worse it looks as if Tina and I have been lying to our employers.'

Tina went pale as the silence that greeted Thea's was underlined when she added, 'As if this isn't bad enough, it has come to my attention today that if we can't reach our goal in time, and on budget, the house and grounds will be sold and never open to the public at all. This was something I was planning to discuss with everyone at a group meeting tomorrow.'

The communal gasp was cut short by Mabel breaking her crab-apple silence. 'That's ridiculous. They wouldn't dare! Anyway, they would have told me when—'

'When you told them about Shaun coming? Well, you're good at phone calls, Mabel, why don't you ring the trustees back and find out?' Knowing she sounded childish, Thea carried on, 'And now, I have to leave the jobs I'd scheduled for the rest of the day to play nursemaid to a celebrity.'

Catching Derek's reassuring eye, Thea adopted a less

combative tone. 'You guys have been great. What you've done is fantastic, but even with the extra folk due to help we were pushing it for opening in August. I've already had to dismiss things like saving the big lean-to greenhouse. If the Open Day has to be two weeks earlier than arranged, even more will have to go. Perhaps the entire mill building will have to be abandoned in favour of the manor.'

Not waiting for this news to sink in, Thea turned on her heels, with the parting words, 'I would very much appreciate it if you'd all leave by five o'clock so that I can show our unexpected guest around in peace. I would also appreciate it if word of Mr Cowlson's presence here did *not* leak out.'

As Thea passed Derek, she heard him mumble, 'Well done, St George.'

With her pulse galloping around her system, her face red and her head thumping, Thea sat at the kitchen table and started to scratch red lines across her plans for the rest of the day. Wishing confrontation didn't always make her feel ill and guilty, even when it was justified, she took some calming breaths. Thea couldn't believe she'd just said all that out loud rather than letting it stew privately in her mind as usual. She wouldn't blame Sam if he picked up his holdall and left there and then.

Thea closed her eyes. *This is your fault John! If you hadn't come to Bath I'd be sitting in my little office there, sorting out artefact exchanges, cataloguing new acquisitions and chatting to the statue of Minerva in the corner.*

The kitchen door opened and Tina stuck her head around

the door. 'Can I come in, or would you rather be on your own?'

'It's safe, I've calmed down.'

Tina waved the kettle up in an unnecessary gesture to see if her friend wanted coffee. 'I've never seen you like that. You were fantastic. How do you feel?'

'Ready to curl into a ball and hide under the bed until it all goes away. I can't stop shaking.' Thea lifted her hands, which were quivering as if she'd got a severe case of stage-fright.

'Here, have some water while I boil the kettle.' Slipping onto the seat opposite, Tina pushed the water jug and a glass nearer her friend. 'I know this is a silly question in light of what you said outside, but has Mabel really arranged for Shaun to open the manor two weeks early and cleared it with the board?'

'Yep. I'd better phone them and explain she was being overzealous.'

'Hell!' Tina was stunned. 'I'm not sure talking to the Trust will work.'

'I have to try. Then when Shaun arrives, I'll say thanks but no thanks to his offer of help.' Thea shook her head. 'I can't believe Mabel's put me in this position. It's so embarrassing.'

'Why don't you deal with Shaun and I'll call Malcolm in the morning. He won't be there now or I'd be on the phone already. It's my job to deal with the trustees after all.' Tina played her right pigtail in her fingers. 'Do you want me to help with Shaun's tour?'

'Thanks, but I'll be okay,' Thea reassured her friend. 'How did you get on with Sam?'

'He's very quiet. Every time I asked him a question he dodged it and talked about the gardens instead.'

'What did you ask him?'

'Normal things. Where he'd come from, what work he was escaping and stuff.'

'Maybe he's extremely private.'

'Maybe he's an escaped prisoner or something.'

'Don't be ridiculous!'

'Well, he might be.'

'If he is, he's an escaped prisoner who knows a lot about gardening, so he can stay.'

Tina unhooked her bag from her chair. 'Are you absolutely sure you don't want me to stay? All I'd have to do is make a quick call and I can stop here overnight.'

Noting the mild heightening of colour on Tina's cheeks, Thea cocked her head to one side. 'A quick call? Have you got a date?'

'Well, umm, yes.'

Thea's eyes widened. 'Really? That's great. Why didn't you say? I'd have left off going on about Sam.'

Tina shifted her bag further up her arm. 'I thought you might laugh.'

Thea propped herself against the edge of the table. 'I'd never laugh at you. With you certainly, but never *at* you. What's the lucky chap like?'

'His name's Leon, but I don't know what he's like. Not yet.'

'How come you... ah, Internet dating?'

'Yeah.' Tina tugged at her pigtails. 'Why aren't you smirking?'

'Because it's a good idea. You're braver than I am. I'd

started to think about joining a dating site, but then John re-arrived and my life tilted in a rather different angle than I was expecting.'

Tina beamed. 'You were? And you aren't saying that to be nice?'

'Thousands of people find their partners that way now. One of my colleagues at the museum met his wife that way. Seeing them together, it's inconceivable to think they may never have met otherwise. They just fit somehow.'

'That's good. Maybe that's how I'll feel tomorrow.'

'This is a first date, then?'

'Yes. I've had a few that haven't worked. I've told myself this is the last chance on this site. If it's a disaster I'll try a different one.'

'Which one is it?'

Tina blushed. 'Superior Singles.'

Thea couldn't help but grin. 'Leon wouldn't be an older guy with a bit of money in the bank, would he?'

'You wouldn't be laughing at me, would you?' Tina smiled despite herself.

'As if!' Thea stuck out her tongue playfully, adding, 'Just make sure you have someone who can rescue you if you need to. I'd offer, but I'd probably be in the wrong place in the house to get your call.'

'Don't worry; my housemate has my back on this.'

'Off you go then. Enjoy your silver fox.'

Ten

As soon as Tina had gone, Thea dashed upstairs to her room. Casting aside her curiosity about Tina's dating experiences, and vowing to ask her about them soon, she forced herself to focus on the matter in hand. If she was going to show Shaun around, she didn't want to do so looking as if she spent the day wading in compost. Her jeans were still damp from her earlier walk in the gardens, and the cloying denim sticking to her legs was doing nothing to improve her mood.

Stripping off, Thea stuffed her work clothes in a corner to be dealt with later, and tugged on her final pair of clean trousers and her warmest jumper.

Ruffling her hair into slightly less of a nest state, she risked a glance in the mirror. Accepting she'd been better off not knowing how tired she looked, Thea dashed downstairs so she didn't miss the expected knock on the front door.

Sitting at the foot of the stairs, resting her pad on her

knees, Thea started to write another list. Not one for the improvement of the house and grounds, but one for herself.

She urgently needed to discover where the nearest launderette was, and then she had to start house-hunting. If Tina had stumbled across her bolthole, it was only a matter of time before one of the volunteers did. Although Thea had been careful to keep the attics off the areas of the house and grounds that required attention, she couldn't guarantee Mabel wouldn't ride roughshod over those plans.

The knock on the door came at exactly five o'clock.

Suddenly nervous, Thea gripped her list to her chest and opened the door to find Shaun Cowlson running a reverential hand over the stone mullion running round the doorway.

'Mr Cowlson, how good of you to come.'

'Shaun, please.'

She nodded. 'Thea. Would you like to come in?'

'I'd be delighted.' Shaun's trademark giant stride crossed the Mill Grange threshold with puppy-like exuberance. 'To tell you the truth I've wanted to have a nose around this place ever since I came across it on a listed properties website years ago. I've never been in the area long enough to make the necessary plans. Then I saw you on the local news. It felt like providence.'

'You saw me on the TV?'

Shaun flashed Thea a grin. 'I told you on the phone I did, and very professional you were too.'

'Oh.' Thea didn't know what else to say.

'As soon as I caught a glimpse of you on screen my curiosity got the better of me. I'd assumed you were going to talk about the Roman Baths.' He held his hands up to the intricately carved wooden porch roof. 'I had no idea your career had changed direction.' Amazed that Shaun not only knew who she was, but that he'd registered where she worked, Thea felt uneasy, until she reminded herself that not all men acted like John Sommers.

Intrigued by how lively Shaun's eyes were as they darted over every inch of the porch's floor, ceiling, walls and furniture, Thea stepped into the main hallway to give him more space. As she watched him, she found herself remembering the conference they'd spoken at all those years ago. The same conference at which he'd broken her friend's heart.

As Shaun reached the bottom step of the wide wooden staircase, he scrunched up his nose. 'Why does Mill Grange smell like a pickled onion?'

Thea couldn't help but laugh at his expression. 'That would be Mabel, or at least, the result of Mabel's labours.'

'Mabel Hastings? The lady who called my agent?'

'Yes.'

Shaun broke off from his loving caress of the balustrade's varnished wood. 'That was a rather loaded "yes".'

Knowing she was being given an opening into the issue of Mabel's accidental invitation to change the Open Day date, Thea dived in. 'Mabel is one of the main volunteers here. She's enthusiastic and umm, a little high-handed.'

'Ah.' Shaun smiled. 'One of those.'

'One of those?'

'Committee mafia. She'll be lost once the manor is finished, unless she finds another project.'

'Oh believe me, there isn't a committee within twenty miles that hasn't got her hand at the helm.'

Shaun stopped in the act of picking up a vase and examining the date stamp on the bottom. 'You did know she'd invited me over, didn't you?'

'To be honest, no, I didn't.' Thea found she couldn't meet Shaun's eyes as she went on. 'Not that I don't appreciate your offer of help, and I'm more than happy to show you round, but the thing is…'

Shaun's bright gaze dulled as he sat on the bottom stair and patted it so Thea would sit next to him. 'You don't want the baggage that comes with having a so-called celebrity in the manor.'

The practicality of his statement took Thea by surprise. She found herself blustering, 'It's not that, it's just that there is so much to do and every pair of hands is welcome, especially when they belong to someone as knowledgeable as you… but…'

'You think I'll be more trouble than I'm worth.'

Dwarfed by his tall, bulky frame, Thea felt the tension that had knotted her shoulders earlier return. 'I didn't say that. But we have so little time, and even less money and…'

Shaun's eyebrows knotted. 'You didn't think I'd ask to be paid to help, did you?'

Surprised, as the idea hadn't crossed her mind, Thea shook her head. 'Not for a second. It's the fan thing that bothers me.' Unsure how she'd lost control of this situation so quickly, Thea dragged a hand through her hair, returning it to its usual tangled mess. 'I would love you to help. We all would, but there isn't time to deal with the fanbase you'd bring with you and—'

'Had it crossed your mind that many of my fans are

only fans because they are passionate about history and archaeology? They couldn't give two hoots about me personally. And that's how I like it.'

'I thought…' Thea's cheeks stung with embarrassment.

'You didn't think at all. You assumed I'd endanger the project and not help it.' Shaun dug his hands into his combat trouser pockets. 'Perhaps I should look around on my own. If you'll excuse me.'

Shaun had leapt up the wide corner staircase before Thea had the chance to open her mouth again. *How did that happen?*

With a growing sensation that she'd completely lost her grip on Mill Grange, and on her ability to manage people in general, Thea sat very still. She could hear Shaun's feet moving around the bathroom above her.

I haven't even mentioned the Open Day date fiasco yet.

Gripping her pad so tightly it dug in to her palms, Thea didn't know what to do. Did she sit there and let him explore alone as he'd requested, or did she go after him and apologise?

The sound of Shaun moving out of the bathroom and into the adjacent bedroom was followed by a low whistle of appreciation from above. Whatever the circumstances, he was clearly enjoying what he was seeing.

Suddenly remembering what her friend Becky had told her about Shaun having a quick temper, Thea swallowed. *Why should I feel guilty? He hasn't given me a chance to explain. Anyway, I didn't dig this hole in the first place, Mabel did.*

Wiping the perspiration from her palms Thea went upstairs. Whatever happened, she didn't want him helping himself to a peep in the attics.

Shaun was in the third bedroom peering out of the window at the garden and woodland beyond. Hovering in the doorway, Thea had a sensation of trespassing.

'You can come in, I won't bite your head off.' Shaun gave her an apologetic smile. 'Forgive me. I get tired of people assuming I'm some kind of luvvie. I'm just an archaeologist who landed a dream job. That's all.'

'I should apologise too. I've no excuse except a very trying day and, if I'm honest, a sense that I've bitten off more than I can chew.'

Shaun said nothing, but gestured for Thea to join him at the window. 'Just look at that view. If that doesn't make you feel better, then I don't know what will.'

Finding herself squashed up next to the archaeologist, Thea agreed. 'It was the view that convinced me to take the job.'

'A sideways step for you away from the Roman Baths?'

'Very much so, although I did study industrial architecture and conservation in my final year at university, so I haven't come into this completely cold.'

'Why the move? You're a good Romano British historian. Military buildings and Romano British society are your bag if I remember rightly?'

Amazed Shaun had taken notice of her specialism, Thea continued to stare out of the window. 'I was looking for a new challenge. My friend Tina is the Exmoor Heritage Trust's business liaison officer. She told me about the job and I wanted to get my career rebooted without distractions.'

'Distractions?'

'Oh you know, a private life and stuff. At the time it seemed too good an opportunity to miss.'

Accepting Thea's side-stepping of a discussion about her personal life, Shaun smiled. 'But not anymore?'

'I'm sorry?'

'You're wishing you'd never come here. This Mabel you mentioned – more trouble than she's worth?'

Thea saw the twinkle in his eye and realised he must be used to handling people like Mabel. 'It isn't Mabel, not really. She and her friends have done marvels here.'

'Despite the vinegar?'

'Indeed. But the trustees have discovered an error in their accounts made quite a while ago. It was a simple mistake anyone could have made, but it means that, rather than save the house and open it to the public, it might have to be sold, restored or not.'

'That would be a tragedy.'

'I think so.'

Shaun was quiet for a moment. 'For you personally as well as the village of Upwich.'

'My job would go, I know that, but I'm more worried about the house right now.'

He turned to Thea, his eyes burnt shrewdly into hers. 'I believe you mean that.'

Thea grabbed the chance to explain the remainder of the problem. 'The Open Day was supposed to be on 4th August.'

'So I heard, but I can't do then, so it was moved forward.'

'And as a consequence, the trustees want me to get everything done, with a fortnight's less time, and under budget, or it will sell. No question.'

'Oh hell.'

'Quite.'

'And if you do pull off this miracle?'

94

'It might still be sold anyway.'

'You did what?'

'Don't speak to me in that tone of voice, Bert!'

Mabel hadn't even taken her coat and shoes off before she'd grabbed a carrot from the vegetable rack and started chopping it into perfect, angry, circles.

'If you don't put that knife down you're going to have a finger off.' Bert laid a gentle hand on his wife's arm and removed the knife as if he was talking down a criminal. 'Now tell me again from the beginning.'

'I've already told you! Why don't you keep your hearing aids in?'

Used to his wife's short temper, Bert usually shrugged it off. Fifty-five years of marriage had taught him when it was personal and when Mabel was letting off steam. This felt different. He could feel her righteous indignation bouncing off the walls – a sign he recognised as meaning she'd overstepped the mark and pride was stopping her from apologising.

Dropping the knife into the sink, Bert counted to ten in his head and then said, 'Take off your shoes and coat and sit down.'

'I'm busy.'

Repeating himself, Bert pointed at the kitchen table. 'Take... off... your... shoes and your coat and sit... down.'

Grumbling under her breath, Mabel did as she was told.

'You went over Thea's head and contacted the trustees.'

'Someone had to. That girl was willing to let a God-given opportunity pass us by.'

'If I understand the situation correctly from the word down the pub, Thea has come in like a breath of fresh air, and things are getting done.'

'Thanks to my idea of a television appearance.'

'Granted. That was an excellent idea. But that doesn't change the fact that Thea has been employed to sort out the manor. She has the final word. This is her livelihood you're messing with.'

'Her livelihood...' Mabel frowned. 'Don't be daft, Bert. Once the house is opened to the public she'll be the manager. She's set for life.'

'Not if they sell the house, she isn't!'

'But—'

'No.' Bert covered his wife's hand with his own. 'Girl, I love you to pieces, and goodness knows when you set your mind to something it jolly well gets done, but this isn't your party. If you can't sort this mess out you will have to live with the fact you've possibly lost Thea her job, and the community their manor house to a private buyer, probably from London or somewhere.'

'But—'

'But nothing.' Bert got up. 'I'm going to make a cup of tea, and first thing tomorrow morning you are going to phone the trustees and put the record straight.'

Eleven

Tina recognised Leon as soon as he swung his long legs out of the silver BMW in the far corner of the restaurant's car park.

Breathing a sigh of relief as she noted he had used a current photograph for his profile, rather than one ten or more years out of date, she brushed a stray hair from her black velvet jacket.

Stepping further into the shadows where she'd been waiting, Tina watched Leon walk confidently through the main doors. His head was held high. He looked neither left nor right. Tina wondered if his lack of curiosity about his surroundings meant he knew the restaurant well.

How many other women has he wined and dined here over the years?

Leon certainly had the whole 'George Clooney' thing going on that she'd hoped for. His charcoal suit was designer, and smart but not too smart. His salt-and-pepper hair was cut into the back of his neck and his shoes positively shone.

If he was fifty-two years old as his profile claimed, he wore it well.

Tina had taken only one step forwards when she stopped and sank back into the shadow of the trees that lined the car park. When she'd checked her reflection before leaving her flat she'd felt good. Silver heels, a tight-fitting white V-neck top teamed with her favourite floral velvet jacket, and a smart pair of black satin trousers. Her glossy yellow hair hung around her shoulders, and her makeup had been carefully applied. Suddenly she felt unusually insecure in her appearance. Leon looked like the stuff of fantasies. Would he take one glance at her and walk out?

Her eyes strayed across the sea of Mercedes, Jags and BMWs to her fifteen-year-old Fiesta. It was lurking, as if ashamed of itself, in a dark corner of the car park. What would Leon make of that if he saw it? Everyone on Superior Singles was supposed to be successful. For the first time since she'd joined the site, hoping to find the financially secure man of her dreams, Tina realised that perhaps her version of having made a success of her life wasn't the same as the owners of vehicles such as these.

Her two previous Internet dates had been with established businessmen. Both were prosperous, but increasingly tired of having nothing in their lives but work. Leon, on the other hand, had the air of a man who'd reached the level of job security which meant he may not have driven himself here. Trying to remember which side of the car she'd seen him get out of, Tina was considering creeping around to see if a chauffeur was in the driver's seat waiting for their meal to end, when an image of Sam arrived in her head.

Shaking the tatty gardener from her mind and telling

herself that Leon was the sort of man she'd been craving for years, Tina strode from the shadows. She only had two minutes until fashionably late morphed into properly late. Telling herself off for making assumptions about Leon before they'd even said hello, she pushed her shoulders back and moved forward.

Acknowledging the doorman with a bat of her elongated eyelashes, the restaurant's glass doors were dutifully swung open on her behalf. Seconds later a crisply attired receptionist greeted her with a white-toothed smirk and a swish of an expensively manicured hand before leading her to Leon.

Classic steel-grey eyes, strong cheekbones, clean-shaven and a nice discreet smile. Leon was the stuff of her late-night fantasies. *Why the hell is this man single? What's wrong with him?*

Rising to his feet, Leon gave an approving nod that made Tina's pulse leap from a trot to a canter.

'Leon?' Tina felt a grin break out across her face, but despite her physical attraction to the man, it didn't feel real. It felt like a work smile. The sort of upturn of the lips indicating good customer service rather than genuine pleasure. Tina was puzzled as to why her brain wasn't gushing in delightful tandem with her body. *It's because you don't know him yet and you're nervous.*

Keen to break the silence so it didn't have the slightest chance of becoming uncomfortable, Tina was about to comment on his choice of dining location, when a waiter swooped between them. Flapping around with pure white linen napkins, the wine menu and offerings of nibbles, which he called 'hors d'oeuvres', he left Tina in no doubt that he was an authentic Frenchman rather than an English guy paid to act out the whole cliché.

As the nerves she'd been so determined to keep hidden began to stir, Tina distracted herself from this unnecessary show by surveying her surroundings. She admired the simplicity of the place. It was a million miles from the clutter of Mill Grange and its hotchpotch of ornaments and paintings which came from a jumble of periods in time and accompanying acetic acid ambience.

Here there wasn't a single item out of place. Even the cutlery appeared to have been lined up with the assistance of a tape measure and theodolite. The art was sparse, incomprehensible, and clearly had come with unjustifiably big price tags. The walls were a crisp duck-egg blue and the chairs were considerably more comfortable to sit in than their skeleton-like twisted metal frames suggested. As she looked closer, Tina found herself slipping from admiration to cynicism, thinking how much effort had gone into making this place appear exclusive.

Leon still hadn't spoken, but all the time the waiter was fussing about, he'd kept his eyes levelled on Tina. She wished she knew what he was thinking. His deadpan expression gave away nothing as he ordered wine for both of them, before she could tell him she was driving.

You're an adult. There is nothing to say you have to drink the wine he has ordered without consulting you.

Put out, but telling herself she could drink the water in the carafe on the table, Tina decided she'd have to make allowances for Leon. He was used to being in control. Might it not, just for an hour or two, be nice to have someone make all the decisions for her?

By the time she had opened the menu the waiter had pressed into her hands, Tina managed to direct a fresh smile towards her companion.

'I like your shoes.'

As opening lines went, it was not the one Tina had expected. *Does that mean he doesn't like the rest of me? Oh God, does he have a 'thing' for feet?*

'Thank you.' Tina glanced down at the glittery heels that displayed the gentle curve of her feet while affording a glimpse of her turquoise painted toenails. 'They're my favourite pair.'

Seemingly satisfied with the answer, Leon gestured to the menu. 'Do you understand what is written here, or would you like me to translate for you?'

Biting the insides of her cheeks together so she didn't respond to his patronising tone, Tina studied her wood-bound menu. Everything was in French.

'I'm fine, thank you.' Disregarding her intention to ignore the alcohol, Tina took a hefty swig from her wine glass. 'I'll have the *cigares de légumes croquants et algues nori en tempura* to start with please, followed by *le pressé de bœuf laqué*. Thank you.'

Enjoying the tiny rise to Leon's eyebrows as he realised she could speak and read French, Tina watched while he clicked his fingers towards the waiter. She would have winced in embarrassment if they'd been anywhere else, but all the other customers were acting in a similarly high-handed manner.

As Leon ordered the same meal as her, Tina picked up a tiny piece of bread and crumbled it in her fingers. It was so crispy it could have masqueraded as a crouton; perhaps that was what it was supposed to be. No one had spoken since the shoe comment beyond the requirement of ordering food, so Tina fell back on the classic blind date opening line.

'Have you been on many dates via the website?'

Leon was appalled. 'Shhh.' His eyes skimmed the room, as if he was afraid someone had heard Tina. 'That we have to stoop to such methods to secure companionship is hardly a matter for discussion in a public place!'

Tina, her own voice low, couldn't believe what she was hearing. 'You're ashamed of being here with me?'

'Come on, you are clearly an intelligent woman. You must see how using such sites or apps signals an element of failure in our otherwise successful lives.' Sitting back up, the stiffness of his movement acting as a very definite signal that that part of the conversation was over, Leon added, 'Remind me, what it is you do?'

Struggling not to gawp like a bewildered goldfish, Tina found herself replying on autopilot. 'I'm the business liaison manager for the Exmoor Heritage Trust.'

'A responsible job for someone so young.'

'Yes.' Tina suddenly had the urge to giggle. She could just imagine how Thea would react when she told her about this in the morning. 'I'm currently helping renovate a Victorian manor, near Upwich.'

Leon's eyebrows rose, 'I saw an appeal about that on the news. That wasn't you though?'

'That was Thea. She's in charge of the renovation as a whole, whereas I work on a broader range of properties and sites.'

'An interesting way to spend your life, I'm sure.' Leon did not sound sure at all.

'How about you? Your profile…' Tina changed her words as she saw Leon's brow darken. 'You said that you were involved in property.'

'That is a rather loose way of putting it.'

'Then tighten it up.'

Leon was spared expressing his surprise at her curt response by the arrival of the waiter with their starters.

Not caring what his views on her etiquette, or lack thereof might be, Tina punched her fork into the nearest piece of tempura. 'Property in the UK or abroad?'

'In the States and Scotland.'

'To cater for the oil industry?'

'Yes.' Again Leon didn't hold back from a show of surprise. 'How did you work that out?'

Tina felt her hackles rising. She couldn't remember the last time she'd met someone who made her angry and defensive like this. 'Well, I have a brain, and I have friends who live in Aberdeen. They are always complaining how property magnates have scooped up all the affordable housing and turned it into unaffordable housing.'

Leon levelled his stern gaze on Tina, but said nothing. Suddenly he looked less like George Clooney and more like a villain from an Alfred Hitchcock movie. *What the hell am I doing here? Why did I think this was the sort of man I wanted?*

With one more mouthful of her delicious starter, Tina picked her napkin off her lap and got to her feet. 'If you'll excuse me.'

As she walked across the restaurant's heel-echoing floor, Tina's heart beat so fast she thought it might break free of her ribs. She wasn't sure where she was going. To the toilets or out of the restaurant, never to return.

It wasn't until she was sitting in her car, glad she'd only had a couple of mouthfuls of wine so could drive, that she registered she'd walked out on Leon. She was prepared to bet that was a first for him.

'It will bloody well do him good!' With her pulse still galloping around her veins, and not looking back in case Leon had sent a waiter to search for her (no way would he go after her himself), Tina drove into the night to find the comfort of a Chinese takeaway and a night with a boxset of *Poirot*.

Twelve

April 9th

There was a message in Tina's neat script waiting on the scullery table when Thea reached her office the following morning.

Malcolm wants to see you in person. Today at 11 a.m. in the Taunton office. Take these.

Thea followed the arrow Tina had drawn to a file of accounts.

'Bang goes another day's work on the manor.' Gripping the mug of coffee she'd carried through from the kitchen, Thea opened the file as she finished reading the note.

PS. Sorry I didn't hunt you down in person. I thought you should lie in after the shocks of yesterday. Gone out for coffee and biscuits.

PPS. I'll tell you about the date later.

While wondering how Tina had got on with her silver fox, Thea scowled at the figures. 'If these are supposed to work in Mill Grange's favour, I'm going to have to wear a low-cut top.'

'Sounds good to me.' Derek gave her an impish wink as he came into the scullery. 'Thought I'd come and see if you were alright.' He gestured to the seat opposite Thea and sat down. 'Mabel has gone too far this time. Even Diane is giving her a wide berth this morning.'

'It's not so much that she asked Mr Cowlson to help us, it's the fact she didn't speak to me first. These things should be group decisions and this one in particular could chime the death toll for Mill Grange as a public heritage centre.'

Thea looked at Derek's grave face. All signs of his previous flirting had disappeared under a cloud of concern. 'Do you want me to carry on outside with the kids, or are we calling a halt? I'd like to keep going if I can. I had a great time with them yesterday.'

'I bet they loved working with you. I'm sorry I had to stop things before you lit your bonfire.'

'No matter. We'll do it this morning. It's cooler today, so it'll be more welcome.'

'Thanks Derek.' Thea closed the file of numbers. 'I have to go into Taunton to try and undo the damage Mabel has done.'

'Would you like me to come? Moral support and all that.'

'I appreciate the offer, but I'd be happier with you here keeping an eye on things.'

Derek nodded. 'Can I ask how you got on with Shaun Cowlson last night?'

★

As she drove across the open ground of Exmoor, alert for stray sheep and ponies, Thea reflected on the previous evening. Despite a shaky start, it hadn't been anything like she'd assumed it would be. For that matter, Shaun was nothing like she remembered him. Although, now she thought about it, most of what she knew about him she'd gleaned from Becky, who in a state of broken-hearted hurt, may not have been a terribly reliable witness.

After they'd cleared the air, and Thea had confessed her fears for the manor's future, Shaun had leapt from room to room like an over-excited puppy. On arrival in each new space, he'd stop, statue-still, taking in everything he could. His examination was almost forensic as he swivelled 360 degrees on the spot so as not to miss a thing. He'd tapped walls, knocked on the woodwork and waxed lyrical about the manor's original functioning Victorian baths and flush toilets.

Thea had felt like a tour guide who'd learnt the script, only to find the audience not only knew all the words, but had memorised the back notes and accompanying stage plans. Shaun talked with enthusiasm about mullions and mortise and tenon joints, soldering techniques and wallpaper restoration. 'So much for my assumption he only knew about buried things,' Thea told a passing sheep.

Shaun's excitement had been contagious, and she'd quickly forgotten that his presence as a volunteer could cause more problems than it solved.

Slowing to let a ewe and her two lambs meander across the road, Thea recalled her sense of surprise when she'd realised they'd visited every nook and cranny of Mill Grange manor, bar her room, which she'd claimed to be locked and victim to a lost key. Two hours had passed in a blur of ideas, appreciation and suggestions concerning how to get the best from each room on the smallest possible budget.

After such a productive tour, it had seemed natural to offer Shaun coffee while they'd swapped restoration ideas. Mill Grange had looked different as she'd seen it through his eyes. The sense that saving the house was perhaps possible after all had wrapped around her like a warm blanket.

'No wonder he's so good at bringing historical sites across on the television.' Thea double-checked for stray animals in the gorse at the side of the road as she negotiated a hairpin bend. 'If only he could stay as some sort of private advisor rather than an onsite volunteer.'

When the time had come to turn down Shaun's offer of help, she hadn't been able to do it. It would have been like punching a kitten, albeit a six-foot-four kitten with gangly limbs and large clear hazelnut eyes.

Thea's phone burst into life as she pulled her Mini into a miraculously empty parking space on the outskirts of Taunton, only a few minutes' walk from the trustees' office. Not recognising the number, she answered with a cautious, 'Hello?'

'Thea, forgive the interruption when I know you're busy. I wanted to thank you for showing me round last night.'

'You're welcome, Shaun.' Thea started to search in the glove compartment, hoping she had enough change for the parking meter. 'Thank you for all your ideas and insight.'

'Are you alright? You sound a bit muffled.'

'I'm in my car. I have a meeting with the trustees this morning. You caught me fishing for parking money.'

'Ah.'

'Ah?' Thea cupped her loose change in her palm, hoping it would be enough. 'What do you mean, ah?'

'That's the other reason I was phoning.' Sounding uneasy, Shaun said, 'I was so enthralled last night that I got wrapped up in hearing your hopes for the place... I really can see it all restored to its former glory.'

Nausea rose in Thea's stomach. 'What is it you are calling to tell me?'

'I rang the Exmoor Heritage Trust people. I didn't want to be more trouble than I was worth. The last thing the house needs is a load of autograph-hunters crowding the place, when all you want is eager helpers.'

Thea felt a renewed hit of guilt at her earlier assumption that Shaun would crave the presence of his fans. 'I have to admit, as I said last night, somewhat clumsily, as much as we would love your help—'

'Absolutely. I get it. My agent told Mabel that I would only come as a volunteer if I could work quietly without fuss.'

'She didn't tell me that.' Thea closed her eyes and leant against the headrest. 'I'm beginning to wonder what else I haven't been told.'

'Ah.'

'Again with the "Ah"?' Thea checked her wristwatch. There were ten minutes until she was due to see Malcolm.

'I think you'll need to prepare yourself.' Shaun sighed.

'Please Shaun, you're freaking me out.'

'The trustees let it slip this morning, in confidence, that the house is likely to go up for sale.'

'I see.' Thea exhaled slowly.

'I'm so sorry,' Shaun rushed on, 'but even if the worst ultimately happens, I'd still like to see Mill Grange restored. I know we didn't get to see the mill building last night, but as I was driving to my accommodation I had a few ideas that might work for the old mill and—'

'You did?' Thea realised that once again her preconceptions about this man had been wrong. Despite his career, she'd pegged him as a 'rip it out and put things in' person. A moderniser rather than a restorer.

'Would you like to hear them? I mean, if you're free for dinner we could talk them over.'

A picture of Becky's tear-stained face flashed into Thea's mind as her brain tried to work out if Shaun had just asked her for a date or for a work meeting. The former was defiantly out, the latter would have to be done discreetly or the whole world would know he was in town.

'Well, I...' Thea read the clock. Five minutes until the meeting. 'Look, I have to go or I'm going to be late. Thanks for the warning, Shaun. I'll be in touch about the volunteering.'

Hanging up before he could reply, Thea knew she'd been rude not to answer his request for a discussion about the mill. Her insides lurched. 'I've been angry and downright rude three times in two days. What's happening to me?'

Her head thudded and she grabbed her bag of notes and Tina's accounts file. Having paid the exorbitant parking fee, Thea headed to the office to face another unwanted confrontation.

★

Malcolm passed her a steaming mug of coffee. 'Tina told me that a strong black cuppa would be welcome, even if nothing else I have to tell you is.'

Thea took the drink with a dip of acknowledgement. 'Does that mean you are about to impart bad news?'

Gesturing to the folder Thea had placed in front of her, Malcolm avoided the question by asking one of his own. 'Are those the figures from Tina?'

'Yes.'

'Can I see?'

'Of course.' Thea knew Tina would have presented all the numbers in the best possible light.

Malcolm opened the sheaf of paper to the summary page. 'Tina is exceptionally good at her job.'

'You sound surprised.'

'I am, but not that Tina is so capable; she's proved that time and time again. I'm surprised because these numbers are not as bleak as I'd expected.'

Determined not let her professional demeanour slip, Thea asked, 'Would you mind explaining what you mean? I'm not clear as to why I'm here. Is this to confirm the house is to be sold or to confirm that it isn't?'

Malcolm closed the folder. 'As I said when we spoke, there was a mistake that was neither Tina's nor yours. The funds to complete the restoration of Mill Grange are not as healthy as we believed.'

'What happened to them?'

'A misplaced decimal point on a spreadsheet.'

'You've got to be kidding.'

'I wish I was.' Malcolm had the good grace to be embarrassed. 'No one noticed until a few days ago. By then all the calculations, which were wrong as a consequence of the original typo, had been made and the long-term plan for the restoration designed.'

'But that was five years ago. Are you honestly telling me this clerical error has only just emerged?'

'If it wasn't for Tina's eagle eye, and her sense that something was wrong, we may never have spotted it.'

'Tina knew?'

'That there was a mistake yes, that it affected Mill Grange, no.' Malcolm pulled a piece of paper towards him and scribbled down some numbers. 'She was doing a general stock-take for me. Thank goodness she did.'

Thea massaged her temples. 'So a mistake was made in the past. What does that mean for Mill Grange right now?'

'That the budget you were given was twice as much as we have to give you.'

'Twice!' Thea felt faint.

'As this was a mistake our end, we are prepared to pull resources from other projects to help bring up the figures, but this still leaves you about £40,000 short of what's required to do a full restoration.'

Thea gulped, burning her lip on her coffee cup as she did so. 'You said Tina's figures weren't as bad as you'd thought.'

'I need to examine these properly, but if they are feasible, she might have shaved that to a deficit of £35,000.'

'Still a fortune.'

'Hence the need to sell.'

'What do the original owners think about this?'

'They washed their hands of the house years ago. It's a money pit.'

'So it will be sold despite everyone's hard work?'

'Unless you can get it finished under budget and on time, then yes.' Malcolm pushed back his seat and stretched out his legs, as if relieved he'd got the sharing of bad news over with. 'For a start, rather than holding the Open Day as a free event, you could sell tickets, plus find ways of making the manor to start paying for itself straight away… and even then…'

Thea held up a hand. 'Malcolm, are you asking me to carry on with my job, or saying that we should just tidy Mill Grange up enough for it to get the best market price? If that's the case, I can't, in all conscience expect people to continue to volunteer.'

'I'm saying that I'd like you to do everything you can to make this work. That I'd like to stand there with my fellow trustees on 21st July and watch Shaun Cowlson cut the ribbon before Mill Grange opens to the public.

'*But* if the house isn't ready and hasn't passed the relevant health and safety checks, it will have to be sold. And even then, it still might be… the mill may have to be sold as a separate building anyway.'

Feeling as though her brain was on a go slow, Thea dealt with one crumb of bad news at a time.

'Definitely the 21st July not the 4th August?'

Malcolm lost his previous apologetic tone. 'I was assured by Mrs Hastings that you were capable of getting the manor ready by then so that Mr Cowlson could open it for you. This would, as you can appreciate, take a little of the financial pressure off as well. Fourteen days less to pay for.'

'You mean fourteen days less for you to pay my wages, don't you?'

Thirteen

Turning her car into the Tarr Steps car park, Thea kept her hand on the steering wheel and the engine running, unsure if she was parking or pausing.

Exmoor stretched out in every direction. Greens and rusty bronzes vied for her attention with splotches of purple heather and blackened gorse. Erratic boulders and clumps of trees spotted the landscape with accompanying random dots of cotton-wool sheep by their sides. For once there were no other cars, no cyclists and no walkers to spoil the view. It was as if she was the only person left in the world.

Suddenly desperate to delay her return to Mill Grange in favour of uninterrupted time to think, Thea kicked off her ankle boots, reached for her faithful walking shoes and took a lungful of fresh air. She felt as if she'd run a marathon rather than been sitting in an office with her employer.

On leaving Bath the previous month, a trip to see Exmoor's most famous clapper bridge had been something she'd promised herself as compensation for leaving so much of her favourite history behind. But life at Mill Grange had been so hectic that a trip to the Tarr Steps had remained a dream.

Now she was here, Thea's rising guilt at not having contacted Tina the minute she'd left the Trust's office had reached un-ignorable proportions. By the time she reached a visitor board displaying the walking routes available, any chance of a relaxed stroll had evaporated.

Retrieving her mobile from the back pocket of her jeans, Thea was about to press Tina's number when she registered both her lack of signal and the time. It was almost one o'clock, but she didn't feel hungry. Her appetite had died with every word Malcolm had spoken.

Tracing a wistful finger along the shortest walk on the board, she told it, 'I'll just take ten minutes to say hello to the bridge today. I'll come back for a proper walk soon.'

With each clump of her boots towards the bridge, the image of Malcolm's increasingly furrowed forehead grew stronger in her mind, dissolving Thea's hope of a few minutes to clear her head.

It hadn't been until Mabel had called Malcolm in the midst of their meeting, to apologise for her error, telling him she'd been swept up in the excitement of her favourite celebrity being available for the opening, that the frosty atmosphere had started to thaw.

Amazed that Mabel had swallowed her pride and done the decent thing, it had still been hard for Thea to hear Malcolm suggest that she'd been holding out on the trustees. Had she and Tina, he wanted to know, been demanding more time than was needed to get the place ready? They were old friends after all, and could have colluded to get as much out of the Trust as possible. The accusation had hurt Thea far more than she would ever admit. She would never tell Tina.

In the end Malcolm had apologised for his suggestion, mumbling about being embarrassed about their financial error and conceding he'd overreacted. He'd also, after a few sips of coffee, accepted that it was in character for Mabel to ride roughshod over common sense in order to get something she wanted. But it hadn't changed a thing. In all likelihood the Open Day would have had to be brought forward a week or two anyway in an attempt to preserve funds, with or without Mabel's interference. At least Malcolm had been pleased about them being able to charge extra for the event's tickets now Shaun Cowlson was to be there, signing autographs and maybe giving a talk.

'I suppose that's something else I'll have to organise?' Thea told a pheasant as it hurtled across her path.

Although she wasn't sure how she felt about Shaun being a fixture of the team, Thea was absolutely certain what Mabel's reaction would be. It would be considered a victory for her interference. 'She'll be worse than ever.'

Glad no one was around to hear her talking to herself, digging her hands into her jacket pockets, Thea attempted to order the crisis into a solvable situation. 'Problem one: it is physically impossible to do what needs to be done in the time given within the budget we have.'

It didn't feel any better saying it aloud.

'Problem two: if I can't achieve a solution to problem one then I'm unemployed.' Thea's sigh turned into a contradictory cry of delight as, turning the corner, she found herself standing before the Tarr Steps clapper bridge for the first time. Its sheer simplicity took her breath away.

The un-mortared gritstone slabs that formed the bridge's platform were bigger than she'd expected. Thea couldn't imagine how they'd been positioned in place, let alone how such heavy weights had been successfully shifted by floodwater on more than one occasion. Today, the River Barle sauntered serenely beneath the slabs as if it has never caused a moment's trouble in its long existence.

Widely believed to have been in use from prehistoric times, Thea knew the stone bridge as it stood now had certainly been there at least since the medieval period. There was something magical about it. The Tarr Steps sat and waited for history to flow around it.

Walking reverently to the start of the fifty-five-metre water crossing, Thea, with a self-conscious glance to make sure no one was watching, crouched on her denim-covered knees onto the smooth stone. 'You've sat here and survived so much. A storm destroys you and you're rebuilt, a war comes and you patiently wait it out, plague arrives and you wash it away. You were here while Mill Grange was built, while it was used and when it emptied again.'

Trailing her fingers across the somehow exaggerated warmth of the weathered bridge, Thea closed her eyes as the spring breeze kissed her face. 'Any inspiration you could give me right now would be welcome.'

Backing her Mini into her usual space on the drive, Thea was in time to see Sam leaving the butler's pantry, a fearsome-looking sickle in one hand and a sack in the other.

'Disposing of a body?'

'Any particular corpse you have in mind?' A gentle grin played at Sam's lips. 'I have something to show you if you have time? I think it'll make you happy.'

'Anything that has the capacity to make me smile is always welcome.' Thea followed their latest volunteer, glad of having a reason to put off talking to Mabel.

Sam lapsed into the silence that he seemed to prefer until they reached the hinterland between the garden and woods; a tangle of brambles, fallen branches, leaves and weeds.

'Here, where the garden slopes into the wood.' He indicated a metre square area he'd cleared to what would have been grass level if the grass had had enough light to grow. 'I'm sure this must have formed part of a path, well, more of a walkway really, which led around the whole garden. Somewhere the ladies of the house could perambulate with friends.'

Dropping down so that her eyes could run the line of the path Sam was indicating with a gesture of his hands, Thea nodded. 'You're right. I have the original garden plan on my desk which has a path sketched onto it, but to say it is vague understates it. It also predates the actual construction of the garden, so it is impossible to know what was completed and what wasn't.'

'Are there no mentions of the path in the house documents?'

'There are, but the precise location isn't stated, although it seems logical to assume it spans the outer edge of the garden.' Thea felt a sense of satisfaction she'd feared would elude her at Mill Grange. 'Do you have archaeological or landscaping experience?'

'No. I just like stately homes and gardening. I've seen such paths before.'

Mentally plotting out where the path might come out on the other side of the house, Thea was delighted. 'Sam, you have no idea how timely your discovery is. Thank you.'

Without looking at her, he asked, 'You've been to the trustees?'

'Yes.' Thea kicked a stray stone into the woods. 'I owe you an apology. You'd only been here two minutes before witnessing me ranting at the volunteers. I can assure you that is not something I make a habit of.'

'I know. Tina delivered some tea an hour back.' Sam pointed to the drained mug. 'She explained the situation.' Crouching down, he stuffed handfuls of cut back brambles into a sack. 'Do we still have a manor to restore?'

'For now.'

'That was neither a yes nor a no.'

'Which is as good as it gets.' Thea looked up towards the manor. 'I would completely understand if you changed your mind about helping here.'

Sam carried on with filling the hessian sack. 'Am I right in assuming that money, or lack of, is at the root of this?'

'That's the main problem, with lack of time coming a very close second.' Thea could see Mabel moving around behind the drawing room window. She couldn't see Diane. 'I'm going to call an emergency meeting in the kitchen this evening. I was going to have one anyway, but now it's more urgent. Will you be able to come?'

Sam hesitated. 'Um, no I don't think I can. Sorry.'

'Not to worry. I appreciate it's rather last minute.' Thea

tugged at the end of her disintegrating ponytail. 'I'm sorry, Sam. I didn't even ask where you were staying.'

'Oh, not far away.' He followed Thea's eye line up to where the sun was reflecting off the manor's window panes. 'You're not going to quit though.' It was spoken as a statement rather than a question.

'No, I'm not.'

'Good. This place deserves more respect than that.'

Surprised by Sam's determined tone, Thea turned so she faced the woods. 'I've just been to the Tarr Steps. I know I shouldn't have taken the time out, but I needed space to think.'

'Always sensible.' Sam regarded the full sack of discarded undergrowth with approval. 'One of my favourite places in the whole world.'

The way Sam spoke suggested that he had seen plenty of the world to compare Exmoor's clapper bridge to. 'You're well-travelled?'

'I used to make Michael Palin look as if he wasn't trying.'

Thea was curious to know more about Sam's adventures, but his expression held up a subject closed sign so she changed the subject. 'I'd better get on.'

As she took a step towards the manor, Sam said, 'Did you know local folklore insists the clapper bridge was built by the Devil?'

'Really?'

'The tale goes that the Devil vowed to kill anyone who tried to cross his bridge in either direction. Nervous, the local population, who obviously wanted to use the bridge as they were tired of wading across the water, sent a cat across the stones. As the cat set a paw on the bridge it vanished in front of their very eyes.'

Thea laughed. 'A black cat presumably?'

'I have no hearsay on that.' Sam tied the sack shut. 'After the cat's abrupt demise, a parson was sent over – willingly or unwillingly, I couldn't say. He met with Satan in the middle of the bridge, and although he threatened and abused the parson with evil words, the churchman stood firm. Eventually the Devil gave in and allowed the local population to cross his bridge.'

'I rather love that.' Thea laughed. 'No wonder I saw no cats down there this morning. They're probably scared of being vaporised.'

'I take it the Devil wasn't sunbathing either?'

'Excuse me?'

'The tale ends with Satan adding a condition to the use of his bridge. Should he wish to sunbathe on the bridge, then no one should attempt to cross or disturb him as he relaxes.'

'You're joking?'

'Nope. It's a clause that stands to this day, so you take care next time you go thinking down by the Barle. The last thing Mill Grange needs is its esteemed leader being turned into a puff of atoms by a tan-seeking demon.'

'Right now, being vaporised feels like the easiest option.' Thea's laugh quickly curtailed as she considered the conversation she needed to have with Mabel.

'If you wanted an easy life you'd never have taken this job.' Sam spoke with a confidence in her that was both touching and disconcerting.

Thea strode back to the house, having decided not to tell Sam that she'd only taken the job because she was hoping for exactly that. Or at least, a career where she could get on with her work without worrying about her ex-boyfriend popping by every five minutes.

Fourteen

April 9th

Tina watched Sam working from the scullery window. Every now and then he flashed out of view, as he carried bundles of cut branches and brambles to the other end of the garden to be burnt later.

There was a self-contained air to the volunteer gardener which Tina couldn't put her finger on. She'd have said it was a contentedness, but somehow that didn't sit right with a man who still hadn't set foot across the threshold of the manor.

Her mind flicked to Leon. No wonder Sam had flitted through her mind while she'd sat in the restaurant last night. He was Leon's polar opposite. Un-groomed and uncaring as to the opinion of the world on the subject. Sam just was. *I bet he wouldn't see using a dating site as failure.*

Sneaking into the scullery via the back door, so she lessened the chances of encountering Mabel, Thea was relieved to find Tina there.

'Thanks for taking Sam out for a cuppa this morning. He clearly appreciated it.'

Her habitual smile strained, Tina pushed thoughts of her non-date from her mind and got straight to the point. 'What did Malcolm say? Did my accounts help?'

Thea's eyes fell on a note on her desk in Mabel's wobbly script. 'We have another volunteer?'

'What?' Tina tucked a stray blonde hair behind her ear. 'Oh yes. A bloke turned up to enquire about helping shortly after you'd left. Mabel gave him the tour as I wasn't here.'

'One thing less for us to do I suppose. Hope he's not too old to swing an axe. The rotten trees at the back of the drive need clearing before they fall on someone's car.'

'Sod that! What did Malcolm say? Come on Thea, I'm worried sick here.'

'I think we're going to need coffee for this one.' Taking off her smart jacket and top, Thea put on the oversized chunky jumper that hung across her chair and immediately felt more herself.

There was no trace of a smile on Tina's expression now. 'We're screwed, aren't we?'

'Unless you came across someone in Upwich this morning with an ability to freeze time, then it isn't looking great. Your figures were good. They did help, but…'

'Too little too late?'

'It was all I could do to convince Malcolm that we hadn't been lying about needing more money and time than we'd claimed after his conversation with Mabel and her conviction we could be ready to open on 21st July.'

'Oh hell.' Tina followed Thea to the kitchen, her need for caffeine accelerating.

'As it happens, it made no difference that Mabel interfered. The trustees are on the defensive. That financial cock-up you uncovered means we were about to have our work time shortened anyway. Ironically Mabel may have done us a favour by bringing the issue to light earlier rather than later.'

'But we're still to keep going? Malcolm didn't mention selling?'

'I'm afraid he did. We have to make Mill Grange pay for itself as soon as we can. We also have to start selling Open Day tickets. Preferably by yesterday. And even then, the house may well be sold.'

'That must mean we're to go ahead with the restoration for now then.' Tina took her coffee cup and held it like a talisman. 'Thank God we have Shaun then.'

'Assuming we still do.'

'What do you mean? Didn't the tour go well last night?'

Thea hooked the biscuit tin under her arm and grabbed her mug as they returned to the privacy of the scullery. 'It went well. Shaun loved the place.'

'So, what's the problem?'

'Problems. Plural.' Thea dunked a chocolate digestive into her mug. 'He's a television personality. If the call comes from his production team, whether his intentions to help are pure or not, then he'll be off in a puff of smoke. A bit like the cat on the clapper bridge.'

'What the hell are you talking about?'

'Ask Sam next time you take him tea.'

Tina rolled her eyes. 'You wouldn't be trying to matchmake in the middle of a crisis would you?'

'Light relief.'

Her smile restored, Tina took a cookie from the tin. 'Have you spoken to Sam today?'

'I caught him in the drive just now. He's found the start of the old walkway the Victorian ladies would have strolled around. Isn't that great?!'

Tina gave a thumbs up as she crunched her cookie.

'I apologised to him for my rant yesterday. He was very good about it.'

'Will you apologise to the others?'

'Derek has already congratulated me on my dragon slaying, so I think he's fine with it. I'll try and see Diane later, then talk to the others at tonight's meeting. Can you email everyone to check who is coming?'

'No problem. What time? Seven?'

'Perfect.' Thea regarded the heap of paper on the desk. 'I should have shifted this lot by then. Honestly, when am I supposed to get some actual restoration done?'

'What is all that?'

'Some of it is quotes for work on the house, but a surprising amount is applications from schools for trips in the future and stuff like that.'

Tina's face burst into its missing grin. 'But that's fantastic. We can start to take bookings and charge a holding deposit. If Malcolm is insisting we get Mill Grange to pay its way, then this is a way to start doing just that.'

'There's no way we'll make the £35,000 deficit he was talking about by booking a few school trips.' Thea grimaced. 'If only Malcolm was definite, one way or the other, about the sale. I think we have to assume the house won't be with the Trust by the end of the summer? How can we take a deposit for something that might be cancelled?'

'Won't it be harder to sell the house if we have loads of event bookings in place?'

Thea laughed. 'You're a devious woman, Tina Martin.'

'Thank you.' Tina raised her mug in salute. 'Shall I draw up a visitors' pre-booking agreement form?'

'Please.' Thea's conscience pricked her palms. 'But make sure it states that if unforeseen circumstances occur, their money will be refunded.'

'I will, but I'll say that only 50 per cent of the money will be refunded. If I make it clear there's a risk from the start, then it's up to them if they go ahead and book.' Seeing Thea's uncertain face, Tina added, 'We need the funds. This isn't for us, it's for the local community.'

'Agreed. As long as it's clear that we aren't trying to con anyone. Goodness knows the local schools don't have money to waste either.' Thea re-read the note from Mabel. 'How many volunteers will this make if Mabel's latest recruit joins us?'

'Eighteen regulars plus the three students helping Derek with clearance until their university term re-starts and… hang on…' Tina rifled the papers on her side of the table. 'From 18th June the students we have now are coming back until we're done, and they are bringing another four with them.'

Thea picked up one of the photographs of the house she had on her desk. It was of Mill Grange in 1882. There was a splendour about the house which shone out of the sepia colouring. A carriage was parked outside its front door. A proud if somewhat puffed-up groom held the horse as Lord and Lady Upwich posed by the carriage door.

'I wonder how long they stood there before that photograph was captured.'

'Anything up to four hours, probably.' Tina glanced up from her laptop screen. 'I'm surprised there isn't a pile of dung steaming beneath the horse.'

Thea chuckled, 'I bet there was a stable lad just out of view, ready to dash in with a shovel.'

Seeing the wistful expression on her friend's face as she stared at the photograph of Mill Grange in its heyday, Tina said, 'We can do this. We can save Mill Grange from being sold.'

'Can we?'

'It won't be easy, but despite any differences we have with one or two of the volunteers, we all have one aim in mind. To get Mill Grange manor house open to the public. To get it up and running.'

Thea nodded. 'You're right.'

'It happens occasionally.'

'More than occasionally.' Thea pulled her clipboard closer. 'Time we stopped with the negative.'

'We?'

'Okay, time I stopped being negative. Every major restoration project has problems. We've just had ours all in one go, avalanche style.'

'Absolutely.'

Pulling her old lists from the clipboard, Thea dropped them in the recycling box. 'New list for new time schedule.' She grabbed a pen. 'We're lucky in that the building is structurally sound. The lion's share of the deep cleaning has been done, and the house retains much of its original possessions, albeit with an accompanying hint of vinegar.'

Eagerly Tina added, 'Once we've cleared your bedroom and emptied this place – because people always like poking about in the scullery – cleaned and made up all the beds, we'll be able to arrange the furniture as we see fit. Then the inside of the house will be good to go.'

'Apart from information boards or folders.' Thea wrote 'info boards' on her new list. 'Sam is already producing miracles in the garden and Derek and team are clearing the ground that has been blocking the way to the kitchen garden at quite a pace.'

'Are you hoping to grow things in the garden? If so, Sam said we need to plant out ASAP. It's already too late for some things.'

'You are getting on with Sam then?'

'I thought you'd given up on the matchmaking.' Tina kept her focus on the school trip agreement she was mocking up. 'I told you, he is not my type and I'm certainly not his.'

'You don't know that.'

'I do. The garden. Do you want vegetables planted?'

'We won't be cooking here, so is it worth it?'

'We could sell the produce?'

'Then let's get planting.' Thea added 'price seedlings' to her list. 'Can you ask Sam if he knows where to get seeds from and if he'll supervise the sowing?'

'Only if you promise to quit the romance hints.'

'Deal. But only if you give me all the gory details about Mr Silver Fox later.' Thea got to her feet. 'Right now, I'm going to the mill. I want to see if we can use it to help earn money to save the manor, or if I should endorse the trustees' idea of selling it off.'

Tina winced. 'I'd hoped it wouldn't come to that. It seems criminal to split the buildings. I had considered suggesting we open the mill as a demonstration space.'

'Likewise.' Thea pulled her old khaki jacket over her shoulders. 'We could have had spinning displays and so on. But, if we need to reduce our budget then, as the mill isn't physically attached to the house, it seems the obvious place to start cutting.'

'Shame though, especially with so many of the villagers' ancestors having worked there.'

Thea scooped up her clipboard. 'I'm going to re-examine every part of the project and start again, as if this is a brand new assignment. Hopefully we can do something with the mill, but as the millwheel doesn't exist anymore, and the water course which drove it has long since dried up and been filled in, I'm not optimistic.'

As she made ready to leave, Thea's eyes caught the note Mabel had left. 'Oh damn, I'd forgotten about the new volunteer.'

'Don't worry. I'll do the honours if he shows up again today.'

'Are you sure?'

'No problem. Everyone Mabel has drummed up so far has been pretty reliable. Ancient, but reliable.'

During the half-mile walk to the mill, Thea's mind teemed with ideas. Tina had done it again. Her natural rebound view of life had got Thea thinking positively. A desire to achieve the impossible sped her footsteps.

As soon as she was free from Mill Grange's driveway and pacing towards the mill itself, her phone burst into life, startling a tree full of crows that'd been peacefully admiring the view.

'What did the trustees say?' Shaun didn't waste time introducing himself.

'Oh hello, I had calling you on my to-do list.'

'I'm honoured.'

He didn't sound honoured, he sounded offended, and Thea realised she'd probably made him sound rather less important than de-cobwebbing the scullery. 'My apologies, Mr Cowlson. It's been a bit of a day so far. Again.'

'Shaun, please.'

'Shaun.' Thea's stomach chose that moment to growl in protest that she hadn't fed it since a rushed bowl of cereal several hours ago.

'Was that you?'

Thea found herself apologising again. 'I haven't had the chance to eat yet.'

'Let me take you to lunch. I'm in the pub now.'

So much for keeping a low profile. Feeling she ought to offer an olive branch, she said, 'You're very kind, but it's rather late for lunch and I've a great deal to do. I wondered if you were free, whether you could come to a group meeting at the manor tonight.'

'Of course. What time?'

'Seven.'

'I'll be there.'

'Are you staying at the Stag and Hound?' Thea didn't

want him to think she was too interested, but at the same time thought she ought to know where their token celebrity was staying.

'I am, but don't worry. The landlady is sworn to secrecy. I'm enjoying a little anonymity in my room.'

Cross with herself for misjudging him again, Thea found herself saying, 'I'm on my way to check out the old mill, so you'd be very welcome to join me if you can sneak out in disguise.'

Fifteen

Thea stood outside the large rectangular building, a quarter of a mile from the manor, and checked the photocopy of the original village plan on her clipboard.

The mill, not large compared to the majority of such buildings from the Industrial Revolution, ran the equivalent length of four terrace houses. Ahead of Thea, stretched out in a curved but linear row, was the village of Upwich itself. At the far end of the village, she could see the sign for the Stag and Hound pub swinging in the afternoon breeze. There was no sign of Shaun walking up the sloping road past the double-sided row of cottages which had once been homes for the woollen mill workers.

Extracting the massive ring of keys from her pocket, Thea unlocked the double doors that had once opened onto the main part of the factory. Despite the lock being released, it still took four hefty tugs before the doors finally unstuck from their surround and allowed her to enter the mill. The smell of damp hit Thea at the same time as a cloud of dust attacked her nostrils, temporarily disabling her with a sneezing fit that made her throat dry and her eyes water.

Heading straight back outside, she took a lungful of fresh air. As Thea held onto the door she noticed that the metal casing around the inside lock had buckled. Opening the door wider, she knelt to examine the keyhole. It wasn't just rusty; the right side had been snapped away, as if something had collided with it at some point. Trying the key on the locks inside, Thea found it was useless. Her keys would let her into the mill, but not out again.

Feeling around the edge of the door, Thea could see why it had been so hard to open. Sticky with lack of use, it needed a sand and repaint as a matter of urgency. Writing 'see to doors and lock ASAP' to the top of her mill to-do list, Thea propped the door open with a brick from a discarded pile of masonry outside the door and turned to face the building's interior.

As the dusty haze cleared, Thea saw she'd walked straight into an industrial-scale collection of spider webs and trapped balls of dust. She couldn't begin to guess how long the mill had been left undisturbed but for mice, insects and arachnids.

Telling herself there was nothing here that a good sweeping out and airing and some humane mouse traps couldn't cure, and thanking her lucky stars she wasn't afraid of spiders, Thea allowed her eyes to adjust to the gloom. 'No wonder the volunteers have concentrated on the manor.'

'Absolutely!'

Thea almost jumped out of her skin as Shaun arrived behind her. 'Bloody hell, Shaun! You could have called out or something. You scared me half to death.'

'Sorry. I'm always being told off for that.' Grinning unapologetically, Shaun pointed to his boots. 'Soft treads for wearing on excavation. Great for not damaging the ground, but silent for moving about.'

'So I see, or hear – or don't hear rather.'

'Did you see the inside of the door? Looks like someone had to break out of here at some point.'

'I did, that's why I propped it open. With that, and the edges of the doors being so sticky, I thought they might be hard to reopen from the inside. It hadn't occurred to me that someone might have broken out rather than in though.'

'I might be wrong of course, but it had that feel to it. Any record of fires or incidents here where employees had to force their way out?'

'Not that I've found.' Thea frowned as she looked back at the damaged lock. 'I'll have a dig through the archives when I have time.'

'Did you know you had a major cobweb network on top of your head?' Unbidden, Shaun reached out, teasing the silken construction from her hair.

Thea's brain told her feet to move away, but her body was too busy reacting positively to Shaun's feather-like touch as he gently worked away the silken threads from her hair.

As common sense won over sensation, Thea stepped backwards. Hoping she didn't look as embarrassed as she felt, she said, 'Oh don't worry. I'm always covered in some mess or other.' She roughly scrubbed a palm through her hair.

'I bet.' Shaun didn't appear the least put out that she'd moved away. 'Occupational hazard.'

Holding her clipboard like a shield, Thea said, 'These are

the original plans. This room was where the giant loom was kept, so in there—' she pointed to a set of closed double doors to their left '—must have been the carding room.'

Shaun followed as Thea, bracing herself to be showered with a new coating of dust, levered open the left-hand door, while Shaun took the right one.

Wiping his grubby palms down his trousers, he strode into the slightly smaller space. 'I'm assuming the carding machine would have stood in the middle here, while the fleeces would have been piled up at the back.'

'According to the records the fleeces were washed and scoured of their lanolin in the larger of the two sheds outside. Then, in the other shed the clean fleece was scribbed before outworkers collected it to be combed and carded into rovings.'

'Scribbed and rovings?' Shaun frowned.

'Scribbed is when the fleeces were torn up into workable pieces, while the rovings are the resulting long strips of wool which were ready for spinning.'

'Was most of the work done beyond the factory? It doesn't feel big enough in here to hold all the people required to complete the entire job?' Shaun outstretched his arms and circled on the spot as if trying to get a mental idea of space.

Thea looked away as Shaun's shirt tightened against his chest while he spun around. *Of course he's got muscles; he spends his life on excavation. Get a grip, woman.*

Her words kept coming, even though her emotions had inconveniently chosen that moment to remind her how long it had been since she'd had a boyfriend. 'It was a real cottage industry. Most of the homes in Upwich housed at least one wool worker, if not a whole family of them. There was a water-powered spinning mule on the right side of the main shed and a loom on the other, but otherwise there were several hand-powered machines which drew out and twisted the individual wool fibres, locking them together to produce a thread known as a single. I'm guessing these must have been used in the sheds outside or, in the case of the most trusted workers, in their homes.'

'I honestly haven't heard of machines being placed in people's homes before. We'll need to check on that. Could be true or it could be village legend.'

Not missing the use of the word 'we', Thea agreed.

'You said about individual wool fibres locking together to produce threads.'

Shaun stared at the space where the mule would have waited, hungry for its constant diet of treated fleece. 'Would that have been strong enough to weave with?'

'No, the single threads then had to be plyed – which means they were reverse twisted. That process turned the single threads into a more stable yarn to be wound onto bobbins or quills so that cloth could be woven on the mule.'

Strolling back into the main factory space, Shaun studied the floor space. 'It would have been cramped with two machines in here, not to mention noisy.'

'Unpleasant working conditions to say the least.'

'Can you imagine how cramped the cottages were with their main rooms taken over by hand carding, spinning and weaving?'

'Plus the stench of lanolin and sheep in the houses where the outworkers who did the roving lived.'

'I bet the whole village had a miasma of dead sheep, sweat and beer.'

'Beer?' Thea caught Shaun's eye and immediately looked away again as her nervous system relived the sensation of his fingers in her hair.

'I'd put money on the first thing the male workers did after work being to spend some of their hard-earned wages on a pint at the pub. Moira, the landlady at the Stag and Hound, was giving me a potted history of the place earlier. The current pub is built on the site of an older one. It was updated in 1842 specifically to serve the growing number of mill workers.'

'Steady trade.' Thea peered up at the grey ceiling, which was built at one level across most of the building, only to slope upwards to the far right towards the wheelhouse. 'The wheel would have been in there then.' She walked to the right side of the spinning room and unlocked the final set of double doors.

This time they were greeted by a taller narrow room, holding little but a deep pit and a wrought iron staircase which no longer had anywhere to run to. The rusted metal fixings that once supported the wheel were the only indicators of how large the wooden structure must have been. There was just enough space around the edge of the room for a few workers to move around the water trough.

Shaun ran a hand over the chipped staircase. 'You can just imagine it, can't you, all black-leaded and gleaming. The wheel turning, the water rushing below.' He paused. 'The water course was filled in when? Do we know?'

'As soon as the mill was abandoned in 1888. It was too small to compete with Coldharbour Mill in nearby Uffculme, not to mention the mills in Exeter and Somerset being built in places where they could expand as necessary.

There's no way you could expand without impacting on the manor grounds. I doubt the family would have wanted to do that.'

'For which we can't blame them.' Shaun stepped back, picturing the wheelhouse in all its former glory. 'The impact on the village must have been immense when the mill closed.'

'I'd love Mill Grange to give something back to the village.' Thea closed the wheel room doors behind them. 'Although in all honesty, I suspect I'll have to recommend selling the mill off separately.'

Shaun groaned. 'Which would mean to a developer, who'd turn it into executive apartments or something similar. Only affordable by incomers from London.'

'I know.' Thea leant against the dusty wall of the main room. 'But unless you have a millwheel builder who doesn't require paying up your sleeve, and you know how to reopen the watercourse with zero damage to people's gardens and bypassing planning regulations, then I can't see an affordable alternative.'

'Point taken.' Shaun ran a reverential hand over the fading plaster. 'But we must be able to do something with it.'

'That's the second time you've said *we*?' Thea smiled. 'You're happy to stay incognito for a while then?'

'If you're happy to put up with me?'

Unsettled by the gleam in his eye, Thea checked her watch. 'There's only just over an hour until the meeting; I ought to get back.'

'May I accompany you? I wouldn't mind a poke around the grounds.' Seeing the doubt on Thea's face he added, 'Don't worry, I'll hide until I've met everyone at the meeting.

Then I'll know who is privy to my appearance, and who isn't.'

'I'm sorry about this, Shaun. It's probably silly, but…'

'You're doing your best for Mill Grange. Don't worry about me. Although,' he paused while Thea relocked the main doors, 'in the interests of me not being spotted by autograph-hunters and such, I wondered if I should sleep in the manor.'

'What?'

'I'd pay the same rate as at the pub. Makes sense, doesn't it? It'll bring in a few more pennies and I won't have to keep creeping around Upwich like one half of Burke and Hare.'

Sitting on the edge of the double bed in Mill Grange's main bedroom, Thea could see out of the large bay window and across the garden into the tops of the trees beyond. She'd intended to make another list. But list-writing seemed to be all she did these days. Better to get on and do something productive. Suddenly all her lists felt like delaying tactics.

Tina was downstairs in the kitchen preparing for the meeting. She cursed herself for not having found time to ask her about her date yet. Perhaps they'd have the chance to chat after the meeting. She could see Sam, pottering away in the garden despite the lateness of the hour. Thea was surprised he was still there as he'd said he couldn't come to the meeting.

A trail of smoke gusted past the window every time the wind got up, telling her that the bonfire she'd smelt as she and Shaun had walked back to Mill Grange belonged to Derek and his helpers. For now there was no one else in view. Shaun was somewhere in the woods, having promised faithfully to keep a low profile if he encountered any dog walkers.

Trying to concentrate on the meeting ahead, Thea realised there was very little to say but what had to be said needed saying emphatically. She didn't want to keep people here as volunteers if they didn't want to stay once they knew the chances of the place ever opening to the public was slim.

Shaun's presence would keep the likes of Mabel and Diane on site, but she was less sure about the others.

'The new timeline, the money situation, the need to raise funds ourselves, introduce Shaun, request their discretion on his presence so it's a surprise when he opens the manor – if that happens – and then send them all home.'

Thea repeated the meeting schedule like a mantra as she smoothed a palm across the bed's Victorian quilt, glad that Mabel wasn't there to tell her off for sitting on it.

Shaun's idea of living in to help pay for the manor's upkeep was a good one, but if she was going to agree to him living in, she would have to move out. It was a miracle she hadn't been discovered by anyone other than Tina anyway.

Thea closed her eyes. All Shaun had done was tease some cobwebs off her hair, but it had felt like an electric shock. A really good electric shock. 'You do not have time for this!'

The sound of the front door opening and closing, followed by the familiar determined tone of Mabel and the accompanying complimentary tone of Diane prevented Thea from admitting what she already knew. She wanted Shaun's hands on her again. 'It's just lust. You've gone without for too long.'

Steeling herself, Thea pushed her inconvenient realisation

to the back of her mind. It was time to start the meeting. Taking pleasure in the touch of the polished oak banister beneath her palm, Thea descended the main staircase, heading towards the aroma of coffee emanating from the kitchen.

From the corridor she could hear Mabel giggling and a man's voice, muffled by the sound of others moving around the room. Thea's spirits lifted. She hadn't heard Mabel laugh before. Perhaps having Shaun here would help far beyond his knowledge of old buildings. Wondering when Shaun had crept in, Thea pushed open the kitchen door.

Her hand froze against its wooden panel.

There was no sign of Shaun.

Between a flushed Mabel and a giggling Tina, sat John Sommers.

Sixteen

Thea held onto the side of her desk and exhaled slowly. Her television appearance calling for volunteers had been ages ago. She'd relaxed. Dared to let herself believe that John had either not seen the broadcast, or had seen it, but sensibly decided not to come here.

I don't have time for this. There's so much to do!

Far from delivering her from trouble, it felt as if Mill Grange had landed Thea neck-deep into the most demanding circumstances of her career. And now, for added devilment, the Ghost of Christmas Past had shown up, and was regarding her as if butter wouldn't melt in his mouth.

Trust Mabel to like him.

Thea tried to dismiss the memory of Tina's expression as she'd looked at John. Her friend's instinct for homing in on men with money was strong. Thea wouldn't wish John on someone as gentle and kind as her best friend though. She wouldn't wish him on anyone.

Thea closed her eyes. She knew she had to go back into

the kitchen. The excuse she'd muttered about needing to fetch some papers had sounded lame and the longer she was absent the lamer it would become.

Lowering herself onto the nearest seat, Thea took a sip of water. *All the effort I went to, to get out of Bath was wasted. And if I can't even save the manor, then what's the point of me staying?*

'Thea?' Tina opened the scullery door. 'Do you need help finding something? You've been gone ages.'

Catching sight of her friend's ashen face, Tina rushed to her side. 'What's happened?'

'The new volunteer.'

'He's mine.' Tina smirked. 'Hands off.'

Thea shook her head so fast her hair whipped her face. 'That's John.'

'That hot bloke in there with the nice eyes and the soft laugh is the man you've come here to escape from?'

'Yes.' Thea licked her lips, trying desperately to get some moisture to circulate around her mouth.

'Oh my God.' Tina was mortified. 'I had no idea. He said his name was John Davies.'

'That's his other surname.'

'What?'

'It's double-barrelled. He is John Davies-Sommers. I've never bothered with the middle bit. Something that he didn't like.'

The uneasy silence was broken by the sound of the back door to the manor being scraped back and Shaun striding into the make-do office with a grin. 'Sorry I'm late, Thea. Couldn't get out of the woods without breaking my cover. Oh… you okay?'

'Yes. Yes, of course. I was gathering myself before the meeting.' Thea plastered a smile on her face. 'Tina, this is Shaun. Shaun this is Tina, my right hand here at Mill Grange and best friend.'

'Very pleased to meet you.' Shaun's palm engulfed Tina's entire hand as he shook it profusely.

Thea, wanting to get the meeting over with so she could work out what to do about John, said, 'Shall we go in? I know Mabel is dying to meet you.'

Shaun lowered his voice. 'Mabel's the one that dropped you in it, right?'

'You could say that.'

Tina turned to Thea. 'Are you okay to go in? Really?'

'Of course.' Not wanting to say anything in front of Shaun, Thea led the small party towards the kitchen.

Mabel was on her feet the second she saw Shaun. For one mad moment Thea thought she was going to curtsy.

'You must be Mrs Hastings?' Shaun, in full television personality mode, kissed Mabel's cheek, turning her fuchsia-pink as he switched his attention to a hovering Diane. 'I'm delighted to be here. What a beautiful manor you have here.'

Grateful to Shaun for taking the limelight, Thea arranged her papers at the head of the table. So far she'd avoided glancing at John, but that didn't stop her feeling his bright green eyes scanning her face. Everyone else was focused on Shaun.

Hoping no one would notice how rattled she was, Thea continued to ignore her ex's presence. 'Thank you for coming along at such short notice.' She turned to Tina. 'If you could relay the minutes of the meeting to Sam tomorrow, that would be good.'

'No problem.' Tina took up her pen, ready to record what was said.

Mabel's hawk-like eyes landed on the pen. 'We never kept minutes in the past. Why now?'

'Because what I have to say is important. The trustees need to have an accurate account of the work we're doing and how much money we spend. They also want a realistic timeframe for our work as we move forwards. In the past things have been relayed to them incorrectly.' Thea kept her gaze on Mabel as she added, 'Such inaccuracies have led to the reason for this meeting.'

There was an uncomfortable shuffling from Diane as Thea adopted a less combative tone. 'However, what's done is done. It is vital to the survival of the restoration project that we draw a line under what's happened – without forgetting all the excellent work many of you have done – and move on.'

Concentrating her attention on Shaun, Tina, and Derek's three students, all of whom stood propped against the dresser, Thea outlined their new timeline. Stressing the increasing possibility that the house might never open to the public and the need for the house and grounds to start to pay for themselves to try and prevent that from happening, she added, 'So, if any of you who've volunteered don't wish to continue, now you know Mill Grange may never become the heritage site you hoped for, then I'd understand. I'd like you all to think it over and email me with your decision. Should you wish to withdraw no one will think any less of you. Your hard work will always be remembered and appreciated.'

Deflecting the heat of John's relentless smile in her direction, Thea watched Shaun. He was running his eyes over the rows of polished pans above the Aga. 'This brings me to our special guest, Mr Shaun Cowlson.'

Shaun smiled, but remained silent so Thea could continue.

'Shaun is here to help out. I'm sure you'll agree we are very lucky to have such an expert on the premises. And, if we are able to pull off a miracle and the house, and possibly the mill, are restored and ready to open to the public by 21ˢᵗ July, Shaun has also agreed to perform the opening ceremony.'

Mabel couldn't have looked more pleased with herself as she told John, 'I invited him, you know.'

Not wanting to give John time to respond to Mabel's gloating, Thea spoke louder. 'Yet this brings problems as well as solutions.' She gestured to Shaun, who dipped his head, showing her he agreed with what she was about to say. 'As we do not need autograph-hunters slowing us down, and as we'd like to keep Shaun's role as house opener a surprise, let's keep his presence as a volunteer under wraps.'

Derek, who'd been regarding Thea with fatherly pride, said, 'That won't be easy, girl. I'm sure *all* of us—' he looked directly at Mabel '—will keep the secret, but Mr Cowlson can hardly be held hostage within the house. Keeping a secret in this village is nigh on impossible.'

Shaun acknowledged the point. 'It will be very difficult. That's why I've suggested to Thea that I live here. Not only will paying rent to the Trust help the funds, it will mean I will be sleeping on site and be able to work the maximum number of hours I can before leaving for the next round of filming.'

'Stay here?' Mabel's eyes widened with a combination of surprise and horror. 'But where? The bedrooms are about the only things ready for opening and what about food? You can hardly call Tesco and ask for a delivery without arousing suspicion.'

Knowing Mabel was right, but wishing she wasn't, Thea said, 'Shaun could have one of the back bedrooms. The work to re-clean one room won't be too much when the time comes. As to food, well, you have a valid point, but if we all pitch in, I'm sure we can get enough supplies smuggled in to keep Shaun going.'

'For how many weeks?' John was incredulous. 'Still wishing for miracles, Thea?'

Mabel swung around to face her latest recruit. 'You've met Thea before?'

He beamed at the old lady. 'We know each other very well indeed. Don't we, Thea?'

Curling her fingers into fists under the table, Thea said, 'Not really, John, no.' Quickly turning to Shaun, whose expression revealed he'd got the situation summed up already, Thea said, 'Would you really want to be stuck here for all your meals? It's a big place, but if we do try and keep you a secret you'll be a virtual prisoner.'

'Perhaps I got carried away by the magic of this place.' A crinkle had formed on Shaun's forehead, but to Thea, it appeared to be aimed at John rather than concern over his culinary arrangements. 'I wouldn't worry. I can make my own arrangements. All I'd ask everyone, if you don't mind, is for you to stay quiet about my presence in the village for now. If someone sees me and works it out, then we'll cope with that as and when. I feel I'd be of more use to Thea, Mill Grange, and therefore yourselves, if I kept a low profile. If anyone has an objection to this arrangement, please speak up and I'll rethink my plans.'

The table resounded with agreements to keep quiet and cries of how lovely it was for Shaun to interrupt his recording schedule to help them. Everyone, including John, was in agreement. Shaun should stay and no one would speak out.

Hoping they'd all keep their word, Thea was relieved when the meeting closed with a feeling of unexpected optimism. Shaun's arrival seemed to have dulled everyone's senses to the fact that the manor might never open at all.

Nearly everyone had gone. Shaun was upstairs picking a bedroom in which to stay once his booking at the pub had run out, and Tina was at the kitchen table writing up the meeting notes. Thea, with her heart thudding in her chest, glad that her friend was only a shout away, had asked John to accompany her to the office.

'An explanation please?'

'I want to help you keep Mill Grange open.' John didn't so much as blink through his lie.

'Bollocks. The real reason please. I'm busy, I'm tired and I don't need this.'

John laughed. 'Devon air has made you feisty. I like it.'

'We're in Somerset.'

'Same difference.' John was dismissive as he pulled out a chair and lounged back.

'I would like you to leave, John.'

'But – but why? I told you, we owe it to ourselves to give it another go. I want to stay. I want to help. This—' he waved a hand around the scullery, not quite being able to disguise his dislike of the crumbling plaster and smell of damp '—is important to you.'

'It is important to me, but it isn't to you.' Thea sighed. 'I appreciate the sentiment, John, but I know this must be your idea of hell. It's one of a huge number of reasons why we are not meant to be together.'

'But you said we should try. In the pub in Bath before you left. I heard you.'

Thea ran a hand through her hair in exasperation. 'What on earth are you talking about?'

'You said you wished you loved me. So here I am, to see if we can make that wish come true.'

Thea couldn't believe what she was hearing.

'I knew I owed it to us to try once more, so I pulled a few strings at work to get time off, and here I am.' He sat back in the chair. Thea had the strangest notion he was expecting to be thanked.

Taking a deep breath, Thea forced herself to look John in the eye. 'One: I said I wished I could love you for your sake, but the fact is I don't and never will. I was trying to be kind. Obviously a mistake. Two: you've given a false name on your safety form.' She waved the paper signed John Davies in front of him. 'And three: one of the reasons I came here was to give you a chance to move on. To find someone to love who will love you back.'

John's expression flicked through various stages of uncertainty, before dismissing Thea's misgivings with his trademark smile. 'You're being unreasonable, Thea. You need all the help you can get here. When I saw your appeal on the television, I realised that sacrificing my annual leave to help get this pile functioning again would be a good way to apologise for my past behaviour.' He placed a palm over hers and gave it a gentle squeeze. 'If more than just a chance to atone comes from my time here, then great. If not, well, I'll know for sure how you feel, won't I?'

Thea stared at the hand covering hers for a second. It felt warm and familiar. Part of her was reacting positively, remembering how good that hand could feel, but her brain told her to grit her teeth and stand firm. 'As I said, John, I appreciate the sentiment, but I want you to leave. Please John, for your own sake. I can't face the thought of hurting you again.'

He crossed his arms defensively across his chest. 'You can't fire me, I'm a volunteer. I've signed the paperwork that says I can stay as I've passed the safety briefing.'

With her sense of exasperation and frustration at John's blind stubbornness growing, Thea all but pleaded, 'But you know nothing about restoration! I can't imagine you getting your hands dirty via manual labour. I know for a fact that the shirt you're wearing cost a fortune. You won't want to ruin that.'

'For you I would!' John leapt to his feet. 'Come out for a meal with me tonight. Just the two of us.'

'You just said you were only here to apologise, and here you are, asking me out again.' Thea picked up her clipboard and held it close to her chest. 'John, I don't think you've heard a single word I've said!'

'Then tell me again over dinner.' He checked his watch. 'If we leave now, then we'll still make our reservation.'

'You've already booked us a table somewhere?'

'Thea,' John's smile stayed in place, as he held out a hand for Thea to take. 'We'll have a nice time. I'm sure you could use some time out from the others. Especially that celebrity—'

Shaun's voice rang across the scullery. 'One of the worst things about my job is being labelled a celebrity. I'm not a celebrity. I'm a lucky archaeologist with a good job. I promise you'll never see me dancing on television with a host of other people who think they're famous, but who hardly anyone has heard of. Nor will I be dashing off to the jungle to eat grubs anytime soon.'

Completely ignoring John, Shaun lounged against the kitchen door and gestured to the paperwork on the table. 'Are you ready, Thea? Our table is booked for nine. It isn't the sort of place that likes you to be late for dinner.'

Recognising a rescue when she heard one, Thea said, 'I'll just make sure the house is empty and change my top.'

'Excellent. I've already escorted Tina to her car. I'll make sure this... gentleman... leaves safely.'

Thea smiled. 'Thank you.'

Thea ran up the servants' stairs. She didn't want to think about what John might be saying to Shaun as he found himself purposefully steered to the back door.

Seventeen

April 9th

'So, it's not exactly the Ritz I made it out to be.' Shaun pulled out a chair so Thea could sit down. 'It could be a McDonald's for all I care.' Thea grabbed the glass of wine that Moira, the landlady of the Stag and Hound, had placed in front of her. 'Thanks for rescuing me, but there's no need to feel obliged to look after me now we've dodged John. I can slip out the back and grab some food from the bar.' She glanced around the lounge-cum-dining room Shaun had steered her into via the pub's staff entrance. 'This is where you're hiding out?'

'It is. Moira has been marvellous. Something of a *Landscape Treasures* fan luckily for us. This is her private living area.' Shaun raised a pint of Owl Bitter to his lips and paused, his expression serious. 'I'm not letting you leave until you've eaten. I bet you haven't had anything since breakfast.'

'There hasn't been time.'

Shaun was unconvinced by this claim. 'As your temporary

Sir Galahad, I insist on feeding you while you tell me what that excuse for a man wanted.'

Thea tried to sound dismissive, taking a sip of wine so she didn't have to look at Shaun as she explained. 'John saw me on the television and decided he'd come here to rake over old times. It was nothing really. I just hadn't expected to see him.'

'It appeared more serious than that. You were shaking and, more to the point, you were willing to come out with me in order to escape going out with him. Not an offer you'd have accepted otherwise, I suspect.'

Shielding her red cheeks with the menu to hide that he was right, Thea spoke into the list of delicious sounding fare. 'Forgive me, I must seem ungrateful. But there isn't much to tell.'

'I could tell that dinner with John was the last thing you wanted, but you obviously need food. You are too pale and shaky for my liking.'

'I shake a lot due to rotten circulation. Nothing to worry about.' Meeting his eyes, Thea saw Shaun regarding her as if she might break and mumbled, 'You're right. I've not been eating enough. Being hungry always makes things seem worse than they are, don't you think?'

'Ummm.' Shaun waved his phone. 'Moira said to text the order and the food will arrive, genie-style, very soon.'

'Wow, you really have got things sussed here.' Finding she didn't want to tell him they'd be housemates, and vowing to find herself a place to stay the next day, Thea asked, 'Are you sure you want to move into the manor? You'll have to cook for yourself and go without home comforts.'

'After three weeks camping on the edge of a field in Wales

in the pouring rain with no toilets or running water and the only source of food being a local petrol station, Mill Grange will feel like Buckingham Palace.'

Thea sounded wistful. 'I remember that sort of adventure.'

'Do you miss it?'

'A bit. Not so much the being frozen and soaked with rain, or the wondering where to pee in the middle of the night, but the camaraderie. Excavation time was always so full of fun and companionship, not to mention the thrill of discovery – or not.'

'That's exactly it.' Shaun's face lit up in understanding, and suddenly he was every bit the TV presenter. 'It's not the work as such, but what it might lead to; what could be found. And the people, they're the best in the world.' Shaun paused, as if he'd realised how enthusiastic he'd become, and held up his phone again, 'Now, do you know what you'd like to eat yet?'

'Chicken and leek pie and chips please.'

'Good choice.' Shaun nodded. 'With gravy, I hope?'

'You Northerner you!' Thea felt some of the tension in her shoulders unknot.

'Don't knock the Northerner, Southern girl.'

'As if I would. My five years in Durham were the happiest of my life.'

'I'd forgotten you were at Durham.' The hint of flirtation Thea thought she'd seen in Shaun's eyes dimmed. 'Why did you give up the excavation circuit to work at the Roman Baths?' He leant forward, giving her a waft of clean skin and fresh cotton.

Fiddling her wine glass in her fingers, Thea watched the pale liquid slosh around inside. 'It was my dream job. Romano-Britain has been my passion since we did the Romans at primary school when I was five. If it hadn't been the Roman Baths, I'd have tried to get a job at Herculaneum or Cirencester or somewhere similar. But Bath…'

'The jewel in the crown.'

'Exactly.' Thea trailed a fingertip down the stem of her glass. 'My job involved a lot of artefact analysis as well as conservation and museum work. I had the best of both worlds. Museum management and historical evaluation, with the occasional site visit thrown in for good measure. I was very lucky.'

'And yet, here you are. On a Victorian site with no qualified staff, bar Tina, and if the trustees carry out their threat, unemployment looming.'

'Yes.' Thea wished she could think of something else to talk about, but her mind had gone blank.

'You don't strike me as someone who'd give up their childhood dream on a whim.'

From nowhere, tears pricked at the back of Thea's eyes. She stared at the menu which rested in her lap, angry with herself for being feeble. Clearing her throat, she pretended to cough. 'Sorry. Dry throats always make my eyes run.' She took a gulp of Pinot. 'There, that's better.'

'You don't have to tell me.' Shaun tilted his head, not convinced that her dotting of tears was the result of one cough. 'Not if you don't want to.'

Suddenly, Thea found she wanted to explain. When Shaun had last seen her, she was one of the main speakers at an international historical conference, and now… now she wasn't sure what she was. It had all seemed so sensible at the time.

'The main reason I came here was because I wanted a new challenge. Perhaps I missed the social side of the dig life more than I realised? I hadn't thought about that until now.' She took another sip of wine to enforce her dry throat fib. 'Working in Bath was great. I loved it. I used to talk to the Goddess Minerva all the time. And yes, I am aware that makes me sound nuts, but I had a statue in the corner of my office and she often gave better advice than anyone else on staff.'

Shaun laughed. 'I can believe that. Frankly, if the Goddess of Wisdom can't help, who can?'

Thea smiled. 'But statues aside, I hardly met anyone. I worked behind the scenes or with transitory groups of people, and well…' Thea broke off. She could feel her earlier blush rising back across her cheeks.

'You were lonely?'

'More tired of my own company really. I'm thirty-two, I suppose I assumed by now…' Revisited by a flashback of Shaun removing the cobwebs from her hair, Thea changed direction. 'The restoration manager job at Mill Grange came along just when I needed it. Tina was already with the Trust, and it is great to be working with her.'

Shaun studied Thea's face, noticing the random flecks of brown that mixed with the blue of her eyes. 'So you fancied a fresh challenge in the hope you'd be introduced to new people and have a more hands-on career?'

'Exactly.' Glad to be back on the topic of her new job, she added, 'If everything had gone to plan, I'd have managed the manor and mill once it was open to the public. Arranged exhibitions, visits, and all that.'

'And now?'

'Until I'm told otherwise, I'll carry on busting a gut to get the manor open on time.' To Thea's relief, they were interrupted by Moira arriving with their food. 'Thank you, that smells amazing.'

The landlady smiled, but said nothing as she scuttled back to her busy bar.

'She'll think we're on a date.'

Shaun's eyebrows rose. 'Would that be so awful?'

'You have your reputation to think of.'

'And so do you.' Shaun's hand hovered over the tiny gravy-boat steaming invitingly on the edge of his plate. 'I have a confession to make.'

Thea tried not to burn her mouth as she chewed too many chips at once.

'I have an ulterior motive for being at Mill Grange.'

Thea's heart sank. Perhaps she should have stuck to her first instincts and not let Shaun anywhere near the grange. 'You do?'

'Do you remember the conference in Bath?' Shaun shifted in his seat. 'The Historical and Heritage Committee one?'

'I remember.' Thea wished she hadn't already drained her wine. 'You were with Becky Gibson.'

'Oh, yes.' Shaun stared into his pint glass. He obviously hadn't expected that name to come up.

'Yes?' Thea felt her hackles rising. 'That's all you can say? You broke my friend's heart and all you give me is an, "Oh yes"?'

'I broke her heart?' His glass landed on the table with a thump. 'Are you kidding me?'

'After the conference, Becky told me what had happened.' Thea's frown deepened. 'You don't deny ending it, do you?'

'No, I don't.' Shaun stabbed his fork at his chips. 'I'm sorry to say this if she's your friend, but there's no denying that woman's trouble.'

Thea was about to defend Becky when she recalled how many times in the past forty-eight hours Shaun had acted against type; at least, the type of man her student-time friend had attributed him to be.

'Becky arrived in my life at that conference like a targeted missile. With hindsight I saw she had it all planned. I was too blind... too flattered and arrogant to see it.'

'Becky's a pretty girl.'

'A little too pretty for my taste.'

'How do you mean?'

Shaun grinned, easing the sudden tension. 'She'd never dribble gravy for a start.'

Self-consciously dabbing a spot of stray gravy from her chin, Thea resisted the urge to stick her tongue out at him as Shaun's smile dropped back into a scowl of recollection. 'Her hair was too neat, her makeup too perfect, clothes too clean and clearly expensive. Didn't you ever wonder how Becky could afford them?' He paused. 'It was like she was hiding something under all the layers of perfection. I was a fool not to see it.'

'See what?'

'That I was nothing more than a challenge to her.' Shaun drained the remaining ale from his glass. 'I'd just landed my second series of *Landscape Treasures*. I was still learning how to act in the public eye. To say I was a rookie who was out of his depth is putting it mildly. Anyway, I discovered later that Becky was a celeb-hunter. The more known faces she slept with the better.'

'You're joking?'

'I wish I was.' Shaun sighed. 'I discovered, purely by accident, that she'd been recording us in bed.'

Thea froze in the act of cutting her pie as an image she didn't want fogged her mind. 'How... ummm... how do you discover something like that by accident?'

'I knocked her mobile to the floor when I turned over to get a glass of water while she was in the shower... afterwards.' Shaun faltered as it dawned on him exactly what he was confessing to. 'The phone was still recording.'

'Oh.' Thea didn't know what else to say.

Intently studying, but not really seeing, a painting of a stag that hung over the fireplace, Shaun hurriedly said, 'I deleted it all before I confronted her, which was stupid because then I had no evidence and, of course, she denied it. Said the video function must have been knocked on by the fall. I told Becky to get out and not come back, and she left – and then apparently painted me as a brute to all her friends as an act of revenge.'

Thea swallowed. 'I'm sorry I believed her. She was very convincing.'

'Fakes often are.' Shaun shifted awkwardly in his seat. 'Anyway, you didn't know me then. I hope you see me differently now we've met properly.'

Finding she couldn't look at him, Thea stared at her plate. 'Yes. Yes, of course.'

Shaun stabbed another chip as if it was entirely to blame for his past mistakes. 'A year later I was chatting to a fellow presenter at a charity dinner and discovered he hadn't been so lucky. Becky had got three grand out of him to keep their night together out of the papers.'

'Bloody hell.'

'I was lucky in that hardly anyone outside of the world of archaeology fans knew who I was at that stage of my career.'

The room became quiet but for the scrape of cutlery on china, until Shaun said, 'I told you I had a confession to make.'

'Wasn't that it?'

'No.' He looked uneasy. 'I've been following your career since that conference. That's why I was so surprised when you stepped off the radar and left Bath.'

'Followed me?' Thea paled. Shaun, as if guessing what she was thinking, quickly added, 'Not in a stalker way, but in a fellow professional spotting a potential colleague sort of way.'

'Whatever for?'

'Because before Becky Gibson blinded me with fake flattery, I was going to ask you out.'

Eighteen

April 9th

Thea realised that her mouth was wordlessly opening and closing before she finally whispered, 'Ask me out?'

'It can't be that much of a shock surely?' Shaun tilted his head and gave her a lopsided grin. 'We have a lot in common.'

'But you don't know anything about me.'

'I'd like to though.' Shaun dropped his gaze to his plate and shovelled up his last mouthful of food. 'You couldn't be more surprised if I'd punched you.'

'I… it's just.' An image of John's grinning face as he sat next to Mabel at the kitchen table elbowed its way into her mind. 'There's so much going on and… well, you could go out with anyone.'

'And yet here I am with you.' Shaun gave Thea a searching look. 'How about we leave it at that? For now.'

'For now?' Thea couldn't decide if she was disappointed or relieved.

'For now you need to sort out the manor and, more

immediately I suspect, John.' Shaun held her gaze. 'After that, I reserve the right to ask you on a proper date. Would that be acceptable?'

'Um. Yes. Thanks.' Thea laid down her knife and fork, not quite sure what to do or say next. She'd spent years with the idea of Shaun Cowlson as the man who'd hurt her friend. Now, she didn't know what to think. There was food left on her plate, but delicious though it was, she couldn't face another mouthful. 'Is it possible to fire a volunteer?'

'Ah.' Shaun glowered over his pint. 'You really don't want John here, do you?'

'No. For his sake as much as mine.'

'Come on.' Shaun pushed back his chair and headed to the sofa. 'Let's sit by the fire.' Seeing the conflicted expression on Thea's face, he held up a palm as if he was a scout making a promise. 'I'll sit as far away from you as the seat cushions will allow. We may as well be comfortable while you explain why you want John away from Mill Grange so badly.'

Thea conceded the point. 'Do you think we could have another drink? This saga requires alcohol.'

After Thea had explained the full story, Shaun insisted on walking her back to Mill Grange.

Protesting for the third time as they crept out of the pub under the cover of darkness, Thea crossed her fingers as she said, 'Tina will be picking me up to take me back to her place for the night soon. And besides, I'll have to move around on my own during the day or no work will get done. In fact, I intend to be so busy John won't have the time to get anywhere near me.'

'I wish it wasn't so awkward trying to fire volunteers.' Shaun hovered at Thea's elbow as they walked up the driveway, almost, but not touching her arm. 'Especially one who hasn't even started work. He hasn't had the chance to make an unforgivable mistake yet, and as he's passed the health and safety thing... I don't suppose anything will come up when his criminal check thing is done?'

Glad that Shaun hadn't asked where Tina had gone to have to collect her so late, Thea shrugged. 'I doubt it. He's annoyingly persistent but he's never hurt me.'

'And you've never reported him for stalking?'

'Well, no, of course not. He's not really a stalker, just a bit fixated.'

'I'm not so sure. Tracking you down in a café, begging you to go out with him, and then turning up at the pub before you left Bath – and now he's here.' Shaun looked angry as he muttered. 'It's a criminal offence these days, for God's sake.'

Disconcerted by Shaun's concern on her behalf, Thea whispered as they turned into Mill Grange's driveway. 'You won't tell the others, will you? I don't want a fuss.'

'I won't say a word, but if you want me to warn him off...'

Despite her resolve not to get too close to him, Thea laid a hand on Shaun's arm, and then quickly removed it. 'Please don't. What if John went to the press saying you'd slandered him or something?'

'Why the hell would the press care?'

'Don't be so naïve! You're a TV personality.' Thea grimaced. 'Look, I'm not sure John'd go through with anything like that, he's more likely to make hollow threats.

But you can't take that risk.' She sunk her hands deep into her pockets as they walked. 'This whole thing is ridiculous. What the hell does he see in me anyway?'

'See in you?' Shaun glanced over his shoulder as they reached the manor's main door, as if he too was expecting to see John lurking in the gloom. 'I assume that's a trick question.'

Picking up on Shaun's less than covert surveillance, a trickle of fear ran down Thea's spine. 'You don't really think he's here now, do you?'

Shaun shook his head, but kept up his vigil anyway. 'From what you've said, John sounds desperate, but not stupid.'

'Thanks… I think.'

'I didn't mean desperate to like you, I meant…' Shaun caught Thea's eye. 'You're teasing me, here, at this time of night, after I've confessed to having dreams about ravishing you.' He winked, his eyes shining with a sudden flush of mischief. 'You're a cruel woman, Thea Thomas.'

Hoping Shaun couldn't see how pink she'd gone in the dark, Thea squeaked, 'Ravishing me? Hang on, you said you wanted to ask me out.'

'I do.' Not looking at Thea as he spoke, Shaun checked over the hedge that ran along the back of the makeshift car park by the butler's pantry. 'But I'm forty years old and I've fancied you for years. I do want to take you out. Often. And then I want to bring you back here and make you very happy.'

'Oh.' Thea was abruptly aware of how tall Shaun was as he stood behind her as she fumbled for the manor's door key.

Shaun's voice had taken on a husky edge as he said, 'You want me to see you inside and wait until Tina gets here?'

'She won't be long. I'll be okay. You should get back before the pub empties and you're spotted.'

He gave her a reassuring smile. 'Lock the door behind you.'

Thea nodded, privately cursing that she'd been too flustered to admit to Shaun that she'd have liked him to come inside with her. It didn't help that she knew she couldn't have invited him in without eventually having to explain Tina's non-appearance.

Double-locking the door from the inside, Thea slumped back against the solid wood. She felt as if she'd run a marathon.

John was here and Shaun wanted to ravish her. The trustees might sell the house and she could be unemployed again by the summer.

'Not the day I was expecting.' The confused but warm glow Thea had felt as she'd seen Shaun disappear, evaporated as she turned into the ray shadowed gloom of the manor.

Normally she'd leave a few lights on if she was due back to Mill Grange after dark, or she'd be safely in her room by ten o'clock, working on her admin from the warmth of her little bed. Tonight, the house felt spooky. 'For the hundredth time, Thea, this house is not haunted. The only thing coming out of the walls is history and experience.'

She tried not to listen to the voice at the back of her mind saying there were a million nooks and crannies where John could have hidden himself. That he may not have left the manor. That after Shaun had escorted him off the premises, he could have escorted himself right back in again, and be waiting anywhere, ready to pounce.

Thea climbed the stairs with more speed than usual. Not allowing herself so much as a peep into any of the many bedroom and bathrooms, whose doors stood wide open to keep them aired, she ran along the corridor to the servants' staircase, and lunged up them and into her room.

Slamming the door shut, Thea took a deep breath as her pulse slowly calmed. Her room was reassuringly familiar. The bed wasn't made, and the heap of clothes which had been waiting to be put away since the beginning of the week glared at her accusingly. Her walking boots were tucked under the desk chair, and a pile of well-thumbed novels sat on the bedside table.

Everything was exactly as she'd left it.

'Perhaps I should let John see how untidy I am. That would probably cure him of wanting to turn me into the next Mrs D-S.'

Changing into the thermal pyjamas and additional old jumper she wore as protection from the cold of the unheated room at night, Thea hid under the bed's blankets. Screwing her eyes shut and trying to block out the prospect of the day ahead, she cuddled a pillow to her chest. Rather than finding her thoughts plagued by John's unfathomable persistence or her possible unemployment, Thea's mind latched itself onto something else. Someone else.

'Shaun Cowlson wants to ravish me.' The image of Shaun being covertly videoed in bed with Becky Gibson invaded her subconscious uninvited. 'That was years ago and she vamped him.'

Beneath the comforting weight of her blankets, Thea considered the implication of the stomach-fluttering sensation she'd experienced when Shaun had de-cobwebbed her in the mill. Despite his huge palms and chunky fingers, the gesture had been gentle. Caring even.

'Shaun wants to ravish me.' The second time she told her pillow about her fellow historian's confession, Thea allowed herself to smile. 'I'm beginning to think I'd like to let him. It's nice to have something to look forward to after this mess is sorted.' Her smile widened. 'I wonder how Shaun wants to ravish me exactly...'

Nineteen

Wiping sleep from her eyes, Tina switched the kettle into life.

Guilt had stabbed at her all night.

When she'd eventually managed to fall asleep, her dreams had been full of images of Thea's broken body lying across Mill Grange's main staircase, a victim of John's unrequited obsession. Or she'd pictured her friend's face crumpled into tears as John dragged her into his car, forcing her into an unwanted gentrified life of motherhood and posh cutlery.

Tina checked her watch. It was half past six in the morning. She contemplated taking Thea a coffee up to her room, but then thought she might scare her friend witless if unexpected footsteps echoed along the corridor at such an early hour, so she stayed where she was.

Telling herself the lack of a body in the hallway proved that her imagination had run away with her, and that Thea was perfectly alright, Tina stared at the place where John had sat. When Thea had talked about him before, she'd left out a physical description, concentrating instead on how guilty the man made her feel for not returning his affection. It had never occurred to Tina that John would be quite so easy on the eye.

Instead she'd been taken in by his classic good looks. His piercing green eyes and expertly cut blond hair. She'd fallen for his smoothly chiselled features and well-tailored but casual clothes. He'd given off an air of confident intelligence and easy-going companionship. *And I fell for it.*

'How could I have let him in? I should have been on the alert as soon as I'd realised he was called John and was our age rather than a pensioner.'

Tina stared at her fingers entwined around her mug and gave a grunt of self-disgust. She'd been charmed by his smile and the air of affluence he projected. To her shame, Tina knew she'd found that attractive. She winced as she recalled how she'd told Thea to keep her hands off because John was hers. But the ugly truth was, however briefly and based on appearances alone, she'd considered John as a more viable version of the man she'd hoped Leon would be.

Leon. His face joined the taunting images in her head.

Tina wished she hadn't left the restaurant without a word of explanation. It had been childish, even though she hadn't planned it. She hadn't thought about anything but removing herself from Leon's company so she could clear her head after he'd belittled her.

'Belittled.' Tina blew the word across her steaming mug. 'That's what it was. He didn't know me – doesn't know me – yet he was hitting my insecurity buttons in neat order.' Until now she hadn't considered what it was that had made her act so out of character. Normally, she'd have seen the date through, politely making small talk, and then afterwards, send a short but honest email saying how she'd enjoyed the evening, but didn't wish to repeat the date experience in this instance. With Leon it was different.

He was so much the image of the man she'd always wanted. Older, experienced, successful, with no money worries. Although she was prepared to accept that such a man would be used to being in control of any given situation, it hadn't occurred to her that he might put her down in order to make himself appear more than he was.

'He's insecure.' Realisation sent a fresh hit of guilt nudging at Tina's conscience. 'Did Leon go all high-handed because he was nervous? Maybe I got it wrong?'

Tina hadn't so much as peeped at the email she'd set up exclusively for use with the dating site. *Is Internet dating really something you only do if you're a failure? If you can't secure a partner by conventional means?*

Telling herself that computer dating *was* conventional these days, Tina hugged her coat tighter around her shoulders. She ought to get on with some work while she was waiting for Thea to come downstairs for breakfast; there was certainly plenty to do.

Knowing she'd be of little use until she'd seen that Thea was alright, Tina checked the contents of the food cupboard the volunteers used for lunches and snacks. A smile crossed her lips. She might not be able to make amends for taking John on as a volunteer, but she could rustle up some pancakes so that Thea could start the day with a full stomach and her favourite breakfast.

*

Lemon juice.

Thea sniffed again as she walked down the servants' staircase. She wasn't imagining it, there was definitely a distinct aroma of lemon juice in the air. She froze on the stairs as, for a split second, she pictured John in the kitchen, cooking lemon cake to try and win her over.

Brushing away the perspiration that suddenly dotted her palms, Thea reminded herself that John didn't have a key to the manor. It had to be Tina.

'That was utterly delicious.' Thea smeared the last piece of pancake around her plate, soaking up as much spilt honey as she could. 'But honestly, you have no need to feel guilty about anything. You didn't know it was John, and he was hardly likely to introduce himself to you as my ex.'

'I know but, it was me who insisted you did the television broadcast and—'

'You did no such thing. It was Mabel's idea, and it was a good one. If it wasn't for the new volunteers, the slim chance we have of getting the house reopened wouldn't exist at all.'

'But if we don't succeed, then John will have found you for no reason and…'

Thea placed a palm over her friend's flapping hand. 'It's no good starting on what ifs.' Sounding more confident than she felt, Thea added, 'Actually, I feel guilty myself, what with one thing and another, I didn't get round to asking how your date with the silver fox went. Was he James Bond without the spying?'

Tina shrugged. 'Let's just say it doesn't seem to be our week when it comes to men!'

Keeping the image of Shaun that had arrived in her mind to herself, Thea decided to say nothing about his intentions of ravishment. After all, they might come to nothing. For now it was enough to have a hopeful dream for company while the demands of the weeks ahead accumulated.

'Leon wasn't the man of your dreams then?'

Tina twisted a pigtail around her fingers. 'I don't know. I walked out on him.'

'You're kidding! What did he do?'

'He made me feel inferior. I don't think he meant to, but before the starters arrived I found my feet marching homeward.'

'If he made you feel like that before the meal had even started, then you were better off out of there.'

'What if I misunderstood him?' Tina twiddled her left plait between her fingers. 'What if he was shy and overcompensating or—'

'He made you feel wrong. We have instincts like that for a reason; listen to them. Trust your gut.'

Tina gave a half smile. 'Like you did with John, you mean?'

'Touché!' Thea snorted. 'If I'd listened to the voice at the back of my head telling me John was too eager earlier on then, perhaps I wouldn't be facing another round of his efforts to prove to me he's the man of my dreams.' The kitchen clock announced the arrival of half past seven. 'I wonder what time he'll show up.'

'He didn't strike me as someone who knows that life exists before eight in the morning on a non-work day.' Tina rubbed her forearms. 'How about we explain the situation to the whole group? If we stand together, we can ask John to leave.'

Horrified at the idea of everyone knowing of her personal business, Thea said, 'I'd rather not. Can you imagine! It would be round the village like wildfire. And, if I do end up working here long-term, I'd always be "the girl who had the trainee stalker", even when I'm ninety.'

'True.' Tina sighed. 'Can we fire him?'

'Apparently it isn't that easy with volunteers. I asked Shaun last night.'

Tina poured a new packet of biscuits into a nearby tin. 'Getting on okay with our celebrity, are you?'

'Don't look at me like that! He's used to working with volunteers, so I asked him.' Thea busied herself with the dirty plates. 'He was very kind and rescued me from John's determination to take me out last night. We ended up having dinner in Moira's living room, but I can hardly expect him to be my bodyguard for the next few months.'

'You went out to dinner?' Tina's face lit up.

'Not in a date way. In a rescue-me-from-John way. Don't go reading anything into it.'

'Yeah, right.' Tina gathered up the mugs and followed Thea to the sink. 'It would help a bit if Shaun did stay here and pay rent.'

'True, although…' Thea hesitated. 'I don't want anyone to know I'm living in as well.'

'What did Shaun say when you told him?'

'I didn't.'

Tina regarded her friend as if she were nuts. 'How will you be able to keep it secret?'

'I don't know. By being extra careful about getting up before everyone arrives and not leaving evidence of breakfast consumption in the kitchen I suppose. Can you imagine how tongues would wag if people knew it was just me and Shaun in this big house at night?'

'Ah.'

'I can see the local headlines now. "Celebrity archaeologist shacks up with restorer at Mill Grange at Exmoor Trust's expense."'

'Bit long for a headline, but I take your point.' Drying her hands, Tina said, 'We could open the manor to others as well. Charge people to stay while having an interactive restoration experience.'

'Wouldn't that mean having to find a caterer and keeping the rooms clean on a daily basis and…?'

Tina raised her hand. 'Scrap that then.'

'It was a good idea, but we don't have the time to run a guest house as well.' Thea added, 'I suppose we could let it be known that volunteers could stay here for a small fee, but that they'd be obliged to look after themselves. But…'

'But John would immediately want to stay.' Tina flapped the idea away with her hand. 'Let's forget it.'

Thea waved at Sam through the scullery window, as he hailed her with a sickle in one hand and a roll of sacking in the other. For a moment she envied the serenity on his face. He was a man who knew what the day held, and was happily embracing its simplicity.

'We have to keep going.'

'We certainly do.' Shaun leant against the scullery door. 'Talking to yourself?'

Surprised by how pleased she was to see Shaun, Thea said, 'I was thinking how much the village needs this project to work, not to mention how much we owe it to the volunteers to succeed.'

'That's an attitude I like.' Shaun crossed his arms over his scruffy Arran jumper. 'So boss, where would you like me to start?'

'Are you sure you're okay with me giving you instructions? I mean, you probably have more idea than me about what to do first and...'

'You know the place, I'm still learning about it. So, where shall I start?'

The firmness of his tone was offset by the friendly shine to his eyes. Thea couldn't help but grin back at him. 'In that case I'd like you to go to the laundry.' Thea pointed along the slim servants' corridor that ran away from the scullery and the comfort of the main house. 'Can you give me your opinion as to the extent of the damp, see if we can do anything both short and long-term to prevent it spreading? If so, I'd like your opinion about if it's worth opening the laundry to the public.'

An imperious voice from behind Shaun suddenly chipped in. 'Of course it has to be opened. Everyone likes to poke about in the old laundry.' Mabel spoke as if even the consideration of the issue was a waste of time. 'Come on, Shaun, Thea's busy running the place. I'll show you.'

Mabel manhandled Shaun away, and Thea fought the urge to laugh as she heard his voice say innocently, 'You clearly know this place well, Mabel. Do you mind me asking why there is such an awful smell of vinegar?'

Twenty

Thea wasn't sure what had pulled off the first small miracle. Whether it was Shaun's arrival and the chance to work alongside someone famous, or whether it was her pleas at how little time there was left if they wanted Mill Grange to reopen on time that had done it, but by nine o'clock the house was bustling with volunteers. Even the students had arrived bright and early, sharing blue jokes with Derek and Bill in the gardens and digging up the weeds as if they were all born to a life of horticulture rather than business management and teaching.

Delighted though she was, Thea could not relax. John hadn't arrived, but she was sure he would. Being marched off the premises might cause other men to listen to common sense, but this was John, who had a rule book all of his own.

Longing to go and hide in another part of the house, Thea cursed the lack of Wi-Fi throughout the manor. It had been a bonus until John had found her, a way to avoid him. Now its lack was a barrier to working on her emails, undetected, in a secret corner of Mill Grange.

Determined that when he did inevitably arrive, John would find her acting every inch the professional, Thea started formatting the information boards she intended to display in each room of the house. She'd got no further than selecting an attractive yet legible font, when Mabel arrived, brandishing a book in her hand.

'Why on earth didn't you tell me that I was damaging things with the strength of my vinegar washes? Honestly Thea, I'd have thought you cared more about the manor's contents than that.'

Thea's brain was still catching up on the fact Mabel was blaming her for a practice that had been in use since before her own arrival at the manor, when a book crashed onto the desk.

'I was working in good faith. That's all I've ever done, and to find I've been potentially harming things…' Mabel looked as stricken as she did angry.

Feeling rather sorry for the pensioner with so many good intentions but no tact whatsoever, Thea picked up the conservation guide, remembering what Tina had said about Mabel's family buying it for her.

'Mabel, I'd be the first to congratulate you on your hard work. In fact, I think I have on a number of occasions.' She gestured for her companion to sit down. 'I have, if you think back, tried to speak to you about the vinegar situation. But on each occasion you've brushed away any suggestion which you saw as criticism or a personal attack on you or your commitment to this project. I have done neither, nor would I. Mill Grange is in trouble, but it would be in a lot more trouble if you hadn't led the original group of volunteers so well for so long.'

Mabel opened her mouth to speak, but Thea held up her hand and kept going. 'I am not sure why you think it's my fault that you either worked out the proportions of the vinegar solution wrong or that the amounts suggested in here were incorrect in the first place.' Thea snapped her lips closed as she registered how close she'd come to shouting. Meanwhile, Mabel just sat as if she'd been stunned.

Adopting a softer tone, Thea sighed, 'I'm sorry, Mabel. I didn't mean to sound so cross, but I can't see why any of what you've done is my fault. As it happens, apart from the stench of acetic acid that hangs around the house, no real damage has been done. Vinegar can indeed be a worthwhile ingredient in cleaning – when used in moderation.'

Avoiding Thea's eye, Mabel asked, 'You're sure I haven't damaged anything?'

'Certain.' Thea smiled. 'Did Shaun tell you about the vinegar problem?'

'Yes. *He* really knows his stuff.'

The emphasis on the word *he* did not go unnoticed. Thea struggled to stop her hackles rising again. 'He does, but so do I. Can I ask why you believed him, but not me?'

This time Mabel blanched. 'Well, because he's, well he's...'

'On television and therefore must know more than anyone who isn't?'

'Well, it must count for something mustn't it? Otherwise you'd have his job and...'

Thea shook her head. 'Mabel, you're an intelligent woman, you can't possibly believe that being on television means anything other than being a good presenter as well as, in this case, being a good archaeologist.'

Rather than pausing to force Mabel to make an uncomfortable reply, Thea moved on. 'However, none of that matters. What matters is what happens next.' She leant forward, her tone earnest and confiding. 'Mabel, I'm very worried about the future of Mill Grange. For whatever reasons, we have little time to get everything ready and fewer funds than we were led to believe to achieve our goal.

'The threat of sale is not going to go away unless we make serious progress and raise at least some money to help cover what needs doing but without fuss. Sticking a large thermometer outside the manor with a donations jar next to it won't even touch the sides. That's why you've found me this morning designing the information boards rather than paying a professional designer to do them.' Thea waved a hand towards the computer screen. 'Even with the extra hands, for which I'm grateful, we're up against it.'

Mabel was silent for a second, and then asked, 'You weren't exaggerating the situation because you resent my help? There really is a chance the manor won't open?'

Thea was shocked. 'You thought I'd made it up because I was cross you'd called Malcolm about Shaun? Seriously?'

Saying nothing, a contrite Mabel shifted in her seat.

'Let's forget it, shall we? You want this place to open, don't you?'

'Of course.'

'Then let's do our best to make sure it does. Let's show the trustees that we can handle whatever they throw at us.'

Sounding uncharacteristically uncertain, Mabel muttered, 'Do you think we can?'

'We owe it to the village to give it our best shot. The pub, café and village shop could certainly do with the extra trade from visitors.'

Mabel's sharp expression returned as quickly as it had disappeared. Thea's heart sank as the more familiar combative glint came back to Mabel's eye. 'You think we owe this to the villagers?'

'Umm... yes.'

'Answer me this, Miss Thomas. How much shopping have you done in the village shop?'

Guilt stabbed at Thea. 'I haven't had a lot of time to go shopping, Mabel.'

'And how many cups of coffee and slices of cake have you had in Sybil's tea shop?'

'Well...'

'Not one. Am I right?' Mabel looked every inch the disappointed headmistress. 'How is that supporting the village? How will they ever know who the person trying to save the manor in their name is, if that person never lifts their head above the parapet? Are you afraid they'll criticise you?'

Thea swallowed. Mabel was spot on. Here she was, busting a gut to try and save a historic part of the community, but she'd forgotten the community itself. Was she afraid they'd find fault with how little she'd achieved so far?

'When was the last time you had coffee in a café?'

'Not since I left Bath.' Relieved that Mabel had dropped her combative tone, Thea tried to explain, 'It isn't that I don't want to go into the village. And as for coffee shops, I love them. But there's—'

'So much to do?'

Thea nodded.

'I know there is, and I'm sorry I've made life more difficult, but you're making it difficult for yourself as well. The villagers are on your side, but you aren't including them.'

'But you're a villager – and so are all the volunteers.' Thea realised she wasn't sure where all the helpers were from. 'Aren't they?'

'Don't you know?'

'Not really.' Thea felt ashamed. 'I suppose I assumed everyone was local.'

Mabel was silent. Her shrewd eyes fixed on Thea, as if trying to decide if she should attack further, or reel in her frustration and help the girl. Before she had the chance to speak again, Thea slouched back in her chair with a thump.

'Look, Mabel, I'm sorry I've gone about this all wrong in your eyes. I made an assumption where the village was concerned. I thought they'd come to me, rather than me making the effort to go to them. I have no excuses. Do you think I'd be welcome if I went now, or have I burnt my boats?'

A rare smile curled up the corners of Mabel's lips. 'I wouldn't worry too much. Moira at the pub was impressed by you.'

'The landlady of the Stag and Hound?'

'Yes. Apparently one of her residents, she wouldn't say who – client confidentiality and all that rubbish – has been talking highly of your work here.'

Privately thanking Shaun for being so kind and Moira for being so discreet, Thea felt two spots of pink highlight her cheeks. 'That's very kind.'

'She's a kind lady. Upwich is full of kind people.'

'People who I need to talk to, so I can discover their hopes for the restoration of the manor.' Thea was suddenly beset by nerves, wishing for the hundredth time that she didn't get stage fright every time she spoke to people she didn't know.

'Exactly,' Mabel agreed. 'But I should come with you.'

'Would you?'

'If you'd like me to.'

'Please.' Thea seized her chance. 'There's something else. If you'd like to do it.'

Mabel was caught between looking pleased and wary.

'I need someone to coordinate everyone: the volunteers and workmen that arrive, any outside visitors who may come by. I'd like that someone to be you. Your organisational skills are superb, so let's make them work for us. If you could take the jobs list and make sure everyone is doing what they said they'd do, or, if they are doing something that doesn't suit their skill base, you could gently steer them in a different direction.'

'I'd be delighted, but are you sure?' Unexpectedly sheepish, Mabel said, 'I didn't think you liked me being bossy.'

'There's helpful bossy and there's unhelpful bossy.'

Mabel laughed. 'You sound like my husband.'

Relief flooded Thea at the realisation that she and Mabel might finally be singing from the same hymn sheet.

'Shall we say coffee in the village tomorrow at 10.30 a.m.?'

Thea could feel her insides swim as she considered how she might be received, but simply said, 'Perfect. Thank you.'

'I'll crack on then.' Pushing herself off her chair, Mabel hooked the jobs list off the wall. 'Any sign of that nice young man yet?'

Thea's moment of optimism was extinguished. She was sure Mabel was referring to John, but instead said, 'I think Shaun's in the laundry.'

'Not him, that nice Mr Davies.' She fixed her astute gaze on Thea. 'He said he knew you.'

'Our paths crossed briefly at the Roman Baths, that's all. And no, he isn't here.'

Sifting through some of the original dockets for the purchase of household supplies, wondering whether to display them as originals under glass, or reproduce them so there was no risk of future damage, Thea picked the three clearest examples, each dating from 1866. One detailed the purchase of a vast supply of onions for pickling, one for oranges for conserves, while the third was a record of the amount of boot polish the butler had agreed the boot boy would require for a year's worth of buffing.

'I doubt those yellowing bits of paper are as fascinating as your expression suggests they are.'

Thea clenched her toes in her boots, determined to keep all emotion from her voice, telling herself if she could call a truce with Mabel, then she could stay strong with John.

'You prove the point I made yesterday, John. You are not suited to working here if you can't see that everything connected to the manor has interest. Are you leaving today?'

'You know I'm not. I'm here to take you out for breakfast.'

'Breakfast?' Thea glanced at the clock. 'It's quarter past

ten in the morning. Everyone else was here ages ago. We are up against it here – or weren't you paying attention last night?'

'I was paying close attention,' John's eyes narrowed. 'Mostly to that giant who everyone seems to think is important because he's on television. It was embarrassing to witness him pawing at you.'

'For God's sake John, Shaun was doing nothing of the sort.' Hoping her reddening face would be put down to indignation rather than the memory of Shaun informing her of his intention to ask her out, Thea added, 'He is a professional who has offered to help here. Someone who *is* passionate about yellowing pieces of paper! Now, please go home, John. I am never going to change my mind about going out with you. You're making a fool of yourself.'

The second the word 'fool' had crossed her lips, Thea knew she'd made a mistake.

John's green eyes flashed and then dulled as he bent closer. 'I'm no fool, you know that. I'm just determined to make you see what you threw away.' He paused, considering.

'How easy it would be to make a fool of *you* though, Thea. To expose the fact you have a celebrity hidden away here.' John lowered his voice, shrugging as he smiled. 'It's such a shame to think that you could let the whole community down only weeks after the Trust started *paying* you to sort this place out. How much could they save I wonder, by not giving you a wage?'

He hadn't mentioned going to the papers, but the implication was there, hanging between them. Realisation hit Thea like a blast of cold air. She was stuck with John until she agreed to go out for a meal… and even then, that wouldn't be enough to get rid of him.

Suddenly exhausted, Thea lowered her eyes back to the nineteenth-century invoices. 'Go and find Sam in the garden. You can help him uncover the old walkway that circuits the house.'

John didn't speak again, but the triumph in his eyes left no doubt that he considered himself the victor of the exchange, breakfast or no breakfast.

Twenty-One

April 11th

For Thea, walking into Sybil's Tea Room was love at first sight. She could have hugged Mabel for bringing her here. Instead, Thea lifted the menu and gave her companion a warm smile. It felt like coming home. Why hadn't she thought to come here before? In Bath, a coffee shop trip had been a daily occurrence, something she did without even thinking.

'Thank you for inviting me here. I love it.'

'You haven't tried anything yet.' Mabel pointed with surprising discretion in the direction of a well-padded woman in a pristine navy apron, half-glasses and a shockingly unflattering short haircut. 'That's Sybil.'

'Looks friendly.'

'Very much so. It's important you make a good impression.'

Immediately self-conscious, Thea brushed her hair with her fingers, remembering what Tina had said about getting it cut.

'What do you recommend?' The menu was the perfect balance of deliciousness, with random token gestures towards good health. 'If I haven't found time to come back here to have an afternoon cream tea within the next fortnight, you have my permission to make me.'

'I'll add it to my list.' Mabel inclined her head a fraction as Sybil glided to their side on silent, thick trainer clad feet.

'Mabel, how lovely. How's that Bert of yours?'

'Potty as ever.' Mabel gestured across the table. 'This is Thea. She's in charge of the restoration at Mill Grange.'

Sybil's eyebrows rose, but her innate customer service skills prevented her from saying what she was clearly thinking. *Why haven't you visited here before?*

Wanting to smooth over any rough edges before they snagged, Thea put out her hand. 'I'm delighted to meet you. I should also apologise.'

'You should?'

'Absolutely. I'm a huge tea shop and café fan, yet I've neglected you. Not a mistake I'll be making again.' Thea held the menu open. 'I'm having trouble deciding. I'd usually go straight for the lemon cake and espresso option, but I wonder... are the toasted crumpets with poached eggs and ham as amazing as they sound?'

'Better!'

The reply came from the occupant of a small round table next to them, where an elderly man was steering a piece of toast around his plate, dabbing up any last traces of fried egg. 'Sybil here cooks the best eggs in the world.'

'Thanks, Alf.' Sybil patted the old man's shoulder. 'Alf's been here for his breakfast every year since time began. I don't think there's anything on the menu he hasn't sampled.'

'Apart from that new vegan nonsense.'

'Got to move with the times, Alf.'

Thea couldn't help but smile as he mumbled. 'Don't see why.'

Sybil rolled her eyes affectionately. 'Are you going to give the crumpets a go then, Thea?'

'Please. And a black Americano if that's okay.'

'No problem. Mabel?'

'The same as Thea please, Sybil, but with a pot of tea.'

As soon as their host had bustled off, Mabel leant in and lowered her voice a fraction, presumably so Alf couldn't listen in. 'Well done.'

Thea smiled. 'This place is truly lovely.'

Clearly once a cottage, the tea rooms consisted of a living room which had been knocked into a dining room, with a large glass conservatory added on at the back. The low beamed ceiling was painted in a traditional white and black style. Pine tables, each covered with serviceable, easy-wipe, Spode-patterned cloths holding matching china, waited patiently for an influx of custom.

The stable-style front door had hardly stopped swinging since they'd arrived. Every time a table emptied, a young waitress would appear like magic from the kitchen, clean the surface, and a new customer would sweep in. They had only been there ten minutes before Thea realised how many walkers visited the village. Far from being desperate for custom as Thea had assumed, Sybil's Tea Room was a hub for hikers and cyclists planning their treks across Exmoor.

'I can see why it's so busy in here, but Mabel, I must ask, why did you make me feel guilty for not bringing my custom here? Sybil is, quite rightly, doing well.'

Mabel gave her hair a satisfied pat. 'I had to tug the heartstrings a little, I admit. But if you are seen in here, then it will be all around Upwich by lunchtime, that Thea Thomas from the manor was here. That you took the time and trouble to come.'

'I get it.' Thea's pleasure at being away from the manor for a while increased as two plates of piping hot crumpets, eggs and ham appeared. 'Thank you Sybil, these smell incredible.'

'I hope you enjoy them. Although, I have to say, the eggs aren't as good as they were when we had them off the manor.'

'You had eggs from Mill Grange?'

'Up until the Trust took the place thirty years back.' Sybil smiled at Thea's surprised face. 'I've been here since I was twenty so that's almost forty-five years.'

Thea looked down at her aromatic breakfast. 'If we reintroduced chickens to the manor, would you be interested in the eggs?'

'I most certainly would. For the right price, of course.'

'Which is?'

Sybil waved a hand towards the cooling plates of food. 'You girls eat up. I'll do some sums and get back to you.'

Mabel, who'd been observing with satisfaction, thrust her fork into her poached eggs, sending golden yolk flowing across her crumpets. 'You see why we're here then.'

'Oh yes.' A few mouthfuls of food later, Thea paused for a swig of coffee. 'Mabel, you don't happen to know of a hairdresser in the village?'

'I most certainly do.' Mabel raised her cup of tea in a salute. 'We'll pop in on Phyllis after we've been here.' She leant forward conspiratorially. 'But don't worry, she isn't the one who cuts Sybil's hair.'

'Chickens?' Sam's approval was unmistakable. 'There's a place in the walled garden which would afford shelter and enough ground for them to run free. If you would like me to, I could build a coop from the old wooden boards stacked at the back of the stables. We'd need to get safety covers for the nails and so on, so the poultry didn't hurt itself.'

'Seriously? You could build one just like that?'

Sam nodded. 'I've seen hundreds of coops. You'd be surprised what some people make them out of. We could put it near to where I thought you could grow vegetables. Tina mentioned that was something else you had in mind.'

'The idea is to sell as much produce from the manor's land as we can, as fast as is feasible. Am I being unrealistic, Sam?'

'For some things possibly, but early spuds and eggs are entirely doable.'

'How much do chickens cost? How many do we need at once?'

Sam laughed. 'I have no idea. A job for Tina's researching skills perhaps?'

'She'll probably welcome the change from pricing waterproof sealant and roof tiles.'

Sam said nothing more on the subject of Tina as he dug his shovel into the soil. 'Shall I show you where I think the chickens would be happy?'

'Please.' Thea followed Sam towards the kitchen garden. 'Have you ever kept chickens?'

'No. You?'

'No.' Rather than feel despondent that this would be something else for her to do, Thea felt enlivened by the idea of having chickens in the garden. 'I have some reading up to do then.'

'Being in the walled garden should keep them safe from foxes.'

Thea blanched, 'I hadn't considered that. I don't think I could cope if I came down in the morning to find the girls savaged.'

'The girls?' Sam laughed. 'And there I was about to advise not getting too attached to them in case of disaster or if you need to sell them for meat.'

'Too late for that. I can already see one called Gertrude, can't you?'

'Isn't that a cow's name?' Sam laughed. 'I thought you'd be calling one Mabel.'

'We seem to have called a truce. At least, I hope we have.' Thea felt her heart lighten as she looked across the garden and Mill Grange's beauty hit her anew. 'I also have Sybil in the village café willing to buy our eggs.'

'Good. Better get Tina to source egg boxes as well then.' Sam stared up at the manor. 'The trustees would be fools to sell this place. It could make a fortune for the whole area.'

'I think so.'

'And in the meantime, it can start to earn its keep.' Sam shifted, uneasily from one foot to the other as if suddenly uncomfortable. 'Actually, I wanted a private word about that.'

'Go on.'

'I wondered if I could camp in the garden. I'd pay a pitch fee. What do you think?'

'Yes!' Thea didn't hesitate. The idea of Sam being on hand if John were to pester her out of hours, and for a chaperone to be around should word get out that she and Shaun were both sleeping in the manor, was a godsend. 'That's a brilliant idea.'

'Really?'

'Yes. You could use the bathroom inside, you know. If you wanted to?'

Sam looked uneasy. 'Thanks for not asking me about that. About the not going inside thing, I mean.'

'Your business, not mine. But if you want to talk, I'm here.' Thea pointed to the back door. 'Just so you know, the room next to the scullery holds an ancient but usable toilet and the only shower in the place. It's a ghastly 1960s thing which the family put in not long before they left. It's literally only three footsteps inside the back door, and there's a large picture window onto the garden.'

'So I wouldn't feel enclosed while in there.' Sam nodded. 'Thank you, Thea. You're very kind.'

'Not that kind. Shall we say that you'll pay the same to camp here as whatever you're paying at the site you're staying at now, minus five pounds per week?'

'Deal.' Sam beamed. 'Starting tonight?'

'Perfect.' Thea, floating high on the positive nature of the day, headed off to source some chickens for sale and to see if Tina fancied helping Sam build a coop. She'd only taken a few steps, when Sam called after her.

'Your hair looks nice by the way.'

Twenty-Two

'I don't want him living here.'

Thea bit her lip and started to mentally count to ten. Her grandmother had sworn by giving life ten seconds before commenting on difficult situations, and often it helped. However, Thea had found herself counting to ten so often over the past week that she was considering reciting the colours of the rainbow or listing the top ten most worshipped Roman gods and goddesses, just for variety.

'And I don't want you working here, so I suppose that makes us even.'

John was sitting on the opposite side of her desk, fidgeting with a pile of paperclips. 'He is clearly after you.' He placed his palms flat against its edge, his legs wide as if trying to make himself bigger. Thea found herself holding back a hysterical laugh as she remembered a nature documentary she'd seen. Sir David Attenborough had been explaining how lower ranking male gibbons attempted to make themselves appear more attractive to the female gibbons. John's current stance was almost identical.

'Did you hear what I said, Thea? I don't want that man…'

This same scenario had played out over each of the last five mornings. And every morning Thea had given the same response. She found the words forming on her lips in readiness. Any minute now John would ask her when she was coming out for a meal with him. Then he'd return to the subject of not wanting Shaun to move in that evening. Well, enough was enough. Today she didn't want to hear it.

It was bad enough that everyone here liked John. At least, the women did. Diane seemed particularly susceptible to his charms, and Thea had heard the girlish giggles of the Biggleswaite sisters undercutting her ex's dulcet tones on a number of occasions.

On the other hand, Thea thought she'd seen Derek giving John a wary eye glance every now and then, although that could have been wishful thinking on her behalf. Sam had passed no comment, but Tina was convinced he was keeping a quiet eye on their less welcome volunteer.

Shaun was polite to John, but then Shaun was polite to everyone. Nonetheless, if Thea was alone in a situation where John could get to her, the archaeologist would magically appear. She was convinced it was Shaun's ability to continually get in the way of his plans that had led John to start showing up so early in the morning.

Ignoring the tingling numbness that was racing down her arms, ready to remind Thea how much she hated confrontation, she slammed her own palms on the table.

'This is the very last time I am going to say this. The only reason you are still here is that we are desperate for hands and I have no legal grounds to remove you. We are *never* going to date again. I do not want to be part of your life. You do not know me. You just think you do. Do you understand?'

John's face flushed. 'Then let me get to know you. I want to, Thea. You're everything to me, you must see that. Beautiful, funny, driven, clever, and I...' He slumped back in his seat, as if all the fight was wiped out of him. Pity hit Thea's kind heart as she looked at him across the table.

'If you want to stay here to work, then I can't stop you, but if you want to get to know me as a friend, then you're going to have to stop acting like this.' Thea bit the inside of her lips, choosing her words carefully. 'You're capable of being a nice man. Start proving it to everyone here. Remember your self-respect.'

'Self-respect?' John pushed his hands into his jacket pockets as he spoke with controlled calm. 'The thing is, Thea—'

'Thea! Are you about?'

The echo of Mabel's shrill voice as she called ahead of herself down the servants' corridor cut John's sentence in half as he rose to his feet.

'Good morning, Mrs Hastings, you're looking most appetising today.'

Giggling girlishly, Mabel beamed. 'Foolish boy.' She gave him a playful push. 'Have you finished with Thea? I have a few things I need to talk to her about.'

'For now.' He almost bowed to Mabel as he turned so that only Thea could see his face. 'I'll be back later to finish what we were discussing.'

'Are you alright, dear?' For the first time, Mabel noticed Thea was looking a bit pale. 'Can I get you some water?'

'I'm fine, thanks. I didn't get much sleep.' Licking some moisture back into her dry lips, Thea asked, 'How can I help you?'

Flourishing a large piece of paper, and a calendar, Mabel sat down. She was clearly very pleased with herself. 'I've made a plan for the volunteers' work structure. It's more efficient than what we had before.'

Glad of Mabel's timely arrival, Thea would have agreed to listen to any plan she had at all. 'Sounds good – let's hear it.'

Thea sat on the edge of her bed. She'd only caught a few parts of Mabel's plan; enough to know she wasn't dooming the volunteers to a Victorian prison-like regime of hard labour.

The whole time the old lady was speaking Thea had been visited by flashbacks of her time with John.

When she'd first seen him, literally across a crowded room, she'd been hit by his amazing smile. It seemed to grow wider the longer he grinned, making you feel as if he was the happiest man in the world, simply because he was talking to you.

How did we get from there to here?

It had been a Christmas party for a local business. The Baths often hired out rooms for such events, but Thea had only been involved on that occasion because half the events team had been hit with a bout of food poisoning after an unwise night out in a suspiciously cheap burger bar.

John had mistaken her for a waitress at first. He'd run out of champagne and wanted his glass topping up, '*by the woman with the most beautiful chestnut eyes I've ever seen.*'

She'd laughed openly at the cliché, but he hadn't minded. They'd got talking, she explaining she was more host than waitress, and he that he was bored with office gossip and welcomed the chance to speak to someone more interesting.

Thea had been so surprised when he'd asked her out for 'some good food and fun,' that she'd accepted without hesitation.

Food and fun. 'And that's what it was for me, John. When did that change for you?'

Moving to the window, keeping back from the glass so no one could see her from outside, Thea surveyed the grounds. Sam was raking over the most recently cleared area of garden. John was near him. He stood out like a sore thumb in his designer overalls and rubble clearance gloves. She wasn't sure what he was supposed to be doing according to Mabel's new rota, but what he was actually doing was piling up branches and weeds for burning.

Deciding to do as much admin work as she could from her room and more practical jobs once everyone else had gone home, Thea sat at her little desk.

Tina would soon be back from a meeting she was having with the trustees, so she could keep up-to-date on the properties she was temporarily neglecting in favour of Mill Grange, and Shaun was due to arrive with his luggage around twelve. All week Thea had been telling herself she had to move out of the manor. She had to find a room to rent before Shaun arrived. Somehow it hadn't happened. There had always been something more urgent to do.

It was going to be impossible not to tell him she was also living in. The best she could think of, was to pretend she'd just arrived; that his idea of paying rent to the Trust was such a good idea that she'd decided to do the same. She was sure Shaun would believe her if she said she wanted to keep the arrangement private because she didn't want John to find out where she was staying.

Dragging herself away from her desk, Thea travelled to the opposite end of the servants' corridor to what would be Shaun's temporary abode. Admiring the view from the window, which took in the other end of the garden, Thea knew part of her wanted Shaun here. 'But do I want him here because I want him to ravish me, or because I want someone to show John I'm off limits?'

'Tina looks happy.' Shaun dropped his oversized holdall onto the little bed. 'Sam tells me she has found some chickens.'

'She has. We get delivery of six Light Sussexes tomorrow.' Thea smiled as she thought of Tina and Sam working together on the construction of the coop with all the care reserved for decorating a nursery.

'What's a Light Sussex, apart from it being a chicken I mean?'

'According to Tina they are one of the easiest breeds to keep. They're hardy, will forage for some of their food around the garden, and they are good layers. We can also use them for meat if we have to.'

Shaun laughed. 'But you're already squeamish about that.'

'Yeah. Stupid as I eat meat, but there you go.'

'Human nature, not stupid at all.'

'Don't forget, if you hear someone moving around

downstairs in the evening or early morning, it'll be Sam. He's started using the downstairs bathroom now he's camping in the woods.'

'He's coming inside?'

'The only time I was around to witness it, he was in and out incredibly fast, but the shower had been used, so yes. I'd love to know why he's so averse to being inside but...'

'But you're wisely leaving it to him to tell you when he's ready.'

'Yes.' Thea frowned. 'You know why?'

'I have my suspicions, but I don't know. And like you, I will not ask.' Changing the subject, Shaun surveyed the room with an air of approval. 'This looks great. Thanks, Thea.'

He sat on the edge of the bed and immediately Thea realised her mistake. How hadn't she seen it before? Shaun's broad frame already dwarfed the slim servants' single bed. No way would his six-foot-plus length squeeze inside the sheets and blankets she'd just used to make it up.

'You are never going to fit in that little bed.'

'I'll be fine. I sleep curled up.'

Finding herself picturing Shaun asleep, his knees under his chin, his arms hooked up over the counterpane, Thea said, 'Even if you were to squeeze yourself up like a concertina, there is no way you'll get a good night's sleep.'

Cross for missing the obvious again, Thea hooked Shaun's holdall up in her arms. 'Come on, let's go downstairs and find you a double bed. We can redo the room before we open.'

Thea was already marching down the corridor when Shaun caught up with her.

'There's no need, I'll be fine. I told you, I'm used to simple sleeping arrangements.'

'Well, there's simple, and there's stupid.' She kept walking down the narrow stairs. 'I'm not having you move out of one of Moira's comfy rooms into an army billet.'

Shaun laughed. 'You sounded just like Mabel then. Good to see you two in harmony.'

'If she'd just see that the sun doesn't shine out of John's butt, she'd be perfect.'

The mention of John cast a cloud over them as Thea pushed open the door to the smallest, and therefore easiest to re-clean, of all the double rooms. 'This do? Not exactly the best bedroom. It belonged to the governess originally.'

'It has a bigger bed, a desk, a window with a stunning view and its own sink. What more could a man want?'

The way he looked at her sent Thea's pulse racing. His eyes made it very clear what else a man might want. Thea gulped. She had intended this to be the moment when she told Shaun she was living there too. No way could she do that now.

Twenty-Three

April 18th

Thea couldn't sleep. Every time she turned over in her rickety little bed, she worried Shaun would hear her.

She'd been so focused on finding him somewhere more comfortable to stay, that she hadn't realised she'd placed him in the bedroom directly below hers until it was too late. Could he hear her? She couldn't hear him, but perhaps he was a light sleeper. Perhaps he didn't toss and turn like she did. Perhaps he didn't have a squeaky bed frame. Thea felt her cheeks flush as an image of helping Shaun make the bed springs protest entered her mind and didn't want to leave again.

'This is ridiculous. You are not in a good place to have a relationship with anyone, let alone Shaun. Especially not with John milling around.'

Switching on the bedside lamp, she looked at the clock. It was one o'clock in the morning. Flicking the room into darkness, Thea plumped up her pillows and tried to get comfortable.

'The walls and floors are so thick in this place, the chance of him hearing anything from below are slim anyway.'

She should have told Shaun she was staying here too. Now the fact she hadn't said anything, felt like a lie, rather than an attempt to prevent gossip before it started.

Squeezing her eyes closed, she forced her mind away from acrobatics with the resident celebrity archaeologist, to consider the manor instead.

'That's supposed to be your passion right now. Not a bloke who's helping to restore it.'

There was no doubt that the restoration was beginning to come together. Sam and Tina had formed a good working relationship. Thea was convinced they liked each other more than either of them showed, but she knew she had no basis for that hunch. It was just a feeling.

'Wishful thinking. You just want your friend to get a good guy rather than a rich guy who's bad for her self-esteem.'

Tina hadn't mentioned Leon since their aborted dinner date. Come to think about it, she hadn't mentioned dating at all. Once the idea of building a chicken coop and preparing for the arrival of their feathery friends had been mooted, Tina had hardly left the manor at all.

Mabel was also performing wonders. By making sure everyone else was working to their strengths, she'd streamlined their days. She had even taken to wandering down to Sybil's Tea Room every other day to collect trays of cakes. Cakes which, Thea had discovered, Sybil was giving to Mill Grange for free as a gesture of goodwill towards the restoration. Thea vowed to go back into Upwich the following week for the cream tea she'd promised herself. 'Maybe I'll ask Shaun to come.'

Idiot. That will blow his cover. Why hide him here if you're just going to stroll around the village together!

Turning over, wincing as the springs squealed in protest, Thea froze. Her ears strained to hear if Shaun made a corresponding noise below.

Nothing.

The garden. Think about the gardens.

The main garden was looking good. Although a fair bit of clearance and general tidying up needed attending to, Derek and his team had made considerable headway. Two days ago, Sam had revealed the full extent of the Victorian walkway which divided the garden and the woods. And today, they'd finished laying fresh gravel along its entire circuit, ready for a new generation of strollers to embed it into the earth beneath the soles of their walking boots.

The greenhouse remained a problem. Thea hadn't been able to bring herself to call in a demolition firm to remove it, but nor had she worked out a way to save it. It couldn't stay as it was though. Health and safety would never allow it.

At least the chickens were coming tomorrow. She was surprised by how much she was looking forward to their arrival.

Thea was finally drifting into a pleasant dream about winning the lottery and saving the greenhouse and the mill, as well as the manor, when a splintering crash echoed through the room, making her sit bolt upright.

'What the hell…?' She clutched the blankets to her thermal-covered chest.

It hadn't sounded like it was coming from outside. Was Shaun up and moving around?

The sound came again. Less a crash this time, more like the sound of something metallic being scraped across the floor.

'The house is *not* haunted. It isn't. No one has ever said it is. It isn't!' Thea spoke quickly, gripping the blankets tighter; images of ghostly figures dragging chains unhelpfully adding to her rush of fear.

She could hear Shaun now. At least, she hoped it was him who was running down the wooden staircase with a clatter of boots on wood. He wasn't bothering to be quiet because he didn't know there was anyone else in the house to disturb. At least anyone who was allowed to be there.

Frozen to the spot, Thea didn't know what to do.

She was in charge. Anything that happened in the manor was her responsibility. But no one knew she was living here.

The fact that Shaun was there suddenly felt like a gift from Minerva. She wasn't going to have to face whatever had happened alone. Okay, so she'd have some explaining to do when he saw her, but she had to get up and find what was happening. She couldn't leave it to him. Then she remembered Sam.

What if Sam's wandered in to use the bathroom and dropped something?

Even as she had the thought, she dismissed it. Sam wouldn't come that far inside, nor would he have any reason to be carrying anything metallic.

Wrapping herself in her outdoor coat and stuffing her feet into her walking boots, Thea grabbed the poker from the fireside set that sat pointlessly next to the dead fireplace. Mentally adding *call chimney sweep* to her list of things to arrange, Thea peered out of her bedroom door.

She listened hard; the noise had stopped, but she could hear movement below. Walking on her tiptoes to keep sound to a minimum, wondering how she was going to arrive without making Shaun jump out of his skin, Thea kept going, her heart racing in her chest.

What if he's walking into trouble? What if it's burglars?

There was another noise. It was similar to the first one but fainter. The metal sound definitely had a scraping sensation to it. But it wasn't metal against metal… more like metal against wood.

Another crash sent Thea's blood to ice. This time the unmistakable sound of smashing china accelerated her footsteps. Her fears about scaring Shaun dissolved as she hurtled towards the noise, poker outstretched before her, images of Shaun being attacked circling her mind. She recoiled away from the thought that she might have to hit someone with her ironmongery, while admitting she felt safer for having its reassuring weight in her palm.

At the foot of the servants' stairs, Thea paused. There was a light coming from the drawing room. The slim door which connected it to the servants' corridor was more widely open than it had been when she'd come to bed. As she took a step away from the safety of the bottom step Thea saw a shadow crossing the room beyond.

Her pulse was thudding so hard in her ears, she felt deaf to everything except the voice at the back of her head telling her she couldn't use her phone to call for help. Even if it had been working for emergency calls, she'd got used to not carrying it around with her. Consequently, it was safely tucked up in her bedroom.

By the time she'd crept to the doorway, Thea could see the

cause of the second crash. Shards of porcelain were sprayed out across the carpet in an arc of destruction. A three-foot antique Imari porcelain vase had stood between the internal connecting doors of the drawing room and living room yesterday. Not only had it been beautiful, it had been worth over three thousand pounds and was irreplaceable.

'Come here, you bastard!'

Shaun's hissed whisper obliterated her fears for the trustees' reaction to the loss of a valuable artefact. Images of who this bastard might be had sent her hands to ice. She had to help him, but her feet wouldn't move.

I'm responsible. Me.

Calling out 'Shaun?' as she moved, Thea held the poker aloft and sidled into the drawing room.

'Thea? What the hell are you doing here?'

'Later. What's happening?' Her eyes darted around the room, which appeared to be singularly free of masked men with swag bags. 'Who did this?'

'Put that bloody poker down, woman, you're going to take my eye out.'

'Oh, sorry.' Thea quickly lowered her weapon. She hadn't registered it had been within an inch of Shaun's face she'd been waving it around so much. 'So…'

'Look!'

Following the line of Shaun's finger, Thea's eyes rested in the far corner of the room. 'What am I looking for?'

'Right at the back. Under the table.'

Taking a silent step forward, Thea twisted her neck so she could she into the shadows below the occasional table that stood beneath the large bay window. 'A bird?'

'A nightjar if I'm not mistaken.'

'A what?'

'They're nocturnal.'

'I got that, thanks. How the hell did it get in here?'

'Shall we work out how to set it free before we worry about that?' Shaun tiptoed forward and picked two cushions off the nearest sofa, whispering, 'Can you go around the other way and open the window behind it?'

Nodding, Thea kept an eye on the small tatty grey bird that had frightened the life out of her. Sidling around the back of the square of sofas, hoping she didn't alarm it, Thea watched Shaun hold the cushions out like soft shields. By the time she'd edged close enough to the window to open it, praying the runners would work and wouldn't make any noise and alarm the creature further, Shaun had thrust the cushions forward, so the nightjar was trapped between them and the window. Now the only way for the bird to go was up and – hopefully – out.

Taking a deep breath, gripping the bottom of the window pane, Thea felt the fear of the bird as it fluttered faster, clearly panicked to find itself in such an environment.

Please open. Please open…

The squeal of wood as the window lifted an inch was painful to the ears, and the nightjar flew upwards so fast Thea feared it would knock itself out on the underside of the tabletop.

'Come on, Thea… a bit more.'

'I can't. It's stuck.'

'You can. You have to…' Shaun winced as the sound of the bird's wings going into overdrive resounded through the room. 'He's going to break a wing.'

Pushing her fists firmer between the sill and the inch gap

she'd made before the pulleys had caught, Thea banished the concept of the ropes snapping and the window falling out and landing on her, and heaved.

As the pane crunched open, Shaun dropped one cushion and tilted the top of the table towards himself, opening a clear path for the nightjar to dart upwards, and into the pitch black world outside.

Slamming the window shut again was mercifully much easier now the long-disused pulleys had been dislodged. Thea sank back against the shut glass with relief and turned to face Shaun. 'Thank God you were here.'

'Forget that, what the hell are *you* doing here?'

Twenty-Four

'How did it get in?'

'I asked you a question.' Shaun replaced the cushions on the sofa and sat down, patting the space next to him.

Thea hesitated, very aware that she was only wearing an old coat and a pair of pyjamas, albeit a super thick, fleece-lined set of pyjamas, cut in a style which cut for comfort rather than flattering the figure.

'Come on, I won't bite.'

Reluctantly sitting, keeping a good foot of space between herself and the archaeologist, Thea noticed he was still fully dressed. 'Hadn't you gone to bed yet?'

'What do you mean?'

'You're not in pyjamas.'

Shaun grinned. 'I didn't fancy confronting an art thief in the buff.'

'In the… oh.' Thea could feel her face reddening. 'Weren't you cold? I mean, it's not exactly tropical in this house.'

Shaun laughed. 'I was fine, thank you, but should you wish to pop by and warm me up, then please do.'

Knowing she'd been thinking about doing exactly that, Thea looked towards the bay window she'd so recently yanked open and pulled her coat tighter over her nightclothes. 'I'm living here too.'

'I worked that one out. How long for?'

'Since I started working here. I didn't intend to. It was going to be a one or two-night thing, before I found a room to rent, but…'

'But everywhere around here costs a king's ransom, or is so far away that you'd be driving constantly. And let's face it, you can get so much more done being here 24/7. Yes?'

'Yes.' Thea sighed. 'I was going to tell you yesterday, but somehow time ran out, and then it felt like I was lying to you… which I wasn't, but at the same time I was. Then I thought, if the others knew we were both staying here, they'd put two and two together and make five. Then there was the danger that everyone would want to start paying rent to stay here, and I'd be running a guest house on top of everything else.'

'And if John had got wind of the situation he'd either insist on moving in too, or go to the papers and tell them we are shacked up together.'

'Exactly.' Thea nodded. 'I'm sorry I didn't warn you I was here, but I'm damn glad you are. I'd never have coped with that bird on my own. I was only brave enough to get up because you were in the manor too.'

'I'm sure a strong independent woman like you could have coped.'

Shaun didn't sound as if he was teasing her, but she

wasn't quite sure. 'Independent I might be, and strong to an extent – otherwise I'd never have shifted that window – but you can be as emancipated as anything, and still be shit scared of an intruder in the middle of the night!'

This time he did laugh. 'Damn right. My heart was thudding, I can tell you.'

'Was it?'

'Of course it was. I was under the impression I was alone in the house with an axe murderer or something.'

Thea looked across to the ruin of the fallen vase. 'That's a problem I could do without.'

Shaun coughed uneasily. 'I'm afraid that's not the half of it.'

'What do you mean?'

'The nightjar didn't get in here, it got in down there. He pointed to the partially opened double doors that divided the drawing and living rooms. 'The far window to the right has slipped open in there. I've only had the chance for a brief glance, but I'm guessing the rope pulley on one side has snapped, leaving the top of the window open a fraction.'

'Oh God.' Thea stared towards the darkened space on the other side of the fallen china.

'We'll need to check for stray bats in the morning.'

'That's not very likely is it?'

'They like attics, why not a warm house with high ceilings?'

Thea groaned. 'I heard a metallic-like crash. Was that the window falling in its setting?'

'No. At least, I don't think so.'

'Then what on earth was it?'

'I think you should come and see.' Shaun got to his feet and held out a hand.

Thea stayed where she was. 'I have a feeling you're going to show me something even worse than the fallen vase. Is it childish to want to stay here and hope it all goes away?'

'Yes.' Shaun reached forward and pulled Thea to her feet. 'But it's very human and I don't blame you one bit for putting off the evil hour. But it's two o'clock in the morning and we need to get some sleep at some point, plus you have to "arrive" for work in time to be told of what's happened in the night as if you've never been here.'

Thea didn't see the damage at first. She was too concerned with locating the offending open window and seeing where the bird had come in. She was half expecting to see a squadron of airborne insects and birds soaring in through the gap.

It took a gentle tug on her arm for Thea to register that, not only was she still holding Shaun's hand, but that there was a metre-long scratch across the far end of the previously unblemished dining room table.

'But how…?' Thea's fingers started to tingle and she tried to pull out of Shaun's grip, but he held her firm.

'You can shout at me for being sexist later if you feel the need, but right now you need to hold onto something so you don't fall over. It might as well be my hand.'

Thea didn't respond. He was right anyway. It didn't matter that holding his hand was a pleasant experience. It could have been John's hand and it would still have been unwise to let go at that particular moment. Her knees were close to buckling, but she'd be damned if she'd let them.

Eventually she gathered her powers of speech. 'This table came all the way from Lancaster in 1880.'

Shaun groaned. 'You're not telling me this is an original Gillows, are you?'

'It is.'

'I was hoping it was just a really good replica.'

'Nope. An original Victorian mahogany table. Seats twenty-four people when fully extended. And, until tonight, it had one tiny blemish on the far left leg where, presumably, something once got dropped on it, chipping the outside edge. A French polisher had made the mark all but invisible. I only know it's there because there is a note of the work in the old accounts.'

'Oh.'

'I had thought...' Thea heard her voice become unnaturally light as she kept talking. If she stopped, there was a danger that panic or hysteria would take hold. 'I had thought of seeing if people could work out which leg was damaged, and giving a prize to children on school trips if they could guess what might have caused it.'

Shaun ran a finger along the fresh scratch. 'It's a surface scratch. A French polisher could fix this.'

'For free? Within the time we have?' Thea grimaced. 'How did a bird do this, for God's sake? Come to think of it, I don't even know what a nightjar is. Until tonight I'd never heard of one.'

'I suspect it was caused by a talon. They're only small birds, but have claws not unlike a kestrel's.' Letting go of Thea, Shaun knelt to examine the underside of the table. 'Could this leaf of the table be dropped?'

'I don't know.' Her free hand felt cold, so she buried it into a pocket as she stared at the semi dropped window.

'Damn, no, it's static.' Shaun examined the scratch more closely. 'Do any of the volunteers do polishing?'

'Not to my knowledge.' As Thea studied the fallen window, a blast of cold night air brought her back to her senses. 'I'm going to fetch some black bags from the kitchen and my staple gun.'

'Why?'

'Because I can't face carpentry tonight. Let's cover over the gap to stop anything else getting in and worry about it tomorrow.'

Shaun smiled. 'You fetch them. I'll get the stepladder from the laundry room.'

The act of doing something helped calm Thea. With only a minor sense of guilt, as she drove staples into the Victorian wallpaper, reasoning with herself that things were not so bad, that a few microscopic holes in the wall weren't going to make things worse, she soon had the gap covered with three layers of black plastic bags.

'You were right,' she called down to Shaun as he held the stepladder steady. 'The pulley is almost completely frayed. Looks like it could have snapped at any time.'

'Very inconsiderate of it to choose the middle of the night.'

Thea slammed one final staple into the bags to hold them taut. 'Does that seem firm enough to you?'

'Come down and I'll look.'

'Can't you tell from there, save me going up and down?'

Shaun growled, 'For God's sake, Thea, it's the middle of the night, you are wearing nothing but pyjamas and, as I may have mentioned, I fancy you something rotten, so don't you dare ask me to look up at you from this angle or I may forget that I'm a gentleman!'

Thea scuttled down the ladder, half wishing she'd stayed where she was and told him to look anyway. 'So, I'm down, what do you think?'

'I think I should have got us a bottle of whiskey for emergencies.' Shaun nodded at her handiwork with the staple gun and turned back to the table. 'This is going to take a bit of thinking about.'

Thea wanted to close her eyes. Suddenly she felt beyond tired, but at the same time she knew there was no chance of sleep until she'd cleared up the debris from the vase. 'I'll get the dustpan and brush.' She pointed at the shattered china.

'Tell you what, I'll get that swept up and sorted, and you put the kettle on. I left some decaf coffee in the kitchen. I could do with a hot drink.'

Too tired to argue, Thea headed to the kitchen, via the scullery, where she picked up the file containing information on all the items of value in the house. She knew the vase was in there, she just hoped that being knocked over by a bird was the sort of accident it was insured for.

Thea knew that the tears she'd been determined not to cry since she'd first seen the fallen vase were causing red rings to circle her heavy eyes.

Oh well, at least Shaun will have no trouble keeping his hands off me looking like this.

The coffee was made, poured and cooling fast before Shaun joined Thea.

'What's that?'

'The artefact catalogue.' She picked it up and flashed the

relevant page at Shaun. 'The vase is – was – a nineteenth-century Imari porcelain vase, of baluster form with flared neck, painted panels of figures and animals in landscape, on a brocade ground.'

'Do I dare ask how much it was worth?'

'Just over three thousand.'

'Damn.'

'Quite.'

'Insured?'

'Yes. Everything listed in this catalogue is covered, but I can't say I'm looking forward to telling Malcolm that we need to make a claim.' Thea cuddled her mug, as she read the additional notes about the piece. 'It was a gift from Lord to Lady Upwich. Apparently she fell in love with the vibrant blues and reds.' Thea sniffed as she lay down the book, 'He must have loved her very much. There's so much in this house that was brought here out of love and now it's all falling apart and however hard I try, I don't seem to be able to stop it disintegrating.'

Shaun's arm was around Thea's shoulders and she was buried into his side, sobbing her heart out, before she'd noticed what she was doing. 'Oh God, I'm so sorry. This is pathetic.'

'It is nothing of the sort. You came here to do a job under stressful circumstances. Not only have those circumstances followed you, but everything that can go wrong seems to have done just that.'

Shaun stroked his fingers over Thea's hair, sending the same sensations of need shooting through her as when he'd de-cobwebbed her in the mill. She wanted to protest that she was ashamed of herself. That she should have been more professional, more businesslike, stronger, but no words would come out. She felt as if she was in delayed shock.

'What you need to focus on is how much you've achieved. The manor is in a much stronger position than when you arrived. Hard decisions needed making, and you've made them. More such decisions are required and you'll make the ones which will work best for the future of this place.' He leant forward and kissed the top of her head.

Frustratingly chaste, the kiss still warmed Thea enough for her to wipe the tears from her eyes. Sitting up, she took a sip of coffee. 'Forgive me, I'm overtired. By tomorrow I'll have pulled myself together.'

'I don't doubt it.' Shaun was regarding her with something very close to pride. 'But for now, how about you cuddle back and rest.'

Not wanting to break the spell, Thea said nothing as she snuggled against his shoulder, inhaling the scent of maleness, Aran wool and the light fragrance of fabric conditioner.

'Because nightjars are nocturnal, they're usually only spotted at dawn or dusk when they're hunting for food. Even then, you have to concentrate to spot them as they are well camouflaged. They're a sort of grey-brown, mottled, streaked colour with barred plumage as well. In the past they were considered unlucky or even supernatural.'

'Really? Why?'

'They fly in silence.'

'Unless they're trapped under tables.'

'Naturally.' Shaun's fingers teased another knot from the lower tresses of her hair. 'They had a mythical ability to steal milk from goats, but I don't know why.'

'They live on the moors?'

'Moors, heath-land, open woodland. Nowhere too enclosed, but with plenty of ground cover. I've never heard of one coming so close to a house.'

'A lost nightjar.'

'Possibly.'

'I hope it's alright.'

Shaun's fingers stopped moving and he turned to look at her. 'That's it. Right there.'

'What is where?'

'The reason why I want to take you out for dinner tomorrow night, or should I say tonight.'

Thea rubbed her tired eyes. 'What are you talking about?'

'A bird gets in and causes thousands of pounds worth of damage, and you're worried about the bird as much as the damage.'

'It didn't mean to come in. I bet it was terrified.'

Shaun smiled. 'So, will you come out with me tonight?'

'I'd like that. But not locally.'

'Deal.' Shaun drained the remains of his coffee. 'Come on, we're going to bed.'

'Are we?'

'We are.'

Twenty-Five

Tina hadn't opened her dedicated dating email inbox since the ill-fated evening with Leon. Guilt nudged her every time she remembered how she'd walked out of the restaurant without a word. If their roles had been reversed and he had walked out on her, she'd have been furious, hurt and confused. After a few days of quiet stewing, she'd probably have emailed him to ask what she'd done wrong.

She was also aware that there might be potential date requests waiting on Superior Singles for her response. Mr Right could be there, right now, in her inbox, being ignored because she was ashamed of her behaviour. Behaviour she didn't understand. Leon had ticked every box she'd wanted ticking…and yet he'd made her feel inadequate.

Or did I do that to myself? Was it my insecurities that took me out of there, not him?

Turning her mobile phone over and over in her palm, Tina trailed a lacklustre spoon around her uneaten cereal and then threw the spoon down in frustration. 'Get a grip, woman!'

Acting quickly in case she changed her mind, Tina switched on her personal email, and scanned down a list of nineteen messages awaiting her attention. Eighteen of them were alerts from Superior Singles telling her that her profile had been viewed and associated messages, likes, winks and communication requests awaited her attention. The final one was from an incredibly optimistic Nigerian company, kindly enquiring if she'd like to benefit from the joys of penile extensions.

Fat chance.

There was nothing from Leon. Nothing at all.

'Serves you right!' Tina placed her phone face down on the table and abandoned the remaining cornflakes. 'He clearly has more pride than you do. What did you think was going to happen? Did you think a man like Leon would be begging for an explanation or another chance? He's probably already found a sophisticated blonde to massage his ego.'

Annoyed by the fact she was hurt by his lack of communication, when she knew he was not the man for her, Tina swept her bag onto her shoulder, grabbed her car keys and marched towards work.

Thea doused her eyes in cold water and stared into the age-spotted mirror. 'Look at yourself woman! The chickens will take one peep out of their travel crate and demand to go back to the farm you've ordered them from!'

The previous night, when Shaun had said they were going

to bed, she'd briefly thought he'd meant together. And she'd been willing to go. Wanted to go. In that moment nothing had felt as welcome as the idea of being curled up next to Shaun's bulky frame. Thea hadn't considered anything happening between them beyond sleep. Not consciously anyway. Too many shocks, too much fatigue, had crept in to want anything other than the comfortable arms of a man she realised she liked far more than she'd intended to.

In the cold half-light of the dimly illuminated bathroom, Thea could admit to herself that, if they had headed to the same bed, something else would have taken over, and the meagre hour of sleep she'd had before her alarm had woken her wouldn't have existed.

Although I suspect I'd feel better than I do now.

The application of a layer of foundation seemed even more of a token gesture than usual. Only grouter's putty would be able to disguise the dark shadows around her eyes and dull the yellow tinge to her complexion.

A vision of the smashed vase, scratched table and broken window pulley attempted to dislodge images of herself and Shaun in interesting states of undress from her mind. Leaning forward over the tiny servants' sink, Thea closed her eyes. 'This is not the time to be falling in love. Especially not with a man who could have his pick of the celebrity world… and then there's John.'

The memory of agreeing to go out for a meal with Shaun warmed her for a while, until Thea saw how impractical it was. He wasn't supposed to be there. How could they be seen out together? The whole thing was impossible.

Sweeping her hair into a ponytail, Thea returned her gaze to the mirror. 'Today you are going to call Malcolm and tell him about the damage done by the nightjar. You are going to work out how to claim on the insurance. You are going to take delivery of six chickens. You are busy. There is no time to think about anything except what you are supposed to be doing. Restoring a manor and rescuing its mill. Nothing else. *Nothing*.'

Tina looked as horrified as Thea felt when they inspected the damage caused by the snapping of a single window pulley and a lost bird. In the early morning light, the scratch on the table was glaringly obvious and the space where the vase had once stood on its wooden plinth loomed large.

'A bird did all this?' Tina stared at the makeshift cover afforded by the black bags.

'Can you imagine what would have happened if two or three had got in?'

'Doesn't bear thinking about.' Tina sat on the nearest dining chair to the scratch. 'At least it's a clean mark. No side cracks. There's a good chance a polisher could hide it and... Hang on, all this must mean Shaun knows you're staying here.'

'Yep.' Thea wiped a hand over her forehead. 'Thank God he was here. I'd never have coped on my own. From upstairs it sounded like a major burglary was in progress.'

Running a fingertip over the wounded table, Tina said, 'I wonder if Derek or Bill knows of anyone who could see to this. They must have come across French polishers, considering their former thatching and carpentry occupations. They may even be able to do it themselves.'

'It's worth asking them and Mabel. She has a vast list of contacts for every occasion.'

'The advantages of living in one place for so long I suppose.' Tina opened her mobile. 'I'd better take a photo of the damage to show Malcolm. Do you have the pieces of the vase?'

'Shaun swept them up. I'm not sure where he left them and as I wasn't officially here last night, I haven't seen them yet. But, unofficially, if you're hoping we can jigsaw the vase back together, then I can end that wishful thinking right now. It all but disintegrated.'

Tina tugged at her right pigtail. 'And there I was thinking the biggest problems today were what we were going to do with the mill, settling in the chickens and deciding if I should unsubscribe from Superior Singles.'

'Seriously? You're going to stop chasing older men?' A yawn overtook Thea.

'I think so.' Tina kept her eyes on the table. 'Can we leave that conversation for now?'

Recognising the anxious expression on her friend's face, Thea, vowing to broach the subject of Tina's private life later, returned to business. 'As soon as we've reported what's happened to the trustees and worked out if we can fix the window ourselves, or if we're going to have to spend more of our budget getting it sorted, then we'll make a decision about the mill.'

'Are you sure you don't want to leave calling Malcolm to me?' Tina studied her friend more closely. 'No offence hun, but you look and sound dreadful. Your voice has gone all low and husky. Did you get any sleep at all?'

'An hour about five til six this morning. Otherwise, none at all.'

Tina gestured to the window. 'Not even before our uninvited visitor flew in?'

'I felt so bad about not telling Shaun I was staying, that I couldn't settle. Ironically, I kept worrying he'd hear me moving about and think I was an intruder.'

'And it was nothing to do with the fact you two have the mutual hots for each other, and you were wishing he knew you were here so Shaun would come visiting?'

Bright red on the instant, Thea blustered, 'We do not.'

'Yeah right, whatever you say.' Tina took her friend by the arm and led her towards the office. 'Let's get these phone calls sorted, and then we can face the day. You can convince me I'm better off being poor but happy, and I can convince you that you're destined to have at least a short fling with a celebrity.'

Thea tried to smile, but the spectre of the phone call ahead stopped her lips curling in the right direction. 'What if Malcolm says that's it? That the extra expense of this new disaster is the final straw and he stops the restoration here and now.'

'He won't.'

'You sound very sure.'

'He'll get more in a sale if the house is fully restored.'

Thea sighed. 'I wish that didn't make sense, but it does.'

'At least it means you'll be employed for as long as possible.'

'I suppose so.' Thea fiddled with her ponytail. 'After that, who knows?'

'Hopefully you'll be managing this place as per the

original plan.' Tina's hands came to her hips in a manner that reminded Thea of Mabel at her most decisive.

'Until last night I was hanging onto that. Now, I can feel the whole thing slipping away.'

Unable to argue with Thea's gloomy outlook, Tina waved her mobile. 'I'm going to call Derek. He's always up early to walk his dog. Let's see if he can fix the window and the table, or knows someone who can. Then at least we can show Malcolm we're already on the case when we tell him what's happened.'

'Thanks hun.' Thea paused. 'Hold on, what about Sam? I'd forgotten he was outside. His tent is pegged in the wood on the left side of the garden. He might know about windows.'

Tina agreed. 'He might well do, but no way would you get him inside to take a look.'

'But he wouldn't have to come in. He could get a ladder from the outside.'

'Do you think he's up yet?'

'Hun, it's eight in the morning, I'd be very surprised if Sam hadn't done an hour's clearance in the garden already. The man is unstoppable.'

'How about felting?'

'Pardon?' Tina dragged her gaze away from watching Derek pass tools to Sam, as he balanced on a ladder and contentedly got on with digging Mill Grange out of its latest pothole.

'Felting. As one of the craft demonstrations in the mill if we open it up as an attraction alongside the manor?'

'Oh yes. Good idea.' Tina paused, 'Did they have felting here?'

'I have no idea, but it's popular and it would fill a gap.'

Tina studied the rough plan of the mill building Thea had drawn. She'd divided it into three spaces, which could potentially be rented out by local crafts folk after the Open Day, but which would also have to provide some form of attraction on the day itself.

'So, we're saying spinning, weaving and felting?'

'If we can find the spinners, weavers and felters to go with them. I wondered about asking Sybil in the tea rooms if she knew anyone that Mabel didn't.' Thea doodled a flower on the edge of her plan. 'Or maybe we should admit defeat on this one. So much needs doing to make the mill usable. Right now, health and safety would close it before it was opened. I reckon it needs about three grand spending on it to make it even vaguely rentable.'

'That's not that much really and we'd make it back in rent money.' Tina jotted some numbers onto her ever present notepad. 'We need to air the place, whitewash the walls and get in some tables, chairs and work surfaces, cupboards and so on. Then we can invite some local craftspeople to take a look. Potentially we could charge a lot of rent for each section. It's in a tourist village on Exmoor for goodness sake.'

'Perhaps we could pop into Sybil's for a cuppa and see if she'd mind putting some cards up advertising the space for rent?'

'Now you're talking. I would kill for one of Sybil's cheese scones.'

'Cheese scones and not lemon cake? Are you quite yourself?'

'I'm not entirely sure I am.' Thea got to her feet. 'There's some whitewash in the stables. I could do with doing something practical. Working out what has to be done all the time, but not actually doing it, is driving me mad.'

'Likewise. Let's go. I could do without thinking about anything but avoiding spiders for a while.'

As Tina spoke, Thea saw her friend glance outside. Sam was talking to Derek. They were fashioning a new rope pulley between them, both laughing, both obviously happy with the day that stretched ahead of them.

'Are you alright, Tina?'

'I wish I knew why he won't come into the house beyond a commando-style raid on the bathroom.'

'Shaun reckons Sam will tell us when he's ready.' Wondering if her friend had started to accept she was interested in Sam, Thea returned the discussion to work. 'Come on, if we're busy at the mill then John won't find me and deliver his daily list of complaints.'

Still watching the men working through the window, Tina nodded as Sam caught her eye, before looking hurriedly away. 'I'll call Malcolm again on the way. I still think I should do it.' She grimaced. 'It's my job after all.'

Not having missed Tina's glances to the window, Thea said, 'Sam looks at you a lot when you aren't looking at him.'

'Does he?'

'You like him, don't you?'

'He's a nice man. Very clever.'

'That isn't what I meant.'

Tina gave a heavy sigh. 'You know he isn't what I'm looking for.'

'He *wasn't* what you were looking for. Now, you're not so sure, are you?'

An image of Leon in his designer suit, gold cufflinks and crisp white shirt flitted across her mind. 'Sam's a bit scruffy and sort of weird.'

Offended on Sam's behalf, Thea couldn't stop herself saying, 'And he's up a ladder, sorting out a problem that would have cost us money we don't have. He's worked his arse off since he's been here, and never complained or caused trouble. Would Mr Silver Fox have done that? No, he'd have waved a credit card and the problem would have gone away with no thought and no effort.'

'But the problem would have gone away!'

'Don't be such a bloody gold-digger!' No sooner had the words left her lips than Thea felt awful. 'Oh hun! I didn't mean that. I'm so tired. It all came out wrong and—'

Tina's round face creased with distress. 'I…'

'Oh hell. Tina, I'm so sorry. I meant—'

'I know perfectly well what you meant, thank you very much!' Tina grabbed her bag from the back of the chair. 'Well, if that's what you think of me, I'll be on my way.'

'Tina! I didn't mean it, I—'

'If you want me, I'll be working from the Trust office.'

'But they've agreed you should work here.'

'And if I need to I will, but when I do, I'd appreciate if you'd keep your opinions about my private life to yourself.'

Thea had taken over an hour to stop shaking. Calling Tina's mobile had produced no response, and so far she hadn't received a reply to the long, apologetic email she'd hammered out.

Wishing it was possible to take back words or erase time, Thea decided the only thing she could do, especially if she was going to have to get Mill Grange sorted without her right hand woman, was tackle something practical and physically tiring.

Hunting through the stables, Thea was beginning to think she'd imagined seeing whitewash there, when she caught sight of two faded tubs in the corner, semi-hidden behind a mound of trestle tables. As she bent down to tug them into view, a male voice cut across her concentration.

'Now there's a view to gladden the heart.' Shaun strode through the open double doors, a broom in one hand and a dustpan and brush in the other.

Despite the new heaviness in her heart, Thea couldn't prevent the grin that crossed her face. 'That's the second potentially sexist remark you've made to me in the last twenty-four hours.'

'Is it sexist to admire a beautiful woman?'

Thea wrinkled her nose. 'Let's just say that, in recent years, the rules have become a little blurred.'

'Don't I know it! Us chaps can't smile at a woman anymore without worrying about a court appearance.' Shaun gave a theatrical bow. 'Do I have permission to tell you I think you look good, whenever I like, providing it's in private?'

'Granted.'

'And that having very little sleep has a very sexy effect on your voice?'

'Maybe.' Thea's grin widened as Shaun battled to keep a straight face.

'Good. So, when do the chickens arrive?'

Remembering Tina's excitement about the arrival of the chickens, Thea felt her moment of optimism dip. 'Not until this afternoon thankfully, so I've a bit of time to crack on.'

'Are you alright? Your smile disappeared very quickly at the mention of chickens. I thought you were looking forward to fresh eggs for breakfast.'

'I am. Just seems like something else to worry about, that's all.'

'Aren't Tina and Sam going to look after them?'

'Tina's had to go to the office for a while.' Looking away so Shaun wouldn't see the sadness on her face, she added, 'I'm sure Sam will cope though.'

'More than likely. He's a capable chap.' Propping up the broom and dropping the dustpan and brush, Shaun took the whitewash from Thea's hand. 'For the mill?'

'Yes. I want to make a start on freshening it up. Even if we have to admit defeat and sell it rather than split it into rentals, it'll need some TLC first.'

'I don't know about TLC But I do know you'll need a ladder and a tall person for those hard to reach places.'

'Are you volunteering?'

'I certainly am.' Shaun hooked a paint tin onto his arm and picked up the broom. 'I want to hear what the trustees had to say about last night.'

'Tina was going to call Malcolm, but I suppose she'll speak to him in person now.' Mentally crossing her fingers that Tina would still honour her promise to liaise with the Trust about the nightjar incident, Thea forced out a smile. 'Thankfully Sam and Derek think they can handle the window, so it's the vase and table that need addressing.'

'Just the vase.'

'What?' Hope clutched at Thea's heart for the first time in days.

'Obviously, Malcolm will have to be told about the table, but you can also let him know that a French polisher has been engaged, and is already on his way. A mate of mine, Richard, will be with us by eight o'clock tomorrow morning.'

'But…'

'I'm sure you are going to say something very dull about money. However, Richard is one of the experts lined up for the next series of *Landscape Treasures*. He is an expert on furniture and its restoration. I gave him a call and sent him some photos of the table. He got all excited about a Gillows dining table being so far from where it was made in Lancashire, and agreed to take a look in return for potentially featuring it in the show. What do you think?'

'Have Mill Grange on your TV show?'

'Yes. It'd be fabulous publicity. It would be a side feature, mainly featuring the interior of the house, but it might help get some interest in the Open Day. Help ticket sales a bit maybe.'

Dropping her paintbrushes, Thea ran to Shaun's side and hugged him. 'That's amazing. Do you really think he'd do the polishing for us?'

'I do. He's good. Used to work for Christies.'

'Bloody hell. I can't wait to tell Tina… Oh.'

'What is it?'

'I upset Tina. I didn't mean to.' Thea sighed. 'She said she was going to work from the office from now on.'

'I'm sorry to hear that. Do you want to talk about it?' Shaun ran a gentle palm over her cheek.

'No thanks. It's my fault. I'll sort it out.' Thea reached out and found her unspoken request for a hug instantly granted.

'If you're sure.' Pulling Thea closer, Shaun's voice was suddenly husky. 'I think we have a few things to discuss when we go out tonight, and not just Mill Grange's potential television show.'

'Such as?'

'Such as why, young lady, you are hugging me, without so much as asking me first? Rules work both ways you know.' Shaun held Thea tighter. 'May I kiss the management?'

'You may.'

Twenty-Six

'**D**o you know why I haven't asked you which room you're sleeping in?'

Thea lowered the spoonful of lemon ice cream that had been on the way to her mouth. 'I assumed it was so you didn't accidentally ravish me without asking permission first.'

'Precisely.' Shaun's teasing eyes took on a more serious sheen. 'Although, I have a confession to make on that score.'

'Then confess.'

Thea, relaxed under the effects of alcohol, good food, lack of sleep and the heat of the pub fire. They were tucked away in a village on the edge of Taunton, far enough away from Upwich for her not to worry about them being seen out together. Her calm state was helped by the fact that, contrary to expectations, not only had Tina honoured her promise to inform Malcolm of what had happened, he hadn't gone mad about the damage to the house. He'd been impressed by their handling of the situation and relieved that the ill wind meant some good in the shape of an insurance payout. The lost vase could now pay for all the materials needed to update the mill before renting it out.

Shaun watched Thea lick ice cream from her lips as he said, 'I am going to find it challenging not to search the attics for your room tonight. That being said, would you rather I stayed here? They have rooms.'

Thea studied his expression, not sure if he was joking or not. 'And what would I do if you were here and another member of Exmoor's wildlife population decided to visit the house in the middle of the night?'

'Call Sam?'

'An impractical suggestion for obvious reasons. Anyway, he's promised to watch the chickens tonight. They are so cute! And as Sam is taking his promise to care for them very seriously, I'm not calling him away.

'Anyway, if you remember, you drove us over here. Hence why you're on lemonade and not beer. If you stayed, I'd have to stay too.' Realising that idea was not unappealing, Thea picked up her spoon and stared into her bowl. 'Now stop being so chivalrous and eat your pudding.'

Shovelling a large helping of Baked Alaska, Shaun shook his head in mock despair. 'Well don't blame me if I get lost going to bed and end up in the wrong room.'

'I promise I will guide you safely to where you belong.'

'Will you?' Shaun placed a palm on her leg. 'Will you, Thea?'

She nodded, her mouth suddenly too dry to talk despite the ice cream.

'I don't want to force the pace, and this isn't just me taking advantage of an exhausted woman in a deserted house.' He winked before becoming more serious. 'Truly. I'm not trying to get my leg over before disappearing in a puff of smoke.'

Swallowing, knowing he was dead right about the exhaustion, Thea said, 'If you happen to be passing my bedroom door, feel free to come in.' She started to laugh. 'Although frankly, I'm more likely to fall asleep on your shoulder than anything else.'

Shaun smiled. 'That sounds rather nice.'

'But not as much fun as what you had in mind.'

'I had it all in mind. Slowly, over a period of years. Including lots of cuddled sleep.'

Thea reached out her hand and laid it over his. 'You mean that, don't you?'

Shaun said nothing, as his eyes filled with desire.

Whispering under her breath to stop anyone overhearing, Thea said, 'There's no way you'd fit into my bed. *I* hardly fit in it. Victorian serving girls were clearly built on much slimmer lines than twenty-first-century heritage managers.'

Shaun's eyes dropped to her chest and back again. 'And thank goodness for that.'

Thea shifted on her seat. 'Perhaps we should talk about something else for a minute.'

'I'd rather whisk you back to the manor right now and test your bed theory, but I do have something else I want to talk to you about.'

'Go on.'

'Come round here and I'll tell you.' Shaun patted the place next to him on the short settle.

'Will I fit?'

'Cheek! I'm not that big you know!'

Shaun budged up a fraction so Thea could squash up next to him. His arm came around her shoulder, half due the lack of space, and half because it felt good to be held and be holding.

'What do you have to tell me? You're being whisked away from the manor and can't help after all?'

The words had come out lightly. A joke. But as soon as they'd escaped her flippant lips, Thea saw how real that possibility was – a fact echoed by the uncomfortable look in Shaun's eyes.

'Oh God, I was only joking. You're not really leaving, are you?' Shaun's earlier words swam back to her. 'You're about to disappear in a puff of smoke?'

Resting his free arm on the table, Shaun fiddled with his lemonade glass. 'Richard, the bloke coming tomorrow to start work on the table, needs to take me away for a few days to give a possible filming location a once-over.'

'Oh.' Thea felt her heart sink. Tina had gone, and now she was losing Shaun too. 'How long for?'

'A week. Ish.'

'Right.'

'Maybe more, but hopefully not.' Shaun shuffled around so he could see Thea properly. 'I'm sorry. I know this is rotten timing with Tina not being around. The production company told me I wouldn't be needed for another month at least. Apparently there is a place in Cornwall ripe for investigating, but the owners need convincing. They want to meet me to reassure them that I won't be riding roughshod over their land just for the sake of it.'

'The perils of being the front man.' Thea tried to ignore

the disappointment that had gripped her insides. 'I'm sure Tina and I will be okay soon.' It was ridiculous. She shouldn't feel this desolate. He was only going for a week. He'd been amazing already, and the fact that Richard was coming to take him away meant that the table was going to be fixed sooner rather than later.

'I'd rather stay.'

Thea smiled up at him. 'This is your job. You have to go.'

'I'll come back as soon as it's sorted.'

'It'll be longer than a week though won't it? There'll be other things that have to be done. You've been away from your post for a while already.' Being more practical than she felt like being, Thea added, 'We've been very lucky to have your help for as long as we have. Mabel will be gutted though.'

Shaun spoke into his glass as he took a drink. 'If I thought you'd agree, I'd invite you to come with me. Your expert eye would be welcome, as well as your company.'

'If you're going to Cornwall, you're hardly likely to need the eye of a Roman historian.'

'I think we both know that you're much more than that.' He flicked back her fringe and smiled into her eyes.

Thea lowered her eyes to her lap. If she looked at him now she'd either kiss him or her fatigue and guilt over hurting Tina would take over and she'd humiliate herself by bursting into tears. Despite her best efforts earlier, she noticed there were still specks of white on her palms. 'We should have the mill whitewashed completely by the time you get back. I can't believe how much we got done today.'

Recognising Thea's determination to stay positive, Shaun squeezed her closer to his side. 'Why don't you visit

Sybil's place tomorrow and get those adverts for the rented space up?'

'A good excuse for comfort food, as well as a sound business move.' Thea gave him a brave smile.

'Talking of mixing business with pleasure,' Shaun said, withdrawing his arm, 'I'm going to drive us home now.'

John sat very still. They hadn't seen him. He hadn't been sure he was going to follow them until the very last minute. Even now, he wasn't entirely sure what he hoped to achieve by doing so. He'd been very careful about where he'd positioned himself. Behind them, and shrouded by a half-draped curtain that divided the restaurant from the bar.

He suspected however, that they wouldn't have noticed him even if he'd paraded in front of them stark naked, they'd been so wrapped up in each other.

This is what Thea was warning me about – about not wanting to hurt me again – but the boring archaeologist is going away.

John scrolled through the emails on his phone. He needed to get back to Bath if he was going to consolidate his promotion.

But without Thea, I might not be able to keep my post anyway.

He drank the rest of his pint of Coke slowly. It was time to come up with a better plan.

April 19th
'Who is that gentleman in with Shaun?'

Mabel, clipboard clutched to her chest, arrived in the office with her usual lack of greeting.

'Richard. He's a furniture expert who is going to try and save our table.'

'Oh.' Immediately satisfied that her territory hadn't been invaded and that her work schedule hadn't been messed up, but merely added to, Mabel referred to her list. 'Aren't you and Tina heading back to the mill today?'

'Just me, Mabel. Tina is at the Trust office dealing with the insurance company about the vase.' Thea crossed her fingers under her desk. 'First, however, I have a mountain of paperwork to sort out. I have to book the health and safety people to come and give the place the once-over in time for Open Day.'

Frowning, Mabel scribbled extra notes on her chart. 'Well, I wish you'd said. Should I rearrange things and get Derek and his team to do the whitewashing in the meantime? The garden is almost there, and I'm sure Sam and that nice John would rather do the outside jobs.'

Thea bit back the urge to ask Mabel why she always referred to John as being 'nice'.

'That would be helpful, thank you. The equipment is there already.' She took the mill keys from the desk drawer. 'Oh, and Mabel, Shaun has to leave today. He and Richard are needed in Cornwall to work on the next series of *Landscape Treasures*, so you'd better take him off your rota for now.'

The old lady was horrified. 'Leaving?'

'Yes.' Thea resisted the temptation to say 'I told you so.'

'But he said he'd stay here. He promised.'

'Only if and when he could get the time off work. We've already had Shaun's help for much longer than I imagined, plus he got Richard here to mend the table, saving us hundreds of pounds.'

The crease on Mabel's forehead deepened. 'It'll take more than today to mend the table. The layers will have to be built up slowly to hide the scratch properly.'

'I'm aware of that.' Thea met Mabel's eyes. 'He will come back with Shaun as soon as he can.'

'So, Shaun will still do Open Day then?'

'I don't know, Mabel. Why don't you ask him?'

'No need to snap!'

Thea exhaled slowly. 'Forgive me, I've had very little sleep for two nights running.'

'You do look a bit tired.' Mabel lightened her tone. 'Shall I fetch you a coffee, dear? We don't need you overworking and getting ill. Whatever time do you get here in the mornings? You're always here before anyone.'

Looking back at her laptop screen so her eyes didn't give her away, Thea mumbled, 'It's as if I never leave.'

'Can I come in?'

'Of course.' Thea gave Tina a half-smile as her friend sat on the opposite side of the kitchen table, perched as if she might run off again at any moment. 'It's great to see you, I—'

'I came to tell you that I should hear about the insurance claim today.'

'Oh, right. Thank you.' Feeling the weight of everything that needed doing crashing down on her, and not wanting to miss this chance to apologise to Tina, Thea leant across the kitchen table, and took Tina's hands. 'I'm so sorry. I didn't mean to hurt your feelings. Please don't go back to the Trust office to work. If you don't want to share the scullery with me, I'll find somewhere else. I miss you so much… I mean, I know it's only been a few hours, but… Look, I don't think you're a gold-digger at all and—'

'You were right.'

Tina's words came out so quietly that Thea wasn't sure she'd heard them properly. 'Sorry?'

'I said you were right. That's sort of how I've been, although all I wanted was someone to take care of me. I hadn't thought about the gold-digger side of it. It isn't like I don't want to pay my own way.'

Getting up, Thea hurried around the table and wrapped an arm around her friend. 'I still shouldn't have said it. I honestly didn't mean it. It's just that you and Sam get on so well. I've seen you working so happily together. It's a shame for you to miss out on something because he doesn't fit the image in your head.'

'Maybe.' Tina looked out of the window. 'How about you and Shaun? You like him, don't you?'

'Against my better judgement.'

'He clearly likes you. Just the way he glances in your direction is enough to tell me that.'

'Do you think so?'

'You know he does, or he wouldn't have invited you out for a meal last night. Did you go? I wanted to ask you about it before but…' Tina swung around to face Thea and sighed.

'I wanted to tell you all about it as soon as I got back, but…'

'But it's hard to talk to someone when they aren't talking to you.'

'I really am sorry Tina. Basically, I was trying to be encouraging and cocked it right up.'

'I know.'

Thea smiled. 'Why don't we climb today's paperwork mountain and then escape for a while? I think we've both earned one of Sybil's scones and some decent coffee. Not to mention a proper catch-up.'

'Yes!' Tina punched the air with her fist before turning to a yawning Thea.

'Success with the insurance company perchance?'

'Yep. It's going to take time to process, but the smashed vase comes under accidental damage. It makes no difference that it was a bird that caused the breakage rather than a human.'

'Thank God for that!'

'And I forgot to tell you, I've finally found a locksmith who is willing to have a go at the mill doors. He'll confirm a date tomorrow.' Snapping her laptop closed, Tina moved around the table to perch next to Thea. 'Now you can tell me about last night.'

Feeling the blush as it hit her cheeks, Thea laughed. 'We went out to dinner.'

'And?' Tina lowered her voice, aware that there was always a chance John might be lurking within earshot.

'And he's leaving.'

'What?'

Explaining the situation to Tina, Thea left out the part

where Shaun had, once again, declared how much he wanted to take her to bed.

'Have you told Mabel?'

'Yes. It went down like a lead balloon.'

'I bet. He'll be back for Open Day though?'

'No idea.' Thea gave an accepting shrug. 'We had a great time together last night, but I'm going to have to accept that that was it. There is always going to be somewhere else he has to be. Not his fault. It's the nature of the job.'

'Did you, you know…?'

'I know perfectly well, thanks.' Thea still regretted her decision to sleep alone the night before. Or rather, fail to sleep. All night she'd lain there, wishing she'd said yes, that she would join Shaun in his bed. She'd wanted to. Very much. But, the notion of sleeping with him and then never seeing him again… it just wasn't her style.

'Of course not.'

'Shame.' Tina gave her friend a hug. 'It would have been a nice memory.'

'Or something to make his leaving even harder.'

Tina lowered her voice further. 'You've gone and fallen for him, haven't you?'

'Maybe.' Thea straightened up. 'Mabel is sending Derek and the boys to crack on with the whitewashing so we can do the paperwork. Would you be a star and check on Shaun and Richard?'

'No problem.' Accepting the change of subject for now, Tina headed towards the door. 'Then I am taking you to Sybil's. Cheese scones and hot coffee! Plus, we can pick her brains about local craft folk who might be up for new premises or a studio in the village.'

No sooner had Tina's footsteps finished echoing along the corridor, than John appeared on silent feet. 'I imagine you're very tired this morning.'

The accusation shot from his lips like a bullet.

Thea closed her eyes. 'John, I'm very busy. If we take it as read that you are about to ask me out, and I'm about to say no, then we can get on with our day.'

'I came to apologise.'

'Apologise?'

'For coming on so heavy with the constant date requests. I hadn't realised your taste in men had changed so dramatically.'

Thrown by the apology, and not quite sure whether she and Shaun were being insulted, or if John was simply stating a fact, Thea mumbled, 'Oh, right then.'

'But he's leaving.'

'For a short time.'

His smile suddenly returned. 'He won't come back.'

John didn't say anything else, but the certainty of his words hit Thea hard as she realised that, just this once, he might be right.

Twenty-Seven

Tina put a bright red cross through the date on the calendar. It had quickly become a ritual since Mabel had hung it up on the inside of the front door on the 1st May. There was no doubt it helped keep people focused, although it scared her and Thea to death.

Mabel was still taking her role as coordinator extremely seriously and, apart from occasional mutterings from a few of the stalwarts about her bossy ways, she was proving an asset. The calendar had been Mabel's way of instilling into everybody else that time really was short. Each day she took up a thick red marker pen, and crossed off the bold black numbers, showing how much – or how little – time they had left. Tonight however, Bert had arrived and taken his wife away early.

Tina smiled at the memory of Bert's kindly face, as he'd steered his far more dominant wife off the premises. He'd manoeuvred Mabel with a soft insistence to which she gave a token effort of resistance, before giving in, just as her husband had probably known she would.

'I wonder what it's like to be happily married for that long.'

Thea tried not to acknowledge the presence of the marker pen in Tina's hand as she came through the front door with an armful of fresh eggs. 'We'll never know. Already too late for us to be married for over fifty years, unless we live to gone ninety and get married tomorrow.'

'That's a depressing thing to say!'

'It must be the effect of that calendar! How can it be mid-May already?'

'Never mind mid-May, where did today go?' Tina rubbed a dust-covered hand over her cheek, leaving a secondary trail of grime in its wake. 'I've been digging out demonstration tables for the mill from the back of the stable block.' She gestured to her hair. 'I take it I'm pickled in cobwebs?'

'Yep.' The memory of Shaun teasing a line of spider's silk from her hair inconveniently planted itself at the forefront of Thea's mind. Had that really been six weeks ago?

Shaun had been away from Mill Grange for thirty days now. Thea had told herself it was inevitable that he'd be longer than he'd hoped, but she hadn't thought he'd be gone a whole month without a word. *John was right. Shaun isn't coming back.*

Guessing what was on her friend's mind, Tina took the trays of eggs from Thea's hands. 'I take it you still haven't heard anything?'

'No.' Tugging her boots off, Thea gestured to the eggs. 'Sybil will be pleased the eggs are coming regularly now Gertrude and the gang have settled in.'

Accepting that her friend didn't want to speculate about Shaun, Tina said, 'When we're finished at Mill Grange, it's going to be a wrench for Sam to leave the hens.'

'Not to mention Tony Stark.'

Tina laughed. 'I still can't believe you called the rooster Tony Stark!'

'The way he struts about and yet remains adorable, it suits him down to the ground. Very Robert Downey Junior.'

'Talking of Sam, he said he'd have the kettle on, and the jacket spuds should be ready by now.'

'Jacket spuds?'

Tina led her friend towards the kitchen. 'Don't you remember? Sam's cooking jacket spuds on the bonfire by his tent this evening. You, me and Sam are going to have a chill with some wine. Celebrating a job well done so far, and a rallying cry to help with the final push to the summit. We have nine weeks until opening, and for the first time ever, we're on schedule.'

'Nine weeks?' Thea stifled a heavy yawn. 'How is that possible?'

'Don't look so dismal. It's working. The chickens are laying, the seedlings Sam and John put in are already mini plants, which will be ready for sale by mid-June, Sam's rent and egg money is keeping us in cleaning materials and snacks, and the mill is almost ready to have its health and safety check so we can invite the spinner and so on for Open Day. The only big decision left is whether to pull down the greenhouse. If we are going to do that, it needs doing ASAP.'

'And professionally. That is no job for Derek, Bill and Sam, however skilled they are.'

'I have the quotes I got weeks ago. Should I chase them up tomorrow? We've saved so much, the loss of one greenhouse shouldn't upset the trustees too much.'

'I'd have still liked to save it.' Thea suddenly held up a hand, as if asking for quiet and whispered, 'Did you hear something?'

'No.' Tina automatically looked around as she replied, 'There's no one here. I double- checked before I marked the calendar.'

'Right.' Thea forced herself not to peer over her shoulder. 'It's such a shame about the greenhouse. It could be so beautiful.'

'I know, but you've worked miracles already. Something was bound not to work out.' Tina studied her friend. 'When did you last get a good night's sleep?'

'Just takes me a while to drop off sometimes. Lots on my mind. At least the trustees have stopped emailing me with demands for progress reports every five minutes. Finally the penny seems to have dropped that I can't get on with my job if I'm answering their queries all the time.' Thea pointed to the mugs on the side. 'I'd forgotten about supper with Sam. Would you like me to cry off so you two can be alone?'

Now it was Tina's turn to sigh. 'I've told you, Sam isn't my type, and frankly, I'm not his. He's never made a single move or said anything to make me think he's remotely interested beyond friendship.'

Suddenly Thea understood. 'And there is no way you'll ask him out because you don't want him to reject you.'

'Of course I don't. No one wants that, do they?' Tina stared at Thea. 'Are you sure you're okay? You seem unsettled.'

Crossing her arms protectively over her chest, Thea said, 'I'm just being paranoid, forget it.'

'John isn't here. I've checked. I check every room every night. And I've told you, you can come back home with me. There's a decent sofa you could sleep on, or we could grab an airbed from Taunton on the way back.'

'I have to be here. After that nightjar got in, I couldn't possibly risk leaving the manor. Anyway, Malcolm knows I'm sleeping here now, so I can keep an eye on the place. He agreed that if Shaun hadn't been here when the bird had got in, and got it out again, then the damage could have been so much worse. It's only the volunteers that don't know I'm living in.'

'Because you don't want John knowing you're here all the time.'

'I can't believe he hasn't worked it out.' Thea looked over her shoulder. 'He's not a stupid man.'

'Bloody persistent.'

'Yes.' Thea had stopped trying to avoid John during the day. He'd turn up at some point during the morning and do a token gesture of work, just enough to be seen as useful so he wasn't asked to leave, then he'd take time to charm either Mabel or Diane or both, before sauntering off again to goodness knew where.

'When he isn't here, what's he doing?' Thea cuddled her arms tighter around her chest. 'I feel as if John is watching me even when I can't see him.' She groaned. 'I sound paranoid, don't I?'

'A bit.' Tina found herself looking over her own shoulder. 'Do you want to check the house again before we go to see Sam?'

'No, it's okay. Logically, I know I'm overreacting because I'm overtired. John's hardly here compared to everyone else.'

'I thought he'd stopped asking you out every five minutes.'

'He hasn't asked me once since Shaun left.'

'That's good, isn't it?'

'Very, but…'

'But what?'

'But the second my… the second Shaun left John stops hassling me. I can't quite believe he isn't planning something.'

Tina crossed her arms as she regarded her friend. 'You were going to say "the second my boyfriend", weren't you?'

'Hardly. Boyfriends don't disappear for three weeks longer than planned without a word. I know the signal here is weak, but it isn't non-existent. He could email me or call the landline.'

'Only if he has a signal his end.'

'He's in Cornwall, not Outer Mongolia. And the landline doesn't need a signal.'

Pulling a face, which clearly expressed her conviction that Shaun was mad, Tina picked up the mugs. 'Come on. Let's take these to Sam. Dinner's bound to be ready by now.'

Picking the back door key off the table, Thea agreed, 'I'm quite hungry actually.'

'I'm not surprised. You've been working like a Trojan and hardly eating.' Tina ran an assessing eye over her friend. 'You've lost weight. I hadn't noticed before. You always wear such baggy clothes.'

'They're warm.' Thea felt defensive.

'It wasn't a criticism. You're looking great.'

'Thanks. Sorry.' Thea gave a weak smile. 'Let's go and find Sam. He'll be hungry as well, and he's such a gent, he wouldn't think of starting without us.'

'He is, isn't he? And so is Shaun.'

'If he was a gentleman, he'd have been in touch.'

'Hun, he'll have a good reason.'

'So you said.'

The aroma of bonfire, cooked potatoes and charred tinfoil hit the girls' nostrils as they crossed the garden. Mill Grange's grounds looked beautiful bathed in the half light of the late spring evening.

Sam got to his feet as they approached. 'They're ready.' He brandished a packet of butter and a knife. 'I'm going for full-on calories myself.'

'Sounds good.' Tina spotted three bundles of foil tucked into the embers at the edge of the fire.

'I wasn't sure if you'd want your potato before you went, Thea? Might be a good idea, as I bet you haven't eaten much today.'

The girls exchanged glances as Thea asked, 'Go where?'

'Didn't you see the message I left on your desk?'

Tina's eyebrows rose. 'You went inside the office?'

Sam poked the fire with a long stick. 'There was no one else about and I'm sure it was a message Thea would want ASAP.'

Thea felt her fingers tingle. 'What was the message?'

'To be at the Stag and Hound at eight o'clock. Same place as last time, whatever that means.'

'From Shaun?'

'The message came from the landlady. Moira, I think she said her name was.'

Tina beamed. 'Same place as last time must mean Moira's backroom. It has to be Shaun. He has to be back.'

'Well, if he thinks he can just waltz back without a word…'

'Oh, for heaven's sake. Don't waste time, woman. It's almost eight now.'

Sam got to his feet. 'Would you like us to walk you over to the pub?'

Tempted to say yes, Thea declined the offer. 'Thanks, but it's not far. You two eat your dinner.'

'Are you sure you don't want yours first? It could be a while before you eat. It's a Saturday night after all.'

'I'm fine, but thanks.' Thea brushed her palms down her jeans, briefly contemplating changing. Then she remembered how long Shaun had been AWOL and changed her mind.

He was bloody lucky she was going to meet him at all. Especially as he couldn't even be bothered to leave a message himself, but had got Moira to do it for him.

Twenty-Eight

'I was beginning to wonder if Shaun would be back for Open Day.'

Sam passed Tina a hot potato, dripping with a heart attack inducing portion of local butter.

'His timing tonight couldn't have been better.' Tina licked stray butter from her fingers. 'Thea has missed him far more than she's let on.'

Giving Tina a fork with which to dig out the hot fluffy potato, Sam balanced his own supper in his hands. 'I have no doubt the feeling is entirely mutual.'

'Did Shaun confide in you then?'

Sam laughed. 'You sounded like a teenage schoolgirl then. All eager for gossip.'

Tina felt hot spots of pink on her cheeks before she realised she was being teased. 'I just want them to be happy.'

'Isn't that what we all want?'

Tina shuffled her legs into a more comfortable position on the travel rug upon which she sat. 'True.' Realising she'd been given an opening to find out a little more about Sam's life, she added, 'How about you? Do you have someone waiting to make you happy in a tent somewhere?'

Sam held her gaze steadily. As his eyes met hers, Tina knew there was no one else. She found herself blustering, 'Forgive me, I shouldn't intrude.'

Pushing up his jumper sleeves, Sam lowered his attention to his potato. 'If there was someone, would I be here?'

'Probably not.' Tina mumbled, taking a mouthful of too-hot spud. Struggling not to spit it out again, she let it burn her mouth as her eyes fell on the bottom edge of a tattoo that had been made visible on his right arm by the rucking up of his sleeve.

'How about you? If you don't mind me asking.' Sam poured some honey into their mugs, followed by hot water from a billycan he'd been warming on the fire. 'I've rather assumed you are also single. It can't just be devotion to your work and your friend that keeps you here all hours.'

Tina felt oddly indignant that Sam had assumed she had nothing else in her life, until she realised that, despite her best efforts, it was the truth. Then she just felt sad.

'Here.' Sam passed the well stirred drink. 'It's honey, hot water and a little tot of whiskey. Goes well with jacket spuds.'

Tina gave a weak smile that expanded into a broad grin as the soothing liquid slid down her throat. 'That's delicious.'

'I am a man of many talents.'

'You most certainly are. I can't tell you how grateful we are that you could fix the window pulley.'

'That was more Derek than me to be honest. He gave instructions and I followed them.'

'Well, you both were heroes.'

'It takes rather more than that to be a hero.' Sam turned abruptly away, hiding his face by looking up at the manor behind them. 'Tell me about your plans. Once the manor is restored, whether it is sold or not, what will you do?'

'Go back to my regular job with the Trust. I'm only here on secondment. I'm their business liaison woman in real life. My days are all accounts and telling people what they can and cannot afford to do with their Trust properties.'

Sam's eyebrows rose. 'I had no idea you were an office girl. That's not how you come across.'

'And how do I come across?' Tina took another sip of her honey drink, cursing herself for asking a question she wasn't sure she wanted an answer to.

'Outdoorsy. Capable, happy and a touch insecure.'

'Oh.' Taken aback by the directness, not to mention the speed of his reply which implied he'd considered the question before, Tina nervously asked. 'Is that good or bad?'

'Very good. Everyone is insecure and we'd be foolish to pretend otherwise, but anyone who can help build a chicken coop at a moment's notice out of random pieces of wood and old tea chests is capable in my book.'

'It was fun.' Tina suddenly felt shy. 'And the chickens must be happy as they're laying well.'

'They're happier still now Mr Stark has moved in.' Sam laughed. 'Such a cracking name for a cockerel.'

'What about you? What will you do once Mill Grange is restored?'

Layering up his fork with potato Sam used it to gesture towards the building. 'Just look at this place. How could anyone bear to leave?'

'It's going to kill Thea if she has to find a new job after all her hard work. She gave up so much to come here to restore it and become the manager once it opened. If it wasn't for...' Tina stopped talking.

'But the reason she gave up what she did is her story to tell, right?'

'Absolutely.' Tina ate quietly. 'I hope she and Shaun are getting on okay.'

Thea checked the time on the mantle clock. She'd been there almost an hour, but there was no sign of Shaun.

The backroom to the Stag and Hound had been empty when Moira, who was clearly expecting her, ushered Thea inside, as if she was on a covert operation for the SAS. Having taken her drink and food, insisting that her visitor would be there soon, but was running late, Moira had left Thea in peace.

The jacket potato and salad that was now history hadn't looked anything like as appetising as the ones Tina and Sam would be tucking into.

'If he isn't here in five minutes, I'm going home.'

No sooner had Thea uttered the words to herself, than the door opened and Moira fussed back in, all smiles, reassuring her that the gentleman had arrived and was on his way.

Thea laughed. 'Why don't you just call him Shaun? I grant you he *can* be a gentleman, but he's kept me waiting weeks without a word and he's an hour late. That doesn't rate high on the gentleman score chart.'

'Because it isn't Mr Cowlson.' Moira's shoulders drooped

as she saw the disappointed expression that crossed Thea's face.

'Who is it then?'

'Mr Sommers. He said it was a surprise, that you would be delighted and—'

'John?' Thea pulled her coat back on. 'I'm sorry Moira, but I can't face dinner with John. Can I leave via the back?'

'Of course, but why?'

'Please Moira. I will explain soon, I promise, but it's best I leave before John gets here.'

Moira was already leading Thea along the corridor that she'd used with Shaun a few weeks ago. All the way she was apologising, 'It was supposed to be a nice surprise, he said…'

'In his mind it would have been.' Thea turned to face her host. 'Will you keep this to yourself? I couldn't bear the villagers to know that I walked out on dinner with one of my volunteers.'

'I'm sure you have your reasons.' Moira's eyebrows met in the middle. 'I've never had one customer run away from another customer before.'

'I'm not running away, I'm just… just so very busy.' Thea's hand was on the back door out of the pub when she remembered she hadn't paid for her food yet. 'The bill. I haven't…'

'Forget it. Just get going. If Mr Sommers asks, I'll tell him you're staying with a friend tonight, shall I?'

'Yes. Thank you, Moira.'

Not sure why she'd agreed to that, and knowing Moira hadn't bought her 'too busy' excuse, Thea rushed back towards Mill Grange. She felt an utter fool. 'Whatever made me think Shaun would come back and surprise me like that? We hardly know each other.'

With every step she cursed Shaun for being away. With every second step she told herself off for expecting Shaun to solve her problems. No one could sort out John's delusions but her.

Visions of John pacing the backroom of the pub filled her head, soon to be transplanted by images of him leaving the pub and striding towards the manor.

Maybe I should have stayed? Guilt raised its ugly head as Thea walked along. *What harm could having a drink with him do? Maybe if I listened to him...* As the path curved towards the garden and woods of Mill Grange, Thea let out a groan. 'No, if I'd stayed, we'd only have gone over the same old ground again.'

'Who's that?'

Sam had leapt to his feet before Tina was aware of anyone approaching.

A trickle of fear washed down her spine as she stood with Sam, holding her fork in her hand as if it was no longer a tool, but a weapon. The trees whose leaves had chatted behind them in the breeze, now felt dark and oppressive. They could be hiding anything, or anyone.

Barely whispering, Tina muttered, 'What is it?'

'I heard someone walking this way. They're close, they... Thea!'

Sam dashed forward, with Tina close behind him. 'Thea? Where's Shaun?'

Thea grimaced, 'Not Shaun. John.'

★

Sam patrolled the perimeter of the manor while Tina took Thea inside and made her a sub-standard, but nonetheless welcome, version of Sam's honey and whiskey toddy.

'I can't believe this. How did John know you met Shaun there last time?'

'Moira, I guess.' Thea rubbed her temples. 'She has no idea about John being my ex – why would she? Moira thought she was doing something good. She was almost girlish about it until the penny dropped.'

'I'm staying here until Shaun gets back.' Tina glanced towards the kitchen window, checking to make sure no one was looking in.

'It's very kind of you both, but I'm not afraid of John, I'm just driven to distraction by him.'

'I'm still staying. I'll make do with the clothes I've got on tonight, and then tomorrow I'll go home and fetch some clean ones. It makes sense for me to be here now we're only two months from Open Day.'

Thea nodded. 'This is so stupid. He didn't do anything. I didn't even see him. I keep wondering if I should have stayed – heard it all one more time just to keep the peace.' Thea massaged her aching forehead. 'I hope Moira's alright.'

'I'm going to go and call her now.'

'Would you? You're a star. Thank you.' Thea held the mug to her chest, inhaling the comforting aroma. 'Tell her she didn't do anything wrong.'

'I'm going to talk to Sam as well. He deserves to know what's going on, if that's okay with you.'

'Yes. Thanks.' Putting down her cup, Thea held her head

in her hands. 'I feel such a fool, but I'm up to here with his delusions about us having a happy-ever-after.'

Tina gave her friend a quick hug. 'If you'd stayed, do you think you'd have discovered if there's more to this than being madly in love with you?'

'If he was madly in love with me, he wouldn't be acting like this. He'd be acting like...'

'Like Shaun does?' Tina smiled as she reached the door. 'I'll have a quick word with Sam and tell him you're okay. Stay right there. Drink your drink. I'll be back very soon.'

Twenty-Nine

May 19th

Thea passed Sam a mug of tea as he stood by the front door. 'I wanted to apologise for my behaviour, and to thank you for looking after me and Tina last night.'

'You have nothing to apologise for.'

'John didn't do anything. I didn't even see him.' Thea raked a hand through her tousled hair, 'He might have been about to apologise and tell me he was leaving.'

'You don't really believe that. He's come this far – why would he quit now? I'm sorry Thea.' Sam shook his head, 'I've met men like John before. They don't give up easily when they don't get what they want.' He sounded apologetic. 'Tina explained the situation. How putting some distance between you and John was one of the reasons you came to be at Mill Grange in the first place, I mean.'

Thea wasn't sure what to say. 'Did you watch outside the door all night, or did you get some sleep?'

'Never mind how much sleep I did or didn't get. You haven't slept, that's very clear. Go back to bed now.'

Thea's voice was laced with panic. 'How can I? No one but you and Tina know I'm sleeping here. If I go to my room now, I'll be a hostage in there all day. Plus it's already almost eight o'clock. There's stuff to be done. The chickens need cleaning for a start, and let me tell you, Gertrude and her gang do not like being out of routine.'

Sam gave her a reassuring smile. 'I have already seen to Miss Gertrude and her cohorts. Tina is in the office looking at quotes for the greenhouse. Until John arrives, I'm going to tackle another long overdue job, which is to clear all the tools out of the entrance to the butler's pantry. If we moved everything to one of the actual sheds, it would be further for us to get what we need, but an extra room of interest would be available to open to the public.'

Thea suddenly felt she might burst into tears. She knew very well that Sam was proposing to tackle that particular job because it meant he could see the main door and the access path to the back door from where he worked.

Sam and Tina's kindness, on top of Shaun's desertion and John's endlessly bizarre behaviour, felt too much and she could only croak, 'When the others arrive, what will you tell them? Where will you say I am?'

'That you are having a well-earned day off.' Seeing Thea was about to object again, Sam held up a hand. 'Now, go up to your room, get enough things for an overnight stay. Tina's going to drive you to her place. You need some time away from here. Twenty-four hours with a modern shower, a modern bed, Wi-Fi and coffee shops.'

'But—'

'Thea, you are going to crack if you don't take a break. Men like John can't be got rid of that easily. They are so used to getting what they want in life, whether it's their dream job, because they know the right people, or a fast car because they're paid way more than they're worth. But don't you worry, I'll keep an eye on him.'

Looking across the driveway at the lack of cars, Thea tried to smile. 'It's Sunday, so at least it'll be quiet this morning, but I suspect Mabel and Derek, if not Bill and Diane, will be here later. I'm less sure about the others.'

'If John does appear, what's he supposed to be working on?'

'I'm not sure. Mabel has the rota.'

'Then he can help me. I need a hand with clearing the debris from the greenhouse before it's removed or saved, or whatever happens to it.'

'It'll be pulled down, I think. So sad. I can picture it full of oranges and lemons and all sorts of heat-loving plants. But, we've been pushing our luck with the budget already. There's no way we can save it all.'

'Well, either way, it needs a tidy up. John can help me.'

'Are you sure you want to work with him?'

'I'm sure I don't, but I will, because I don't want him near anyone else.' Sam paused. 'Shaun would never forgive me if he got near you for a start.'

'Shaun?'

'He asked me to look out for you. Fine job I've made of that!'

A flutter of hope sparked inside Thea, but she batted it away. Shaun could have been in touch. But he hadn't been. End of story. She'd already decided to give him one more week to get in touch; if not, she'd start to hunt for new celebrities to open the manor and mill. It would be a nightmare explaining to everyone who'd already purchased an Open Day ticket why their guest star wasn't going to appear, but needs must.

'John's weird behaviour isn't your fault, Sam, nor is it your responsibility to watch over me. It was kind of Shaun to show concern, but he's clearly moved on.' Thea, realising she sounded ungrateful, gave him a tired smile. 'I think you're right. Perhaps a day away from here would be good for me.'

Unruffled by Thea's objections, Sam shooed her away. 'Go and pack a bag. Let's get you out of here before John arrives.'

'Are you sure your housemate won't mind?'

Tina rolled her eyes. 'How many more times are you going to ask me that?'

Thea allowed her friend to tuck her up in her own bed, and fuss around her. 'Sorry.'

'I'll be back this evening and we'll go to the pub for dinner. We can both stay here overnight, and then we'll head back to the manor tomorrow with enough stuff to live at Mill Grange until opening. Until then, sleep, lounge about, watch crap on the television. Do whatever you like, but don't work.'

'Thank Sam again, won't you?'

'I will, now go to sleep.' Tina placed a door key on the bedside table as Thea's head hit the pillow. 'My housemate will be at work all day, so you'll have total peace and quiet.'

Thea's reply of 'Thanks, Tina,' was overtaken by instant blessed sleep.

★

For a few blissful minutes on waking, Thea had forgotten why she was cosy under a soft king-sized duvet in a room with central heating.

The cruel interruption of recent memories sent her eyes snapping back shut and a long groan escaping from her lips. *John.*

Even if he got what he wanted and she gave in and went out with him, she couldn't see how that would make him happy. He'd always have to live with the knowledge that she'd given in to him for a quiet life. That she'd never love him, that she'd always resent him and that she'd do anything to keep him at arm's length. Where was the victory in that?

Reaching for her phone, Thea braced herself to face the screen. She only wanted to know the time, but there was a high chance that there'd be text messages and emails flashing for her attention – and at least one would be from John.

It was a quarter to four in the afternoon.

Thea sat bolt upright. How the hell had she slept that long? The day was all but gone.

She rechecked the phone, to make sure she wasn't imagining things, just as the digital display changed from 15:45 to 15:46.

Ignoring the envelope symbol that declared she did indeed have texts waiting, Thea swung her legs out of bed, ready to rush to the bathroom for a shower and crack on with what was left of the day.

She sat down as soon as she'd stood up. Where did she think she was going? Tina wouldn't be here for another couple of hours, and she had no transport to get back to Upwich.

A grumble from her stomach urged Thea towards the kitchen. Hoping it would be obvious what food belonged to Tina, so she didn't accidentally steal anyone else's supplies, she went in search of food and coffee.

Thea needn't have worried. On arrival she found a cake tin with a piece of paper placed on top, held down with a mug and a tin of coffee. Addressed to her, it instructed Thea to help herself to as much of the contents as she wanted, as well as to anything on the lowest shelf in the fridge and the third cupboard along above the oven.

Opening the tin, Thea inhaled deeply as the familiar waft of lemon cake assailed her nostrils. She hadn't realised how hungry she was until the scent of Tina's baking hit her.

Ten minutes later the entire cake and a knife sat on the coffee table. With a steaming mug of black coffee to hand, Thea curled up on the sofa in front of the television. It was so long since she'd watched television that she was momentarily thrown by the number of channels showing so little worth watching.

Trying not to feel guilty about her time away from the manor, she aimed the remote control at the screen, channel-hopping away from the third true crime show she'd found and onto the fifth reality makeover programme. The only good thing she could say about them was that however bad things got for her, at least she wasn't the victim of humiliation on reality television.

Flicking onto the next channel, Thea froze as Shaun crossed the screen. A lump formed in her throat, but she couldn't pull her eyes away. It was an old episode, one of his earliest appearances on *Landscape Treasures*. She'd seen them all, although she'd never told him that. His hair had been more foppish then, with a fringe hanging over his eyes, which he continually swept aside so he could see the cameras or the archaeological site in front of him. That was how he'd looked at the conference. When Becky had tricked him into bed. When at the same time, Shaun had claimed, he'd been getting up the courage to ask her out.

But you didn't, Shaun. You didn't ask me. Just as you haven't been in touch for weeks.

Watching as he moved around an Iron Age hillfort, Thea tried to be glad that she hadn't given in to her baser instincts and slept with Shaun before he'd left for Cornwall. But she couldn't. She'd wanted to and couldn't see how it would hurt more if she'd done what she wanted.

'At least I'd have a nice memory. One better than saving me from a rough night with a lost nightjar.'

Even as she'd said it, Thea knew she was being unfair. Not many people would have helped her as much as Shaun had. And as she watched him walking around the excavation, she was reminded just how much he loved his job, and how good he was at it.

He's as dedicated to Landscape Treasures *as you are to Mill Grange.*

Putting down her coffee, she picked up her mobile. 'Maybe he's been waiting for me to get in touch. Maybe he's in Cornwall wondering why I haven't called him?' Thea sighed. 'No. He knows how hard it is for me signal wise, and he said he'd be in touch. And he hasn't been.'

Her eyes fell on the envelope symbols. There were four of them now. They could be from John, but equally, Tina could have been checking on her. Taking a deep breath, Thea pressed the receive button on her phone and forced herself to look at the small screen.

One text was from Tina saying she'd booked them a table at the Lamb and Flag for seven o'clock.

The other three were from an unknown number.

Thea sat on the edge of the sofa, her heart thudding almost as fast as when she'd been running away from the Stag and Hound.

She read the first text.

It's Shaun – got new phone number. I've spoken to Sam. I'm on my way.

'What? On your way to the manor, or did Sam tell you I was here?'

The second text answered her question.

I've been a fool. I believed the messages were from you. I'm on my way. Tina says she's booked us a table at the Lamb and Flag.

'Messages? What messages?'

Thea? Are you getting these messages? You should have a signal at Tina's. Are you okay?

Thirty

Thea had showered at top speed, dragged a borrowed hairbrush through her hair and dressed in the only clean clothes she'd taken to Tina's. Her oversized jumpers and faded out jeans weren't particularly smart, but as they were here and immensely comfy, they'd do.

'I don't want Shaun to think I'm dressing up for him anyway.'

Thea's attempts to call Shaun had failed, but she'd hammered off a selection of texts telling him she was okay, that she'd be at the Lamb and Flag waiting for him, and that she was looking forward to seeing him.

She'd hesitated before sending the last message – but as she knew it to be true, and as Sam had said Shaun was concerned about her, she'd sent it anyway.

Now, sitting nervously by the pub's front window, an unpleasant idea struck Thea.

What if it had been John on the end of those texts and not Shaun?

Cursing, she grabbed her coat from the vacant seat next to her, but didn't move. Stuck in indecision, Thea didn't know whether to flee, or stay where she was, in a public place and therefore be safer than if John cornered her alone. It would at least get the showdown over with.

If there was a showdown.

She took a deep breath and muttered, 'Think logically.'

It must have been Shaun. But I don't recognise the number.

'Messages?' Thea mumbled as she slipped her coat on and cuddled herself with her arms, cold despite the warmth of the room's central heating. She hadn't sent Shaun any messages, which must only mean… 'Has John texted Shaun pretending he's me?'

She sank back against her chair with a jolt. It was ridiculous. *He couldn't have…* But she knew that, on a practical level at least, John was perfectly capable of such an act. *But morally, would he do that?*

Cursing herself once more for running out of the Stag and Hound before she'd had the guts to ask him what was really going on, she considered the possibility that his pointless persistence had more to do with his standing at work than Thea herself.

But how? Thea scanned the pub for signs of Shaun, aware she was either letting her imagination run away with her again, or was clutching at straws. Either way, enough was enough. She was not going to allow John to turn her into the sort of woman who ran out of pubs or hid behind locked doors on a regular basis. Mill Grange needed her, and whether the trustees sold or not, she was never going to put herself in a position where anyone could blame her for what had happened.

Gripping her arms through her thick coat, ignoring the glances she was getting from some of the diners at nearby tables, a renewed determination to succeed at Mill Grange took hold of Thea. A determination she was not going to let John Sommers ruin.

For now, she would stay put. Tina and Sam both knew where she was. So, if tonight was just John trying to trick her into a date again then, as long as she didn't move from where she was sitting, on the settee in the window of the Lamb and Flag dining room, then she was safe, and she could ask him what his agenda was. And, if it did turn out to be Shaun, then she'd find out what was going on and why he hadn't been in touch.

Thea planted her feet harder against the dubiously patterned carpet. 'Time to stop running.'

Her relief as she saw Shaun stride, head and shoulders above everyone else, into the busy pub, was only dwarfed by the desire to throw her arms around him. Somehow, she stayed where she was although the grin that spread across her face gave away how pleased she was to see him.

Shaun, however, had no such restraint. He'd engulfed Thea in his arms before they'd exchanged a single greeting. Her nostrils filled with the scent of his old Barbour jacket and indefinable deodorant, as overloud whispers of, 'Isn't that the man from *Landscape Treasures*,' echoed around the room.

'Thank God it's you.' Thea held him tighter.

'You were worried my message was a trick and that John was going to show up.'

'It crossed my mind.' Thea's heart sank as the reason for Shaun's unexpected arrival crept between them.

Shaun searched her face, as if looking for minute signs of damage. 'You didn't send me those messages, did you?'

'Until tonight I didn't know about any messages. I've sent nothing.' Thea picked up a fork from the table and fiddled it between her fingers. 'You said you'd be in touch within a week. You weren't. I assumed you either didn't have a signal or you'd changed your mind about me. As the days stretched on, the lack of signal seemed less viable, so I assumed you'd changed your mind about me.'

'Are you insane!?' Shaun realised he'd raised his voice, and instantly lowered it to a whisper, ignoring every set of eyes in the dining room that had swivelled their way. 'I've fancied you since... well, you know all that. Then I had to go to Cornwall. I must have driven Richard mad on the way south. I hardly shut up about you. I was a man who couldn't believe his luck! The girl I'd been too nervous to ask out all those years ago was right in front of me. And, miraculously, she seemed to like me too. A kindred spirit. Someone kind and capable and clever and funny and who's interested in the same things as me. And who gets that I don't like the fame thing and... well...' Shaun paused as he reached forward to take Thea's hands in his. 'Who's damn hot if I may say so.'

Thea couldn't help but smile. 'So why—'

'I hadn't been in Cornwall for more than a few hours

when I had a text saying you'd dropped your mobile in the sink and that you'd got a pay as you go phone.'

'I did no such thing!' Thea pointed to her mobile on the table. 'Same phone I've had for the past two years.'

'But I didn't know it wasn't true. I sent texts to the new number, thinking I was reaching you.' Shaun held her hands tighter. 'I was all for getting back in the car and driving to Mill Grange as soon as I'd seen the site in Cornwall was suitable, but the production team were waiting and the appointments to see the owners of the house in Cornwall were booked. Coming back at that point would have meant walking out on my job. If I'd done that I wouldn't have been the celebrity draw you need for your Open Day, would I?'

'You stayed so you wouldn't get booted off *Landscape Treasures* to keep your promise to open Mill Grange.' Thea's forehead creased.

'I'd promised.' Shaun gestured to the phone he'd laid on the table. 'I sent texts to the new number explaining the situation, but no one answered. I even tried calling, but no one answered.'

'And you didn't call the landline because?'

'Because you didn't answer my texts. I know the signal is bad, but there are some hotspots around Mill Grange, so you'd have got my messages eventually. I thought you'd lost interest in me.'

Thea couldn't help but smile. 'We're as bad as each other.'

'That has to be a good thing.' Shaun's eyes crinkled at the edges as he returned her grin. 'I think we need a drink. Pinot or lager?'

★

Ten minutes later, just at the point when she was on the verge of joining Shaun at the packed bar and begging him to put her out of suspense, he returned with two bottles of lager. Thea immediately dived back into the conversation. 'I was beginning to wonder if John had lost the plot completely and hacked my email as well, hence not hearing from you that way.'

'No, the dead mobile phone story was much simpler.'

'And effective. Gave us both time to start doubting ourselves and each other.' Thea sighed. 'Assuming it was John.'

'Of course it was.'

'Can we prove it though?'

'Only if we catch him in possession of the phone he contacted me with, pretending to be you.'

Taking a swig from her lager, Thea said, 'I wonder how he got your number in the first place?'

'Wouldn't have been difficult. As the signal's so bad at Mill Grange, I often left my phone in my room or the scullery.'

'Or I suppose he could have searched the file of health and safety forms on my desk. Everyone's personal details are recorded there.' Thea swallowed hard. 'I assume you changed your number so John couldn't contact you again?'

'I went into Taunton and got it switched this morning.'

'I hesitate to ask, but what did the texts you sent me say?'

Shaun shifted uncomfortably in his chair. 'Umm... I sent a couple saying how glad I was to have found you, and how much I was looking forward to returning to Mill Grange. Although not using those actual words.' He took a long swig of his drink. 'It's embarrassing to think that John read them and not you.'

Thea hated the idea of John reading private messages meant for her. 'I'm sorry I didn't get them.'

'So am I, believe me.' Shaun took a mouthful of beer, before adding, 'I'm even sorrier that he'll have seen the messages I sent after I got drunk with the team a few nights ago.'

Thea reached a hand out across the table, laying it over his. 'Tell me.'

'Like I say, I wasn't worried about your lack of replies at first, because I know how hard it is to get a connection at the manor, but when my texts were completely ignored, I was hurt. In my alcohol-fuelled self-pity I assumed you'd been leading me on and sent a text accusing you of just that. Then two or three texts begging forgiveness for being an idiot.'

Thea shifted her hand from his palm to his thigh. She could imagine how much John would have enjoyed reading Shaun's drunken texts.

'I'm sorry.' Shaun felt his body respond to the hand on his leg. 'I don't really think you led me on.'

'I know. It's okay.'

'It isn't though, is it?' Shaun sighed, 'because John has stepped over the mark from being a nuisance to being a liability.'

'John hasn't been at the manor much this month. He must have been staying in places with a good phone signal. You were gone, so it seemed logical he'd be around more. Making himself indispensable, trying to wear me down. But apart from popping in for an hour here and there to help in the grounds, he's been very quiet. Until last night.'

'When he pretended to be me and arranged a meeting in Moira's backroom.'

'Yes. Well, no. He didn't pretend to be you. I just assumed it was you, and then, when it wasn't, I ran away. Sam told you all about it?'

'He did. I didn't like leaving you at the manor with John about in the first place, so I asked Sam to keep his eyes open, although I didn't tell him why. Last night he and Tina were worried, so he called me.'

Thea looked at Shaun properly for the first time since he'd sat down. 'What do you think John's motivation for all this is?'

'It has to be hurt pride.'

'Is that enough though? And why now? The only thing he cares about is his image at work. I can't see how this is helping with that. He must have used nearly all his annual holiday up by being here.'

'Maybe he has, and he's running out of time. He's getting desperate, hence the phone con.' Shaun raked a hand through his hair.

'Although that still doesn't answer the question – why all this in the first place.'

'Jealousy is probably the immediate answer.' Shaun stared into Thea's eyes, 'John came to Mill Grange, convinced of his abilities to win you back. Then I arrived, and suddenly he had a rival as well as a challenge on his hands.'

Thea exhaled with a drawn-out groan of incomprehension. 'It's so mad. He's clever, handsome and, when he isn't being an obsessive arse, a decent, if somewhat self-centred, person.

278

He could have joined a dating site or something and met someone perfect for him. There are so many options, why this way? Why me?'

'Why you? Well, that's obvious,' Shaun's eyes spoke volumes on the subject, while no words left his lips. 'Why like this? God alone knows. The real question is what do we do about him? And, even more important, can I still open the manor, have the trustees made a decision about selling yet and, most vital of all, can I have a kiss right now please?'

'In public?' Thea coloured.

'Have you sold many tickets for the Open Day?'

Thrown by the question, Thea nodded. 'Over fifty at the last count.'

'We kept quiet to help the manor, but if we've already sold loads of Open Day tickets, then I don't care. Actually, I didn't care in the first place, but you did, and what you want matters to me, so…'

Thea placed a finger over Shaun's lips and silenced him further with a long overdue kiss.

Having texted Tina to assure her that they were okay, Thea declared a John-free conversation zone over dinner. Instead she heard about Shaun's adventures in Cornwall, while he caught up on news from Mill Grange.

'Are you going back to Cornwall now?'

Thea hadn't wanted to ask the question, but it loomed large in her mind as their pudding plates were cleared away and the question of her return to Mill Grange could no longer be ignored.

'I don't have to go back until we do the official filming

in August. Richard is almost done down there too. He'll be back at the manor soon so he can finish the table.'

'That's brilliant. Thank you.' Thea suddenly felt shy. 'Are you coming back to the manor to stay, or would you rather sleep at the Stag and Hound? I know Moira would be pleased to see you. She feels guilty about last night, although it wasn't her fault.'

Shaun smiled. 'If you think I'm letting you out of my sight until we've sorted out the John issue, then you have another think coming.'

'Thank Minerva for that!' Thea sighed, before remembering she'd arranged to stay at Tina's for the night.

'Don't worry, I've spoken to Tina. She knows I'm bringing you back to Mill Grange. Let's be honest, you have to be seen to be there, not just for the sake of the volunteers, but to show John he hasn't driven you out.'

'You think he'll be waiting there?' Thea tried to keep the trepidation from her voice, but failed.

'If he is, then he'll need to get past Sam and me.'

'Sam camps in the woods – pretty easy to pass.'

'Not anymore. He's moved onto the patch of grass by the car park, bang on the path between the two entrances to the house.'

'That's so kind.'

'He is. Sam's a lovely man.'

'I wish Tina would—'

'Shall we sort out our own mess before we start matchmaking for them?'

Thirty-One

May 20th

'Coffee, madam?' Shaun placed a mug of coffee on the table next to his bed.

'Thank you,' Thea mumbled as her eyes came into focus. 'What time is it?'

'Only half six, but I thought you'd want to get out of my room before Mabel arrived.'

'Good point.' She felt sheepish. 'I can't believe I fell asleep in your bed. I'm so sorry.'

Shaun laughed. 'Believe me, I'm sorry too, but only because I rather hoped that the first time you slept in my bed I'd be in it with you.'

Thea blushed. 'Me too, actually. I must have been more tired than I realised. I remember sitting down on the edge of the bed and talking to you, and…'

'…and how much fun we had almost getting into bed together.'

'Oh yes.' Thea pulled up the blanket, clutching it to the chest Shaun had inspected so attentively the previous evening, as if trying to trap in the memory of the heat of his fingers. 'Then common sense intervened and you dashed off to check on Sam before we...'

'Got under the covers?' Shaun grinned at Thea's coyness. 'When I got back you were spark out across the bed at right angles. A fine compliment to my seductive skills I must say!'

'I'm so sorry.' Thea reached out a hand to take his. 'I really did want to.'

'I know. I did too, but there will be other times. Lots of them.'

'Why didn't you nudge me over and get in too?'

Shaun shook his head. 'I suspect you haven't slept well since John's arrival. I didn't want to risk waking you, so I tucked the linen around you and had a go at sleeping in your attic bed.'

'How the hell did you fit in that?'

'It was both an adventure and a challenge.'

Suddenly conscious of her rumpled clothing, Thea pulled the bed linen up even further to cover all of her bra. 'It's been a very long time since I slept semi-dressed.'

'Since you were on excavation?'

'I was on Lindisfarne, helping uncover a Saxon farmstead. The air off the North Sea was cripplingly cold, especially at night.'

'You want to go back to that life?'

Thea wasn't sure if Shaun was looking wistful or concerned she was about to flee for the thrill of discovery in pastures new. 'I'd do a new excavation like a shot, but I'm not sure I could face the rough sleeping conditions at my age.'

'Even if you had someone to keep you warm at night?'

'Perhaps.' Thea smiled. 'If the Trust sells I might try to get back on the circuit. It would give me time to think out my options while hunting for something else. You however, are a hot shot TV star. Hardly someone who needs to sleep in a tent.'

'True.' Shaun grinned. 'But *Landscape Treasures* has an archaeology team, and as it happens, I'm well in with the person who selects the diggers.'

A flicker of hope stirred in Thea's chest, but reality quickly squashed it. 'And be known as the one who got the job because she's sleeping with the boss? I couldn't. I'd love the job, but I couldn't.'

'The excavation job or the sleeping with the boss job?'

'Both?'

Swinging his long legs up onto the bed, so they were sat side by side, Shaun took hold of Thea's covers, his voice husky. 'That looks a comfortable blanket.'

'It is.' Thea licked her lips. 'But right now, it desperately needs to come off.'

Tina threw her arms around Thea as she walked into the scullery. 'Are you okay? Is Shaun staying? What's happening?'

Having explained about the fake phone number, the broken engagement, and that Shaun was back until Open Day Thea added, 'Sam's been wonderful. If he hadn't phoned Shaun, I dread to think what would have happened. How is he today?'

'I haven't seen him this morning. Why?'

'Oh, you know. You two were having a nice cosy evening and then John ruined everything.'

'Thea, honestly! I've told you he isn't—'

'Your type. So you keep saying. But the thing is, he is. So there.'

Tina's eyes narrowed suspiciously. 'What's with you? I expected to find you worried sick about John turning up here this morning, but you're positively aglow.' Before she'd even finished the sentence, a knowing look spread across Tina's face and she all but punched the air. 'At last!'

'What do you mean, at last?'

'You and Shaun. I'm so pleased.'

Thea couldn't stop her own smile widening. 'Is it that obvious?'

'Afraid so.'

'Oh hell, we didn't want anyone to know. It won't exactly help the situation with John, will it?'

'My lips are sealed.' Tina pulled a face. 'Talking of John, what are we going to do about him?'

'We've decided to act like nothing has happened. I know that sounds like we're burying our heads in the sand, but I can't think of another way to stop him. He's a bully who's not worth wasting energy on. If you react to bullies they keep going, if you ignore them, they get bored. Eventually.'

'I bet you rehearsed that speech in the shower.' Tina wasn't convinced. 'And now Shaun is here you feel more able to cope with John's presence.'

'There is that, yes.' Thea's eyes fell on the pile of paperwork that appeared to have doubled in size over the last twenty-four hours. 'How about we try pretending he doesn't exist for a while. Any news on the home front?'

'Not much beyond what we already know needs doing.

Oh, Sam was saying something about the manor maybe getting beehives.'

'Great idea.' Thea made a note on her ever present pad. 'I'll put that on the forward going list. Things to suggest as future money-making enterprises.'

'Do you think it would be worth asking Malcolm what the current status is? I'm almost scared to ask in case asking makes it more likely to happen.'

'I know what you mean. Don't poke the bear seems a good policy to me.'

'Well, whatever happens, the chickens need feeding. I'll go and see if Sam has done them, if not I'll see to them while you get on with that lot.' Tina pointed to the offending paperwork. 'Where's Shaun anyway?'

'He's gone up to the mill to see how we've managed without him. I thought I'd head to Sybil's later to see if she's had any interest in our advert to be one of the three Open Day creatives.'

The sound of approaching footsteps caused the girls to pale, as they simultaneously wondered if the feet belonged to John. Two seconds later, they exhaled in relief as Mabel arrived with a flourish of her clipboard.

'Thea, you're back.' She almost managed to sound pleased. 'Are you feeling better?'

'Thank you, yes. Just a twenty-four-hour bug.' Thea saw Tina nodding in approval of the lie, before she disappeared in the direction of the hen house.

'Many thanks for holding the fort, Mabel.' Thea slipped onto her desk seat. 'I have good news for you. Shaun is back. He's looking around the mill.'

'Oh, that is fabulous news.' The old lady beamed. 'I'd heard rumours that he wasn't going to return, I'm so glad it wasn't true.'

A cloud passed over Thea's face. 'Where did you hear that?'

'When I was having dinner with Bert in the Stag. John was there. He said he'd heard a whisper that Shaun had decided not to bother with us now the manor was likely to be sold.'

Thea bristled with indignation. 'I promise you, that was never the case. I would be very careful of believing anything John says.'

'But he's such a personable young man. No, he must have heard it from somewhere. The gutter press probably.'

Not wanting to pursue the point, Thea asked, 'Anything to report from yesterday?'

'Well yes. I've got some news which I've taken to be a very good sign.'

'Really?' Thea gestured to Tina's empty chair, inviting Mabel to sit down.

'The trustees have asked if we will prepare the attics to open to the public as well. People are always fascinated with servants' living quarters aren't they.'

Fixing a grin onto her face, hoping her sudden panic about where she might live didn't show, Thea confirmed, 'They want us to restore another four rooms on top of everything else with no more budget or time?'

Mabel waved the issue away. 'You're missing the point. If they want the rooms opened, surely it means they are less likely to sell?'

'Or they want us to do them up so they can get a better price for the house on the market.'

'That's a very cynical attitude.'

'Sorry, Mabel.' Thea sat up straighter. 'I think we'll leave the attics for now. They are in a fairly good state. They all have the original little beds and some furniture in them. It'll be a case of sugar soaping the walls, not repainting. I think we can afford to leave them for another fortnight and concentrate on the tasks we have in hand.'

In an attempt to divert Mabel's attention from the attics, Thea added, 'I'm going to walk up to see Sybil this morning to see if she has had any interest in our advert for weavers and so on. Would you like to come with me? We could call in on Shaun at the mill on the way?'

'Good idea, we can talk about the attics on the way.'

As Thea watched Shaun and Mabel chatting as if they had been friends all their lives, one thought dominated her head. She was going to have to move out of Mill Grange. And soon. If Mabel realised she was living in at the same time as Shaun, she'd jump to conclusions. It didn't help that those conclusions were accurate.

She phased back into conversation as Sybil arrived with a mound of piping hot cheesy scones, catching the end of Mabel's report to Shaun. 'The volunteers are all getting on really well. The students have been a blessing, although I'll be honest, I thought they might be a bit of a waste of space. They seem to have got the restoration bug and love working with Derek and Sam.'

Pulling an extra chair up to the table, Sybil joined them. 'I've noticed an uptake in younger customers chatting about their daily attacks on giant spider webs. You wouldn't believe the quantities of coffee and hot chocolate they consume! I'm grateful to you all.'

Thea smiled. 'Not as grateful as we are for your amazing cakes. Your sugar injections are keeping us going. Have we had any interest in the Open Day craft spots?'

Fishing a hand into her apron pocket, Sybil pulled out two cards. 'There's a potter who is interested in a long term let, but not the Open Day, and a hand knitter and spinner who'd like to chat to you about Open Day.' She tapped the card in question against the table. 'She uses wool taken off the moor after the sheep have scratched it onto gorse bushes and such like.'

'Really? Well, okay, why not? Local would be good after all.'

Mabel didn't look convinced as she asked, 'You don't fancy a place yourself then Sybil?'

'Oh, I don't think so. It's been way too long since I played that game.'

Thea and Shaun swapped glances, before Thea asked, 'What game?'

'Sybil here is a fabulous felter. Used to do craft fairs and everything.' Mabel gestured to the felt work pictures on the walls of the café. 'You did those, didn't you, Sybil?'

'Ages ago.'

Shaun stood up to examine the work. 'You're clearly very good at it. I'm sure you'd have fun on the Open Day, but only if you wanted to do it.'

Sybil bit her bottom lip, clearly torn between what she

felt she ought to do and what she wanted to do. 'Can I think about it?'

'Of course.' Thea let Sybil escape to the safety of her kitchen as Mabel started to share the 'good' news about the attics with Shaun. Staring at her scone as Mabel talked, Thea considered the wisdom of moving into a bedroom at the pub. But she wouldn't be able to afford that for long; nor did she want to as John clearly used the Stag and Hound.

She could come clean and say she was living at the manor, but with Shaun being there too… No, she didn't want the rumours to fly. Although, did it matter now she and Shaun had been seen together at the pub in Taunton?

There'd been no sign of John so far that day, but it was still early. Thea knew he didn't get up before ten o'clock if he could help it. She gulped back a groan as her thoughts continued to tumble.

There was only one thing Thea was sure of. John hadn't given up yet.

Thirty-Two

June 1st

While Thea had mentally prepared herself for John's anger or righteous indignation, what she hadn't been prepared for was nothing.

It had been almost two weeks, and there had been no sign of John. At least, *she* hadn't seen him. Some of the others had.

This lurking inaction, this tactic of making sure Thea knew he was around, but not when or if he was going to reappear at the manor, felt worse than when John was pestering her in person.

Derek and Bert had reported seeing him in Upwich, and Tina had seen John on a bench opposite Sybil's Tea Room on a number of occasions glued to his mobile phone, but when, two days ago, she'd got up the courage to ask him what he was playing at, John had replied with a curt, 'It's none of your business.'

Despite Shaun's comforting presence, she couldn't relax. Thea felt trapped in a perpetual state of waiting.

She was waiting for answers from the Trust. She was waiting for something she could afford to rent to come on the market, while running out of excuses to delay the renovation of the attics. And, worst of all, she was waiting for John to pop up behind every hedge or from around every corner and declare his undying love. It was exhausting. But not as exhausting as pretending she was alright to everyone other than Tina, Shaun and Sam.

That morning, having come downstairs via the opposite staircase to Shaun, to make it look as if she was simply in early, and had arrived as he'd got up, Thea met Mabel on the porch. With far more pomp and ceremony than Thea thought the event warranted, Mabel turned the calendar over to July, circling the fifteenth day of the month with three strokes of her red marker pen.

Despite it being only eight-thirty in the morning, the older woman had been in high spirits. 'That's our aim then, Thea. 15th July. That's one week from Open Day. We'll have seven days to do the last-minute things.'

'If we even *have* an Open Day, Mabel.' Thea had grown tired of this discussion. She'd tried hard to stay optimistic about the future of the manor, but with each passing day with no word from Malcolm, she felt increasingly like she was decorating a house just so she could move out of it.

Conversely, over the last week, with no evident logic employed beyond wishful thinking, Mabel had decided that as the Trust hadn't announced the sale, then it wasn't going to happen. She'd wasted no time in spreading this idea around the volunteers, who'd lapped the news up, despite Thea's repeated warnings that there was nothing to suggest Mabel was right.

But, as far as the volunteers and most of the village were concerned, Mabel was always right. What she wanted, she got. So, if Mrs Mabel Hastings said Mill Grange would be alright, then it would be.

With an enthusiastic energy Thea could only envy, the old lady tapped the calendar, saying 'Seven weeks to go, then,' before dashing off to the laundry to check Diane was doing what she'd told her to.

The days were passing so quickly. As Thea walked towards the walled garden she thought of all the hours she'd wasted worrying about what John's next move was going to be.

'Do you think he's going to come back to Mill Grange?' She threw a handful of seed to the chickens as she sought Gertrude's wisdom.

The hen cocked her head in Thea's direction as if giving the matter serious consideration, before shaking her bony shoulders and settling down to peck her grain at drill-like speed.

'Well, you're a big help I must say.'

'She's not big on communication that one.' Sam crossed to the coop as he entered the garden, smiling at the brood affectionately. 'Intelligent woman, our Gertrude. When there's nothing good to say, she says nothing.'

'Unlike Mabel, who seems to be concocting fiction out of thin air. Tina phoned the Trust yesterday to get an update, and the situation remains the same. No decision about the ongoing position at Mill Grange had been made.'

'I assume you reported this to Mabel.'

'Twice. I even got Shaun to tell her. She tends to listen to him more than me.'

'He's a bloke.' Sam shrugged. 'It's a generation thing. She can't help it.'

'I know. Doesn't stop it being damn annoying though.'

'True.' Sam pointed to the cockerel as he paraded across the coop as if he not only owned the place, but that he occupied the penthouse. 'Tony is on fine strutting form this morning.'

'I bet Mabel would believe him if he could talk.'

'I wouldn't be at all surprised.' Sam turned from the chickens and pointed towards the greenhouse. 'Tina tells me the men are coming to pull that down tomorrow.'

'Yes.'

'You don't want them to, do you?'

Thea pushed her jumper sleeves up past the elbow in the morning sunshine. 'I can't help but imagine how it used to be. Oranges growing in large terracotta pots. Grape vines lining the wall of the garden, nurtured by the sun and protected from the winds and frost. Exotic flowers brought back from the Victorian residents' Grand Tour expeditions.'

'Shaun didn't mention you were a romantic.'

'I'm not. I just wish I could save the greenhouse.'

Sam gestured to the empty wheelbarrow parked by the space where the main entrance to the greenhouse had once been. 'We finished clearing the broken glass yesterday. Another couple of hours and it should be clear of rubble and rubbish.'

'Just in time for the men to make even more mess tomorrow.' Thea stretched her arms out in front of her, flexing them towards the sunshine. 'I sound defeatist, don't I?'

'A bit, but it's hardly surprising.' Sam was quiet for a moment before asking, 'Where's Shaun this morning?'

'On his way to Taunton.'

'He's going to tackle the trustees about the sale?' Sam's eyebrows shot up. 'Do you think he can persuade them to stop them going ahead?'

'No. We talked it over last night.' Thea sighed. 'In fact, we've talked about little else for the past few weeks. If it isn't, "when will John turn up", it's "can the Trust be persuaded to find funds from elsewhere to save this place?"'

'But you've decided that he shouldn't bring the subject of the sale up while he's there?'

'Shaun's mate, Richard – the guy that saved the table – wants to film some of the furniture for a side feature of an episode of *Landscape Treasures*. The filming fee would help us big time. I'm not sure it will be enough to prevent the sale, but it would help.'

'And being able to say "as featured on *Landscape Treasures*" in future marketing and souvenir guides won't hurt either.'

'Fingers crossed they see it like that.'

'I can't imagine they won't. This is the sort of publicity most stately homes can only dream of.'

'That's what we're banking on.'

'Yet you don't sound convinced.' Sam kept his eyes on the dilapidated greenhouse.

'I'm not hopeful. This house could make money, it could bring in a reasonable monthly rent from three independent sources at the mill, and there's no reason why the gardens can't go some way to pay for their own upkeep. We have school trips, WI and U3A visits tentatively booked in for the whole of next spring and summer, not to mention that the village fete committee is keen to start up where it left off before the house went to the Trust, but they're still considering selling it. Tina's convinced there's some underlying reason for the proposed sale that we don't know about. If there is, then it might take more than a TV appearance to save us.'

'I take it you haven't spoken to Mabel about any of this, or Tina's suspicions?'

'I tried, but she told me I was being negative.' Thea looked up into the clear blue sky. 'I rather hope she's right.'

Mabel pursed her lips and crossed her arms as she stood in the doorway to the final bedroom on the attic corridor.

The bed was unkempt with only a token gesture made towards the covers being folded back to air the crumpled sheets below.

A heap of clothes overflowed from a large carrier bag in the far corner of the room, and an open rucksack revealed a mess of jumpers – jumpers she recognised as belonging to Thea Thomas.

Having decided that Thea was wrong about leaving the attics for so long, especially as the Trust had specially requested that they be included in the restoration, Mabel had taken matters into her own hands. Armed with her clipboard, pen and a large feather duster to bat away any lurking spiders, she'd moved from room to room making notes on the extent of mould, dust and damage to window sills, with a mind to assessing the size of the job in hand.

'So, young lady, this is why you didn't want to tackle the attics.' Not wishing to view Thea's pile of laundry any longer, Mabel closed the bedroom door with a crisp click and an accompanying tut.

Her hand was still on the door when her mind switched from wondering how long Thea had been living at the manor in secret, to whether Shaun knew she was there. Or, worse, had she arrived *because* Shaun was there. Maybe Thea wasn't sleeping in this room, but merely storing her things there.

Appalled at the idea that the man she admired so much would be living in sin with Thea, Mabel considered going down to the room Shaun was renting to see if there were signs of Thea there too, but she decided against it. She didn't want to see. Instead, she decided to talk to them both together. This might be modern times, but this was not a modern house, nor was it their house. They had no right whatsoever to use it like some rent-by-the-hour hotel!

Disappointed in Shaun and feeling the sense of respect she'd had for Thea slipping away, Mabel marched towards the scullery to make her views on the subject plain. As she reached the bottom of the stairs, she saw Tina pass the hall window, and Mabel rushed outside.

'Did you know? Did you?'

Taking a step back in alarm at Mabel's raised voice, Tina asked, 'Did I know what?'

Mabel looked around her, suddenly aware she was close to shouting, and perhaps didn't want everyone to know what she'd discovered. 'Don't play innocent with me.' Her words hissed through her teeth. 'She's your best friend, of course you knew.'

Guessing that Mabel had discovered Thea's living quarters,

Tina mentally crossed her fingers it was the room in the attic she'd been nosing around in, rather than Shaun's bedroom. Grating the mud off her boots on the scraper by the front door, Tina felt cross and defensive on her friend's behalf.

'If you are referring to the fact Thea has been staying in the attic for a while, then yes, I did know.'

Mabel opened her mouth to protest further, but Tina hadn't finished.

'Thea wants this place to work, Mabel. How else would she be here so early and work so late? And where is there for her to live locally anyway? The rental prices in Upwich are extortionate and there aren't many of them. Isn't it better that she pays the Trust a rent she can afford? Every extra hour she's here improves the chances of this place not being sold. Since Thea learnt the attics were going to be converted she'd been trying to find somewhere to live. But what with the Trust still being vague on the sale of the house, not to mention John…'

The minute she'd mentioned the name John, Tina could have bitten her tongue off.

Mabel didn't hesitate, and pounced on the chance to find out more about Thea's relationship with John. 'What about John?'

'It doesn't matter.' Tina tried to change the subject. 'The point is, if the manor does get sold, Thea doesn't want the Trust or anyone locally for that matter, to think it was because of any shortcomings on her front. She is lodging here so that not a single hour of the working day is wasted!'

★

'Yes, sir, I'm sure she would.' John wiped a few dots of perspiration from his brow as he took the call from the managing director of Sure Digital. 'But as I've explained, she travels a lot, so my wife may not be able... Yes sir, of course I understand. Yes, yes... of course. The figures have been done. They will be in your inbox by tomorrow morning. Absolutely, I'm looking forward to it too. Goodbye, sir.'

John pushed his back tighter against the opposite side of the porch as he listened. He thought he'd heard someone walking towards him, but now there was nothing. He must have imagined it.

He licked his lips as he stared up at the stag's head above the door. Its hollow eyes seemed to look right into his soul.

Today had been the day he was going to sort things out with Thea. He'd already been there for hours, watching and waiting for Sam to get up from his pathetic little tent and go into the woods for his morning walk. He'd waited for Shaun to leave the premises and for Thea to arrive.

He thought somehow he'd missed her arrival. But he hadn't. She'd never been going to arrive, because she hadn't been anywhere but here.

Thea had been sleeping in the attics.

A sense of relief filled John. She wasn't sleeping with the archaeologist. Thea had a room in the attic.

Sliding back into the shadow of the porch, John barely dared breathe. He felt as if he was outside of himself watching a stranger, who looked just like him, acting in a way he never would.

He, John Davies-Sommers, didn't do things like this. He

didn't send fake texts or spy on women. That's what failures did, and he wasn't a failure.

If she'd just let me explain, I could have gone home by now!

John glanced back up at the stag. 'You failed, but I'm not going to.'

Thirty-Three

Thea took a step back to examine the door that had once formed Mill Grange's servants' link from the kitchen corridor to the outside world, and admired her handiwork.

Working the runny preserving oil into the grain of the wood had been satisfying and therapeutic, as well as essential. The liquid had absorbed into the surface so fast Thea could have sworn she'd heard the wood sighing with relief after years of dehydration. It had been good to do something that required no thought beyond the rhythmical circling of a cloth.

She'd just laid down the tin of oil and was scrubbing pointlessly at the pattern of dotted brown splodges that now adorned her jumper, when Shaun's car turned into the drive behind her. Noting the grim set to his face, Thea brushed her dirty hands down her thighs and went to greet him. 'They said no to the television appearance, didn't they?'

'Yes and no. It is dependent on the decision to sell.' Paying no attention to Thea's grubby state, Shaun wrapped her in his arms as he explained how he'd underlined how much the Trust would get paid, how good the publicity would be and how, as they already had a trained historian on site, they wouldn't have to employ someone to oversee the filming on their behalf. But they hadn't budged. No decisions were being made about the future of the manor until they've had a meeting about selling, or not.

From the cocoon of Shaun's side, Thea asked, 'And did they tell you when the meeting is going to be?'

'Today.' Shaun looked at his watch. 'Now.'

'Oh my God!' Thea's breath hitched in her throat as she broke free from his arms. 'Today?'

'You might want to stay in the office so that when the verdict comes you're in the right part of the manor to receive the call.'

Thea nodded. 'Tina thinks the Trust's up to something. This behaviour is so out of character; Malcolm isn't usually anything but crystal-clear in his instructions apparently.'

'She may be right.'

Returning her attention to Shaun, Thea took his hand. 'Did Malcolm say something then?'

'Not as such. I don't know Malcolm, but I could tell he wasn't comfortable with the non-answers he was giving me.' Shaun registered his girlfriend's sticky jumper and hands as he accidentally brushed against a blob of sealant on her sleeve. 'You've been keeping busy then.'

She gestured half-heartedly to the pristine servants' door. 'For what it's worth.'

'Don't give up, love.'

'Come on Shaun, I'm not stupid. They're going to sell. I just wish I knew why.'

Wishing he could argue, but suspecting Thea was right, Shaun stroked a hand through her hair. 'Well, we can't do anything until we know the outcome of the meeting. The income from the filming might be the ammunition we needed to tip the balance in Mill Grange's favour.'

'Let's hope so.' Thea kissed his cheek. 'Thanks for trying. I think I'll go and change. If I'm going to face the firing squad, I think I'd like to do it without looking like a sticky scarecrow.'

'And the verdict?' Sam paused in the process of tightening the hinges of the gate that divided the walled garden from its main counterpart.

'The Trust is in discussion about the sale now.'

Giving the gate an experimental swing, to make sure it was hanging level after years of being cockeyed in its settings, Sam said, 'Let me guess. They withheld a discussion about the filming pending a decision.'

'You are quoting them almost word for word.' Shaun glanced up at the attic window where Thea would be changing. 'I think I'd like to be with Thea when the call comes through.'

'Quite right.' Sam pocketed his screwdriver. 'But before you go, could I show you something?'

'Thea's changing her clothes, so I've only got five minutes. That girl doesn't hang about on the clothes front.'

'It'll only take two.' Sam gestured towards the rough slope of land between the back of the garden and the woods.

*

With every step towards the little attic room she'd called home for the past three months, Thea felt increasingly incensed at the Trust's behaviour towards her, and more importantly, towards her volunteers.

The creak of each stair seemed to echo her thoughts and imprint images of the work her team had done at the manor. She could see Derek and Sam battling against the broken window pulley. Diane, doing her best to clear out the stables, despite her hatred of spiders. Bill and Derek, laughing with the students from Exeter University, as they piled branches and brambles onto the latest bonfire. Tina handing out slices of lemon cake during her early attempts to gain the volunteers' support. And Mabel… Mabel, both the bane of Thea's life and Mill Grange's saviour. Thea knew the manor and mill house would never be as advanced in its restoration without Mabel's unstoppable gusto. At least nothing stank of vinegar anymore.

Reaching her room, Thea sat on the bed and rested her head in her hands. Mabel was going to take this news harder than anyone.

It might not be sold.

The voice of hope that Thea had been so determined to keep hold of since Tina accidentally discovered the possibility of the manor being put on the market, was becoming fainter by the minute. Peeling off her jumper, she threw it into the corner to join the others. She had hardly anything left to wear that wasn't coated in some sort of paint or grime. Cross with herself for living in such a mess, Thea muttered, 'I might as well be back on excavation after all.'

Picturing Malcolm and their fellow trustees sitting around

a table playing God with the manor's fate, Thea moved to the window. She could see Shaun and Sam walking up from the woods, deep in conversation.

Relieved that Shaun was softening the blow for Sam, who despite having never progressed further into the manor than the bathroom nearest the back door, held an obvious affection for the place, Thea closed her eyes.

'There must be something I can do. Something I haven't contemplated yet, that can stop the Trust selling. There must be…'

'Maybe there is.'

Thea swung around, her heart thumping in her chest. Her mouth went dry, while her brain screamed accusations at her for not paying attention to who might be lurking in the other rooms as she'd come up the stairs. 'John.'

'You were expecting someone taller? Someone who must have enough money to buy this place for you?'

Thea turned back to the window. There was no one in sight; not even a rogue student with an armful of brambles for burning. 'What do you want John?'

'I want to talk to you, just like I wanted to talk to you when I booked the meal at the pub.' John crossed his arms over his chest, a determined smile set on his chiselled features.

'Go away, John.'

'Not until you've heard me out.'

Thea's mind raced as she stared at John. It hadn't crossed her mind that Shaun could buy the house. Surely television presenters weren't paid that well. And even if they were, she'd never ask him to buy the manor in a million years. They'd only been together for two minutes. If they'd been married fifty years, she'd still never have asked. 'Have you any idea how pathetic you look standing there like a Bond villain? Surely you see that you're being here is pointless.'

'I wouldn't be so sure about that.'

Thea was amazed at how steady she was managing to keep her voice. 'If you're about to threaten me with outing the fact that Shaun is staying here, then you're too late. People already know. And if you're going to start yelling the news that I'm lodging here too, then I hope you have fun doing so. In fact, it would save me a job, as I intended to tell everyone at tomorrow's staff meeting.'

John's eyes narrowed. 'If there really was a staff meeting tomorrow, I would have been invited to it.'

'No you wouldn't. You haven't done any work here for weeks. Your safety check has expired.' Thea kept talking, hoping he'd believe her lie. 'Hanging around the village and generally making people wonder what you're up to is not helping your cause. All you've done is create suspicion. Even Mabel is beginning to wonder what you're up to.'

John didn't even blink. 'There isn't a meeting tomorrow, is there?'

'There is.' Thea grabbed the nearest semi-clean jumper from the chair and tugged it over her head. 'Why are you still here? Do I really need to tell you again what a fool you're making of yourself?'

'A fool?' John raked his hands through his blond hair. 'Yes, that just about sums it up.' He sighed heavily, looking rather defeated. 'My plan today was so straightforward. I'd come up here, ask you a favour, which you'd agree to, and then I'd leave. I never meant to be away from Bath for so long, nor for things to get so out of hand.'

'Out of hand? That's an understatement.'

'I want to explain why I'm still here. But as I walked up the stairs just now the answer came to me – it's so obvious!'

'Hold on, did you say you were going to leave as soon as you've spoken to me?'

'Yes! I'd have gone back to work ages ago if you'd listen to me. I only wanted to ask a favour.'

'A favour?' Thea sank onto the edge of her bed, 'John, you asked me out five times in the first twenty-four hours of your stay here.'

'That was before I realised how much your taste in men has deteriorated.' John waved a hand, as if his previous badgering was ancient history. 'Anyway, like I said, I just thought of the answer – a way to get you out of the mess you find yourself in. A way to convince the locals that you aren't the total failure they're bound to take you for once word of the sale gets out.'

'Total failure?' The words left Thea's lips at barely a whisper.

'You came here to save their manor and open it to the public, but you can't do that. Despite how badly you've treated me, I don't want them to consider you a disappointment.'

Blind to Thea's shocked expression, John ploughed on. 'I will buy the manor from the Trust. I have plenty of savings and had a decent inheritance from my grandparents.'

Speechless, Thea watched John as he spoke. He didn't appear to be talking to her. It was as if he was reciting something: an act in a play, with him as the hero.

Thea cleared her throat. 'You can't buy me, John.'

'Not you, the manor. *For you.* To say thank you for the

favour I need you to do. Then you could let that blonde bimbo you hang around with run it for you, and return to Bath and civilization generally. You never know, we could go back to having the occasional dinner together, like when we first met.'

An image of her best friend flashed through her head as John kept talking. 'This way, the village gets its precious manor restored for free, I can make a steady income from the events and opening it to the public, and you can be the heroine you want to be in the eyes of these village idiots. On top of that I... Well, let's just say everyone is happy.'

'Happy?' With the words 'bimbo' and 'idiots' ringing in her ears, Thea pointed to her desk chair. Something inside her snapped as she shouted, 'Sit down, John!'

Thea could feel a nervous shake in her shoulders, but ignored it as she gave her temper free reign. 'I've had enough! Tell me, what favour is *so* important that you're willing to blow your life savings on a house you don't want? And, I warn you, if you say it's to make me fall in love with you, I swear I'll lock you in here until you come to your senses.'

As John sat down, Thea added, 'And no more lies! I want the *real* reason you've been pursuing me to such a ridiculous degree. I feel like I'm stuck in a Shakespearian farce!'

'Farce?' John blustered, rising back up from the chair as he did so.

'John, all you've ever cared about is your career. You've just got a promotion, so why aren't you in Bath doing it?'

'I told you, I took some holiday so I could come here and...'

Thea was already shaking her head. 'I know for a fact you never take more than two weeks off at a time, because you're paranoid someone might steal your position in your absence. So, please John, tell me the truth.'

'And me.' Mabel appeared on the threshold of her room, a stack of papers in her hand and a very peculiar expression on her face. 'And while you're at it, you can tell us who this wife of yours is.'

'Wife?' Thea had never been so pleased to see Mabel in her life. 'John's married?'

'He is. Or at least, he told someone, his boss I assume, as he kept calling them sir, that he was.'

John looked furious, 'You've been listening to my calls, you nosy old—'

'Shut up Mr Sommers.' Mabel closed the bedroom door behind her and leant against it. Crossing her arms firmly over her apron, she took in Thea's stunned face, 'This young man is going to tell us precisely what he's up to. That's if he thinks a village idiot like me can understand his sophisticated reasoning.'

John's face flushed pink as he reached his hands beseechingly towards Thea, 'I'm not married, I promise, I'd never cheat on you.'

Mabel's hawk stare switched from John to Thea. 'Cheat on you?'

'I'll explain later.'

'I really don't think…' John made to get up, but Thea pre-empted him.

'Well, I do.' Positioning herself next to Mabel, copying her determined crossed armed stance, Thea said, 'You were about to tell me what you wanted to say at my "surprise" meal. Something about a favour?'

'Meal?' Mabel's wrinkled face creased further as she regarded John with increasing distaste.

'I'll tell you that later too.' Thea patted her friend's shoulder. 'After we've discovered when John found time to squeeze a fake marriage into his busy schedule.'

'It was a misunderstanding.' Glancing at the door, John accepted he was trapped with a groan. 'There seemed no harm in it at first. But, suddenly, the companies were merging and I was sent back to Bath and …'

'Hold on.' Thea interrupted, 'You told me you got your new job through an old school friend.'

'I sort of did.'

'Sort of?'

'My best mate from school has worked for Safe Hands Digital in Newcastle for years. He recommended me as the one to liaise between the two company's COs as I'd worked for them both. And as the new HQ was to be in Bath…'

'And this misunderstanding?' Mabel demanded.

Licking his lips, John mumbled, 'My boss in Newcastle thought I was married – an assumption I never got round to correcting. But he told the managing director in Bath that I'd got married, and as he's keen on promoting Sure Digital as a family-centred company…' He swallowed. 'I needed a wife and…'

'Hang on.' Thea raised her hand. 'Are you telling us you played along, inventing yourself a wife, to impress the management?'

'It's worse than that.' Mabel's eyes narrowed as she focused on John, 'He's told them that wife is you, Thea. Haven't you John?'

'You've done what?' Thea went white as she stared at her former boyfriend. 'That was the favour? To pretend to be your wife every now and then?'

'Just once! Just at the merger celebration party.' John gestured his arms wildly around the room. 'And in return, I'd buy you all this!'

Brandishing her papers as if they were a weapon, Mabel kept her eyes fixed on John as she addressed Thea. 'Why don't you sit down, my dear? Have a look at these while I escort Mr Sommers from the house?'

Dropping the pile of local house rental details she'd been clutching into a shaking Thea's lap, Mabel placed a strong bony hand on John's shoulder. 'You're coming with me.'

Thirty-Four

June 1st

'What the hell is going on?' Tina held her pigtails as she sped into Thea's room. 'Mabel told me you needed me.'

Leaning against the little desk by the window, Thea stared out across the Exmoor countryside. 'How did Mabel know I was living here?'

'She decided you'd left the restoration of the attics too much to the last minute, and went poking round. Never mind that now. I've just seen her frogmarching John out of the door. What's happening?'

Thea turned to face her friend. 'Well, for a start I shall be buying Mabel a huge bunch of flowers.'

Tina sat on the edge of the half-made bed and patted the space next to her. 'I think you should sit down, you're shaking.'

'I am. But not with nerves or fear or any of my other hang-ups. This is fury.'

'What did he do?'

'John offered to buy the manor so that Upwich could still have its heritage site once it was out of the Trust's hands.'

'Blimey.'

'On condition that I occasionally accompany him to corporate functions.'

'Mabel interrupted him trying to buy you off?'

'Oh, it's far more interesting than that.' An unexpected smile prickled at the corner of Thea's lips. 'Actually, Mabel came to tell me John was married – as well as to give me some house details.'

Tina's eyebrows shot upwards so fast, she looked like a cartoon character. 'Married!'

'Except he isn't.'

'You've lost me.'

Tapping the bed next to her so Tina would sit down, Thea explained how John's new and old companies were merging, and how he'd backed himself into a corner by claiming to have a wife he'd never had, to secure his new position within the enlarged Sure Digital empire; and how he'd chosen Thea to be that wife.

'I suppose I was an obvious choice. As an archaeologist, my long absences due to travel, and regular inability to attend any "bring the wife" events, were believable.' Thea gave a huge yawn. 'I think I need a cup of coffee.'

'I'm surprised you don't need something stronger!' Tina led the way along the attic corridor and towards the back stairs. 'Why would John's career depend on him having a wife in this day and age?'

'I doubt it would. I think he was afraid of being caught out in a lie.'

'He could have said you'd split up.'

'John rarely stops to consider the obvious when he's desperate not to lose face.'

Following Thea into the kitchen, Tina asked, 'So, when he first arrived at Mill Grange, did he want this favour granting, or did he think he could actually get you back and marry you fast?'

'Initially, he may have thought that we could have some sort of whirlwind marriage. It explains why he was so persistent after he'd found me in Bath.'

'But it doesn't excuse the Facebook stalking or the hassle he caused.'

'True.' Stirring coffee granules into two mugs, Thea inhaled the aroma, its familiarity a comfort.

'It's weird then, as soon as Shaun went to Cornwall, John more or less disappeared.'

'I suspect that he'd given up on me as a partner by then. He'd seen Shaun and me together. Hence the meal. That's when he wanted to ask his favour – although he hadn't come up with the idea to buy the manor at that point, so who knows what I'd have been offered in return!'

Tina poured milk into her coffee and blew across the surface. 'So he's been hanging around just so he could talk to you?'

'He's probably been working while he wasn't on site. His job is new after all, and he can do it remotely.' Thea shrugged, 'I'm only guessing, but that might be why you saw him sat around the village in places that have mobile connection.'

'Makes as much sense as anything else John has done, I suppose.' Tina opened the biscuit tin and pushed it towards Thea.

'Just as Mabel took hold of his arm ready to march him off the premises, John blurted something out about a merger party in two weeks' time. I suspect he's meant to be there with a wife on his arm.'

'Hence his desperation lately? The pub meal, the stalking air he was giving off, and all that?'

'Precisely.' Thea pulled a cookie from the tin. 'It's so pathetic. I feel a bit sorry for him.'

She sighed as she crunched into her biscuit. 'But what if me being with John was the only way the villagers could have their manor restored and kept for the public? If the Trust does sell it as a private house, I'll always know that if I'd accepted John's offer, Upwich could have kept its manor in the public domain and…'

'No.'

The force of Tina's response took Thea by surprise. 'No?'

'Do you honestly think that the people of Upwich, especially the volunteers here, would want the manor knowing that was the price? That you'd sacrificed yourself for them? Now that *is* pathetic. This isn't a bloody Roman tragedy, Thea. This is your life. Can you imagine how miserable you'd feel to have to trot off to play John's wife whenever he snapped his fingers when you are in love with Shaun?'

Thea opened her mouth to speak, but Tina was in full flow.

'How could you even think of agreeing to John's weird gesture when Shaun is so potty about you? Have you any idea how lucky you are to have someone so on your wavelength and…'

As the penny dropped, Thea put her hand out to her friend. 'You've fallen for Sam, haven't you?'

'I can't have. He isn't part of the plan. He doesn't even come close to fitting my plan.'

'Then you need a new plan. You deserve more than a man who would have treated you like a trophy – the equivalent of the latest Jag or a new iPhone.'

'I'm sure not all wealthy and successful men are like that.'

'Probably not, but you haven't met any of them. On the other hand, you have met a scruffy gardener with claustrophobia.'

'So much for the big house and swimming pool. We'd have to live in a tent.'

'Some people don't even get a tent.'

'True.' Tina moved to the window to see if she could spot Sam. 'Do you think Mabel's thrown John off the grounds?'

'Probably with a belly full of advice he may or may not have the common sense to take.' Thea gave a half smile, which disappeared as she looked at her watch. 'The Trust's meeting about the future of the house is happening now. Did you know?'

'Shaun told me before he went to help Sam with something.' Tina looked grave. 'But I didn't know before then.'

'You ought to have been told, surely?'

'Yes. I would normally be sitting in that sort of meeting myself.' Digging her hands into her pockets, Tina glanced back outside. 'Perhaps they think I'm too close to this project to be objective.'

'I don't suppose we can argue with that.' Thea joined her

friend at the window. 'What are the boys doing? I can't see them.'

'I've no idea. Something beyond the gardens I suppose.'

Hurt that Shaun hadn't come straight back to make sure she was alright after finding out that the Trust was deciding the manor's fate, and hers, and then telling herself off because she was either a strong independent woman or she wasn't, Thea got to her feet. 'I'd better get to the office. If the Trust is meeting now, then we can expect a call soon.'

Following Thea down the corridor, Tina said, 'I can't believe they didn't tell me this was happening today. Despite their promise that my job was safe with them, I'm beginning to have my doubts about the truth of that too.'

'They wouldn't be so stupid as to get rid of you.'

'Why not? They're stupid enough to be considering getting rid of this place and you, when together you're a money-making combination.'

Thea trailed a finger over the polished oak table. 'Do you think Mabel's alright?' Suddenly Thea was alarmed. 'I should have gone with her. What if John's hurt her?' Thea leapt up. 'I'm not thinking straight.'

'If Mabel had needed your help, she'd have made it very clear.'

'True.' Thea sat straight back down again. 'She had house rental details with her. When did she find out about me staying here?'

'Today. She said she had to nip into the village after we'd spoken about it. I was quite cross with her actually. As you can imagine, her first assumption was that you were here as Shaun's bit of stuff. So I told her that the village couldn't expect miracles from you if you weren't on hand to produce them. Or something like that.'

'Thank you.' Thea hugged her friend as they reached the scullery-come-office. 'She must have gone straight to the estate agent's near Sybil's and picked up the details.'

'Mabel has a kind heart underneath all that bossiness.'

'She's so convinced the manor won't go into private hands. If they do sell, it is going to hurt her as much as us. More probably.' Thea jumped as the phone rang. 'Do you think that's them?'

They stared at the phone as if it was an unexploded bomb.

'Only one way to find out.' Tina put out her hand towards the receiver. 'Do you want me to do it?'

'No. This is my responsibility. Thank you though.' Thea reached for the phone. 'Can you spread the word that they'll be a staff meeting tomorrow morning at ten?'

The journey to Taunton seemed to take only half the time as it had on her last visit to the trustee's office.

Thea hadn't bothered to change, nor had she gone to find Shaun. She had no idea where Mabel was. Despite Tina's promise that she'd track her down and call the minute she'd made sure the old lady was okay, Thea felt guilty she hadn't gone after Mabel herself.

Malcolm had been very firm on the phone. Thea was to leave whatever she was doing and report to the Trust office within the hour. With the state of traffic in and around Taunton, and the lack of parking in the area, this was pushing it, even with the fact that she'd dived into her car before the phone's handset had had the chance to cool from the heat of her palm.

On her third circle around the nearest roads to the office, Thea started to mutter under her breath, 'Minerva, I could so do with a bit of that famous wisdom right now. And, while you're at it, a parking space wouldn't go amiss.'

Tina found Mabel in the laundry room with Diane calmly folding huge Victorian linen bed sheets.

'I've been searching everywhere for you Mabel, are you alright?'

'I am.' Mabel passed the crisply laundered sheet to Diane. 'Is Thea okay?'

'She's been summoned to Taunton. The Trust appears to have made a decision.'

Diane placed the sheet on the pile of similarly pristine linen and automatically turned to Mabel. 'You said they wouldn't sell.'

Uncertain, Mabel said, 'They aren't that foolish. This place could do so well for them. And anyway, John said...' She stopped talking and took a sharp inhalation of breath. 'He lied to me, didn't he?'

'If John was the one who made you believe that the manor would be alright, he wasn't exactly lying. He had a plan to buy it from the Trust himself.'

Mabel frowned. 'At what cost?'

'Thea was to pretend to be his wife whenever he required her to.'

'Too high. Far too high.' Mabel brushed her palms

together to remove any dust and lint from the sheets. 'I have no time for anyone who tries to impress me with money.'

Diane agreed. 'Mabel was telling me all about it. What a creep! Well, we won't be seeing that young man again.'

'How did you get rid of him?'

'I got Derek and Bill to escort him to the hotel he's been staying in. They have strict instructions to watch while he checks out and oversee the packing of his belongings into his car.'

Tina hugged the startled older woman. 'Mabel, you are marvellous.'

'He'll drive off with a flea in his ear, make no mistake about that.'

'At least that's one thing we don't have to worry about now.' Tina grimaced. 'As long as he doesn't come back.'

'His pride's been hurt. He won't come back.'

Mabel sounded so sure that Tina didn't like to argue.

Diane was looking worried as she patted the remaining pile of antique linen waiting to be pressed and folded. 'Is there any point in carrying on with this?'

Tina and Mabel exchanged a look of uncertainty, before Mabel reasserted herself. 'We keep going unless we hear otherwise.'

'Absolutely.' Tina smiled. 'I'd better go and find Shaun and Sam. Thea didn't have time to tell them she had to go to Taunton. Could you tell Bill and Derek when they get back, and let them know there will be a staff meeting tomorrow morning at ten?'

Sam found Tina before she found him.

'Do you happen to have the phone number for the greenhouse guys? I need to ask them if they'll want to take the lead. If not we could sell it for the manor.'

'What?' Tina had been so psyched up to break the news about Thea's summons to Taunton, that she felt confused.

'The greenhouse. It's being demolished tomorrow. Remember?'

'Oh yes, so it is.' Tina looked beyond Sam towards the woods. 'Have you seen Shaun?'

'He's in the woods. What's going on?'

'Thea's on her way to Taunton. In fact, she's probably almost there by now.'

'The Trust has made a decision?'

'Apparently, but they wouldn't tell her over the phone. She was ordered to be with them within an hour.'

'That doesn't sound good.' Sam tossed the trowel he was holding from one hand to the other. 'Come on, we should tell Shaun, and I really need that number.'

'Umm.'

'Tina? Are you with me?' Sam reached an arm out to her, and then hastily lowered it before he made contact. 'Do you have the number for the greenhouse people? It's important.'

'What? How is that important now?'

'Because, if we are going to lose the manor, then why should we spend the budget we have on pulling down something the new owner may want to keep?'

'But you said something about the lead.'

'That was before you told me Thea had been summoned. I think we should delay the demolition by a week. That way, we can still get it done if the Trust isn't selling, but we can save the money if it is selling. Yes?'

'Oh yes. That makes sense.' Tina dug her mobile out of her pocket and scrolled through her contacts. 'I'll call them in a minute.'

'I'll do it. You find Shaun and tell him what's been happening.'

'If you're sure. Here you go.' She passed her phone to Sam. 'There's no signal here, you'll have to go into the scullery, or walk down the drive towards the village.'

Sam turned to face the path towards Upwich. 'How was Thea when she left?'

'Not great. I wish Shaun had been there. There's more going on than the Trust making a decision. John tried it on again.'

'Shit.'

'Mabel stopped him and Bill and Derek have marched him out of town.'

'Good.' Sam nodded in satisfaction. 'You'll find Shaun where the garden turns into the woods. I'll be back as soon as I've made this call.'

Thirty-Five

The car park was almost empty. The daily rush of afternoon ramblers had yet to give way to the Tarr Steps' evening strollers and dog walkers.

As Thea made her way towards the bridge, determined to complete the short walk she'd missed out on before, she lifted her face to the sunshine. The sky was so blue. She could almost hear her Nan saying, 'More than enough to patch a pair of sailors' trousers up there, my girl.'

Taking a swig from the bottle of cold water she'd grabbed from the car park kiosk, Thea stood at the brow of the bridge and exhaled slowly. There was no sign of the devil sunbathing, despite the heat of the day. Not even a passing black cat hinted towards the legend that, until she'd met Sam, she'd never heard of.

Waiting her turn, as a family of pushchairs and assorted toddlers gingerly crossed the stones, Thea was struck once again by the bridge's sheer resilience.

Like Mill Grange. People come, people go, but the house is still there. And thanks to Mabel, Derek, Bill, Diane and their helpers, it will be standing in better condition from now on.

Taking her turn, Thea walked forward, pausing in the middle of the bridge. Watching the water flow sedately beneath her feet, she peered into the far distance. If she took her socks and shoes off, jumped into the water and walked, she'd be at Mill Grange in less than half an hour.

Mill Grange.

She'd given up a lot to help restore and run it. But would she have gone if John hadn't been back on the scene making her life difficult? Probably not. She'd have relished the challenge, but never have been brave enough to apply for the job, even if she'd known Tina would end up sharing it with her.

I'd never have met Shaun again.

As another party of walkers appeared on the opposite side of the bridge, Thea hurried on, off the ancient stones, and along the tree lined walk bordering the run of the river. She felt no guilt about being there this time. The only promise she'd made herself before coming to Upwich was that she'd take time to explore Exmoor, and she hadn't so much as glimpsed it beyond the manor lands or via the window of her car. Delaying telling everyone the outcome of the meeting wasn't going to change anything, and she needed to be alone to think.

Exchanging greetings with fellow walkers as she passed, Thea breathed in the beauty of the place.

It had been worth coming.

John may have found her, but Mabel had kicked him into touch – and she'd made new friends in an amazing place. Friends she hoped to keep.

After twenty minutes of gentle meandering, Thea saw a wooden bridge in the distance, patiently waiting to take her to the opposite side of the water for the return walk to the car park. Not quite ready to go back, she sat on the first empty bench she came to, tilted her head to the sunshine and closed her eyes.

The house had been sold.

Malcolm had been kind enough not to beat about the bush, telling her the worst as soon as her backside had hit the office chair.

On the journey to Taunton, while bracing herself for the news that Mill Grange and its lands were to go up for sale, Thea had dreamt up a final straw idea of putting together a local consortium, so the villagers could buy the manor together. The idea, although possibly unworkable, was redundant before she'd even mooted it.

Unknown to anyone beyond the trustees, the decision to sell hadn't been made that day, but several weeks ago. The meeting they'd had that day concerned the sale itself, and how to break the news to Thea and her team. The house had gone on the market at nine o'clock that morning. A private sale had been agreed, subject to surveys and contract, only three hours later.

Thea's first reaction had been to be consumed by panic. John. John had to have bought the house and grounds.

Then common sense had kicked in. No one at the house had known about the stage of the sale. John was still in

Upwich at eleven, being evicted by Mabel and her team. With mobile signals weak and Wi-Fi non-existent beyond strategically placed hubs, there was no way John could have found out about the sale. *Unless he had an insider...*

Had she really been so assertive with Malcolm? Looking back, it felt as if she'd been watching someone else responding to the news. She hadn't shouted or growled, but said with a forceful certainty that would have made Mabel proud, how disappointed she was with the underhand manner in which this situation had been handled. That the lack of information from the Trust was questionable.

Then she'd asked what she needed to know, even if she'd already rationalised it as impossible within herself.

'Has a Mr John Davies-Sommers bought Mill Grange?'

Malcolm had shaken his head. Thea felt it was the only time during the whole meeting he'd acted with honesty when he'd said, although he was not at liberty to disclose the name of the vendor, it was not anyone of that name. Nor, to the best of his knowledge, was there a Sommers connection.

Then she'd asked Malcolm what it was they weren't being told.

He'd shifted uncomfortably in his chair, just as he had on her previous visit to his office. All he'd said was that an unexpected situation, which he was not at liberty to share with her, had arisen and that he was truly sorry for the inconvenience he'd caused her. He'd gone on to waffle about giving her impeccable references, but Thea had stopped listening.

The word 'inconvenience' had been ill-advised. Thea,

who was ten times more assertive than she'd been prior to her arrival at the manor, had raised her hand slowly before stating precisely what she'd sacrificed to pursue a new career at Mill Grange. She'd politely underlined how much the long-term volunteers had given in terms of time and unpaid labour, how much work Shaun was missing, risking damaging his reputation just so he could be at the Open Day. She'd spoken about Richard doing several hundred pounds' worth of furniture repair to the table free of charge, and how Sybil had provided free tea and cakes for weeks in the expectation of an upturn to village trade once the manor opened to the public.

Malcolm's mouth had fallen open, but whether he'd been intending to speak or not, Thea didn't know. She hadn't finished. She'd gone on to inform him that she would be emailing him the list of local schools and groups who'd paid a deposit for a tour around the house once it was reopened, and that he'd have to sort out refunds and apologises. Oh, and he'd need to re-home six hens and a cockerel.

Although instinct had told Thea to run at this point, she'd ignored it and asked what the Trust expected from her from that moment on, and what their intentions for Tina were. She'd folded her arms and crossed her legs and sat there, staring at Malcolm, hoping like hell that her nerve didn't give way.

With a promise to herself that she'd come back and walk the much longer circuit of the Steps before she left, Thea pulled herself away from the bench and headed to the car. Her friends would be worried. She couldn't keep them waiting any longer.

Talking to herself, Thea strolled back to reality. 'Should I take Shaun up on his offer of working on his travelling excavation team?'

Thea addressed a low hanging branch as she walked along, rustling it through her fingers. 'People would talk, but at least we'd be together.'

A warm contentment, at odds with her anger at the loss of the manor, made Thea smile. Perhaps it would be alright? Perhaps the new owner was local and would open the house to the public as they'd hoped. She might have to hunt for a new job, but at least she could leave Upwich knowing that Mill Grange was in good hands, and the village would benefit from its renovations. Or perhaps it had been purchased by a multinational corporation, who intended to turn it into a conference centre for suited city people, who'd arrive to escape the stresses of the metropolis, only to moan when they realised they were almost entirely off the grid.

Less thrilled by this latter idea, Thea paused as she placed a palm against a wooden stile. 'Unless…'

John's accusatory words came back to her. He'd declared he was going to do what Shaun should have done. What if Shaun *had* done what John had suggested? Shaun had been the only other person who'd known about the meeting. Not only that, but he'd been there, with Malcolm, when the announcement of the meeting had been made. What if he'd learnt about the house already being tabled for sale and acted on that information?

'If he did, why didn't he tell me?' Thea started to walk faster. *No, he couldn't have. He'd have told me, or at least asked my opinion.*

With every step closer to her car the idea that Shaun might have stepped in, Sir Galahad style, again took a firmer hold.

'We've only been together two minutes. Surely Shaun wouldn't have saddled himself with such a lifetime of responsibility on a whim?'

Would he?

Thirty-Six

All her attempts at phoning Shaun from the Tarr Steps car park had failed. Now she'd had time to compose herself, Thea was desperate to talk to both him and Tina. But how was she going to tell them that all their hard work had been for nothing?

Driving up through the village, towards Mill Grange, Thea noticed that one of the mill doors was wide open, and pulled her car to a halt. Hoping it was one of her volunteers inside, and not an uninvited guest, Thea approached, reasoning with herself that the mill's doors were so solid they'd be very difficult to break into, and there was nothing inside to steal anyway.

Grateful that, thanks to Mabel, she knew it couldn't be John inside, Thea stepped into the gloomy half-light. 'Hello?'

Tina's head peeped around the door to the connecting room. 'Oh Thea, it's you. I'm so glad you found me.'

'What are you doing here? Are you on your own?'

'I was getting fidgety waiting to hear from you, so I've left Sam with my phone. He's pruning the hedge on the driveway in that spot where there's a mobile signal. He was going to run here as soon as you called.'

Knowing she wouldn't have been able to wait idly for news either, Thea understood her friend's desire to keep busy. 'I'm sorry I've been so long.'

'Just tell me.'

Thea followed Tina into the old spinning room. A wave of guilt and sadness hit her. If she'd come straight back after the meeting, then perhaps Tina wouldn't have spent so long turning this room into the ideal demonstration area for the Open Day's guest spinner.

'This is amazing. How have you done all this so quickly?'

A small row of tables had been erected along the far wall, each covered with fleeces in lieu of tablecloths. Upon those were baskets ready to fill with wool skeins and any other small sale products. Next to the hefty bunch of mill keys, a tray of candles flickered in the dim light, throwing the room into a gothic mix of light and dark.

The floor had been not just swept, but polished, and there was a large wicker-backed chair in the corner next to the only modern item in the room; a large Anglepoise lamp.

'The lamp needs new bulbs, but otherwise, apart from sorting the lock on the door, I think we're nearly there.'

'It's wonderful.' Thea peered up at the high ceiling. The old electric lights were feeble to say the least. 'Decent lighting, or a lack of it, is going to be our only issue once the locksmith has worked his magic tomorrow.'

As she heard the words come out of her mouth, Thea

gave an internal groan. Better lighting wasn't going to be their issue at all.

'That's why I have candles to help with that tonight.' Tina pointed to the three flames across the room. 'We can't have those once we're open. Health and safety and all that, but they're helping for now.' Tina started to pick at a piece of stray fleece wool. 'It's bad news, isn't it? If it was good news we wouldn't be talking about the candles. You'd have bounded in here, all smiles, and told me everything was alright. But you didn't.'

Thea's sigh was so deep it made the nearest candle flame gutter. 'The house has already been sold.'

'Sold!' Tina's face creased into a map of lines. 'I thought they were going to tell you if it was going to go on sale or not. How can it already be sold?'

'That's what I've been wondering. If Malcolm was telling me the truth, then the house officially went on sale at nine this morning and was sold by noon.'

'Is that even possible? Don't you have to have surveys and mortgage meetings and stuff before you could buy a house?'

'I should have said sold subject to survey, but even so it's quick. Must have been a cash sale, but who has money like that in this day and age?' Thea picked up one of the baskets as she voiced a suspicion that had been niggling at the back of her mind since leaving Taunton. 'You don't think it could have been Shaun, do you?'

'Shaun? The buyer, you mean?'

'No one else could have known about the sale so fast. He saw Malcolm first thing this morning to talk about his show. If he was told about the sale, he could have put in an offer before it went public.'

'And a private sale would save the Trust a lot of hassle and a fair bit of money on agents' fees.' Tina examined the display critically as she added, 'Could Shaun afford it?'

'John seemed to think he could.'

'Oh hell, it wasn't John after all, was it?'

'That was my first thought too, but he couldn't have known. Anyway, I asked Malcolm outright if there was a John Sommers involved, and he swore not.'

'I suppose that's something.' Tina looked around the room she'd spent the last few hours cleaning. 'I suppose we'll have to work out how to give everyone back their Open Day ticket money.'

'Well actually, that's happening. After that it's all over.'

'Why? What's the point of giving a child a sweet and then taking it away once the wrapper's off?' Tina slumped against a freshly whitewashed wall.

'Malcolm made it sound as if he was doing the community a favour, but I suspect it's more to avoid the bad press of cancelling after so many tickets have been sold.'

'I suppose the new owners might have insisted it went ahead.'

Thea put the basket back on the table. 'What makes you say that?'

'If I was about to buy a place that was tabled to be a house the locals were hoping would bring Upwich as a whole extra income, I'd want to do anything to keep them on my side if I'd taken that hope away from them.'

'Makes sense.' Thea grimaced. 'There's something else.

Malcolm asked me to give you a message. He wants you to come off secondment from Monday.'

'What? But that's in two days! The trustees agreed I should stay until the Open Day.'

'I know.'

For a second, Thea thought Tina was going to cry, but then she tilted her chin up and said, 'We'd better finish this room now then. You'll have too much to do after I'm gone to fiddle with this.'

'There's no need. You've done loads and it's getting rather dark. I ought to go and tell Shaun and Sam what's happening.'

'I've only got to arrange the last of the fleeces. I thought I'd pile a few in the corner of the room on that table.' Tina pointed across the room to an empty table behind the door. 'If you hold a candle up so I can see better, it won't take a moment.'

Lifting a candle from the table, Thea stood in the open doorway, casting as much light as she could in Tina's direction. 'Do you know where Shaun is?'

'Probably with Sam in the driveway or waiting in the office so he's in range of a call.'

'As soon as you're done, we'll go and find them.'

'Have you heard from Thea?'

Shaun had grown tired of waiting in the office. There were only so many emails he could face answering in one go, and his mind wasn't on the job. With his phone held optimistically out in front of him to catch any stray signal in the ether, he'd gone to find Sam.

'Not yet. I was going to go to the mill to help Tina, but it'd be sod's law that Thea would call the minute I left this spot.'

Shaun checked his watch. 'It's almost half six. She should have been back ages ago. Let's fetch Tina. She might have Malcolm's private number.'

'You're worried something's happened to her?'

'John might not have gone straight back to Bath.'

A dark cloud crossed Sam's countenance. 'Let's go.'

The fleeces were so heavy that Tina could either pull them into position or talk, but not both. With Thea nodding encouragingly, she draped the final one over the table in a manner she hoped appeared as if they were waiting to be carted off and turned into wool.

Just as Tina stepped back to admire the display, the mill plunged into a deep charcoal gloom.

'Hell. A power cut.' Thea moved the candle she was holding as close as she dared to the display so she could see Tina. 'Are you okay?'

'Yeah. Let's get out of here before we trip over something and—'

A sound in the dark made them jump.

'What's that? Is someone there!?' Stepping back as she twisted towards the sound, Thea knocked her arm on the wall behind her, sending the candle flying, the motion blowing it out and plunging them into pitch black obscurity.

'Is someone there?' She shouted louder, but there was no reply.

Tina grabbed Thea's hand and pulled her towards the door. 'Come on!'

'But I dropped the candle.'

'I can't see it, so it must have gone out. Come on!'

Following the glint of light coming through the part-opened main door, Thea stopped again.

'I definitely heard something.'

They froze to the spot, their pulses racing as they listened. 'I can't hear anything, I...' Thea sniffed. A new acrid scent was coming from behind them.

Wishing she hadn't left her mobile with Sam, Tina tugged on Thea's arm. Her voice barely above a terrified whisper, she said, 'The fleeces were on paper tablecloths. The candle can't have gone out after all.'

'Oh God...' Thea started to fumble for her phone, and then remembered she'd left it in the car. She was so used to it being little more than a timepiece here.

As the stink of burning paper filled Thea's nostrils, she gripped Tina's arm tighter and pulled her forward, following the fleeing figure towards the doors.

They were closed.

'The noise must have been them swinging shut.' Thea felt nausea rising in her stomach as she spun around to look back the way they'd come.

An orange glow grew on the far side of the mill.

'Oh God!' Thea stumbled towards the spinning room Tina had set up.

'No!' Tina tried to pull her back. 'You can't save anything.'

'I'm going to shut the internal door, trap the fire in there.'

Tina immediately helped tug the connecting doors shut. 'Faster...'

Running back to the main door, Thea tugged at Tina. 'You have the keys.'

'Keys?' Thea couldn't see the colour drain from Tina's face, but she felt her friend's fear.

'You do have the keys, don't you?'

'They're... they're in there. I left them on the table.' Tina banged on the inside of the main doors in the hope of being heard. 'Is there another way out? An unlocked door?'

Suddenly remembering through her panic that the lock was broken, so the keys probably wouldn't get them out anyway, Thea thumped her own fists against the doors, shaking her head into the dark.

Thirty-Seven

John stared back across the moor. The lay-by in which he'd been parked for the past few hours gave a perfect view of the village he'd left.

He'd needed to think. Mabel had told him to tell his boss the truth or invent a divorce, and learn to live with his lies. He wasn't sure which was the worse option: explaining that his three-month marriage was already over, and looking an idiot and a failure, or explaining he'd lied, which made him look untrustworthy, *as well as* an idiot and a failure.

Mabel's parting words echoed in his mind as his eyes scanned the village, from the pub at one end, to the mill at the other.

'Thea is under the impression you're an intelligent young man. You could prove it by setting up your own company. Prove yourself better than Sure Digital. But of course, I'm just a village idiot, so what do I know?'

'My own company. My own boss. Maybe I could, perhaps I...' He broke off as something caught his eye.

337

Is that smoke?

John squinted harder. Wisps of grey smoke were seeping out of the mill building.

For a split second he froze. *What if someone's in there?*

A telephone box sat, neglected and alone in the lay-by. Muttering under his breath, praying that the phone would work as he didn't have a mobile signal, he dived along the track.

Trying not to inhale the stench of stale urine, and avoiding the inevitable long abandoned lager tins, John banged in the numbers and responded to the receptionist's calm request.

'Fire Brigade, please.'

'What the hell?!' Sam was running towards the mill with Shaun fast on his heels.

Puffs of grey smoke were wafting beneath the main doors. A jumble of arrhythmic bangs and faint indiscernible shouts could be heard from within.

'Tina!' Sam pushed his face up to the door and yelled, but the structure was so thick, he couldn't be sure he was heard.

'Christ!' Shaun was already calling the fire brigade when he spotted Thea's car pulled up on the side of the road just beyond the mill. 'Thea's in there too!'

'Do you have keys?' Sam had started to tremble, his voice betraying the fear he didn't want to confess. As Shaun shook his head helplessly, Sam pulled at the doors, his shoulders heaving with the effort.

'The doors were stiff before, but Tina got in, so we should be able to.' Shaun joined in with the tugging. 'Something must have shifted and jammed in the lock's catch across when the door shut.'

Sam glared at the lock as he struggled to regulate his breathing. 'How far away is the fire service round here?'

The men exchanged a glance that said it could be miles. Upwich was at least fifteen miles from anywhere of any size.

Hoping the girls could hear, Shaun yelled, 'Help is coming! Hang on!'

Sam's knees buckled as the voices he battled to keep at bay every day of his life arrived all at once. The screaming accelerated in his brain until they were so loud he had no choice but to clap his hands over his ears, his face a picture of agony.

Shaun grabbed his friend's arms and shook him hard. 'Not now, mate. Tina and Thea first, panic attack later. We can save them.'

'Tina?' His voice was a whisper at first, and then something in Sam clicked into place. Whether it was the years of training, Shaun's terrified expression, or the thought of the trapped women – a trapped Tina – that broke through the nightmare, it didn't matter. Sam stood up so straight he looked as if he was on parade. 'There must be other doors.'

'There's several, but the mill was designed to keep things in. Thea told me the original owners were paranoid about theft from within as well as from outsiders.'

'Show me.'

Running around the side, passing another large set of double doors, they reached a smaller single door at the back of the building that would have been used by the outworkers to deliver spun wool ready for weaving.

'This one.' Sam was already putting his shoulder to the

thick wood as Shaun joined him, crashing their combined weight against the wood.

'What's that?' Thea spluttered the words, but she wasn't sure if they'd actually made it out of her mouth. Her lungs felt heavy as their banging on the door subsided into effort filled taps.

Coughing, scrubbing at her stinging eyes, Thea strained to listen above the threatening crackle of the fire in the next room. There it was again, a faint thumping, but not from the door they were crouched by.

Grabbing a slumped Tina's shoulder, Thea looked towards the spinning room door. It was barely visible for the smoke that billowed beneath it although, mercifully, no flames licked under the gap. Yet.

Trying to say they should move, Thea's words turned into a coughing fit, and she was forced to communicate by pushing and pulling Tina through the mill.

Shaun scrambled around to find something he could use to help lever the door open and break the lock, but Sam was ahead of him.

Penknife to hand, Sam jammed it into the space between the frame and the lock. Then, leaving the tool in place, he took three strides from the door, before running full pelt at the wood.

There was a sound of splintering as Sam collided with the building, but it didn't open. 'Shit!'

Abandoning his hunt for some sort of jemmy, Shaun joined Sam as he rallied to run at the door again.

The third time, just as their shoulder blades were showing signs of giving way, the door did. With a groan of defeat, it fell open. Headlong, Sam careered inside with Shaun landing spread-eagled at his feet.

Their eyes met two pairs of booted feet. The two women were curled up together on the floor. Neither of them was moving.

The whole village had arrived with the sound of the fire engines' sirens. Thea could see Mabel and a blur of other worried faces she recognised, but hadn't the energy to acknowledge them.

The firefighters had made short work of the blaze which, thanks to the dampening and smothering qualities of the fleeces, was more smoke than flame.

'Thank you.' Thea gave another rasping cough as a soot-smeared firewoman placed a second blanket around her shoulders. Her solicitous presence was probably the only thing keeping Mabel and Sybil at bay, and Thea was glad of the delay before the inevitable questioning began.

'You were lucky your blokes were here.'

Thea could see a blanket-covered Tina sitting next to Sam on the grass. Close, but not touching. She didn't bother to say they weren't a couple, as they so obviously were. Or ought to be.

'You were also lucky that someone called the fire brigade earlier than Mr Cowlson did, or we'd have been another ten minutes. Would have made a lot of difference to the state of the ceiling in there.'

'Someone else?'

'Anonymous call from the phone box on Millside Lane.'

The firewoman was joined by a policeman, who was holding a small pad ready to write everything down. 'Can you remember what happened, Miss Thomas?'

'The power went. I jumped and dropped a candle.' Thea felt herself start to shake. 'It's all my fault. If I hadn't held the candle...'

'You were holding a candle while the power was still on?'

'It was getting dark in the corner, and the bulb in the lamp had gone and...' Thea's throat felt like it was closing in and she slowly formed each new word. 'We wanted to finish the job and...'

'Take your time Miss Thomas, no rush.'

Licking her lips, Thea sipped some water. 'We wanted to finish the display, so I held a candle so Tina could see better, then the main lights went out, I jumped in surprise and the candle fell. We thought the flame was out. Then the door blew shut and we couldn't get out and...'

The policeman held up a hand as Thea's words sped towards panic. 'It's okay, we can do this later. Miss Martin has told me the same thing and the initial report from the firefighters endorses what you say. I'm sorry I've had to ask at a time like this, but we always have to in case of arson.'

As the police constable departed, Thea asked the firewoman, 'And the mill?'

'You'll need to get a structural surveyor in. The damage

is contained to the left side, but apart from smoke, soot and water damage, the majority of the building is untouched.'

'And?'

'The room where the fire started is in a very bad way. The ceiling especially. As I said, ten more minutes and it might have come down and then…'

'Then we'd have been in real trouble.'

The firewoman smiled. 'Are you sure you don't want to go to hospital?' She pointed to where the paramedics were in discussion with Shaun further down the road. 'I know you've been checked over, but there's a possibility of delayed shock.'

'I just want a bath.' Wiping her filthy hair from her eyes, Thea stared at the mill. 'No one would ever think we'd spent weeks making it look as good as new.'

The firewoman followed Thea's line of sight as she took in the smoked-marble effect walls and the stench of burnt paper and wool. She spoke softly, but with a finality that told of experiences she didn't wish to share. 'I've seen a lot of fires. They make a hell of a mess, but I'd rather see a thousand smoke-damaged buildings than a single corpse.'

Thea hadn't known she was crying at first. It wasn't until the tears dripped from her cheeks to her chin, stinging her tired red eyes, the action making her cry harder, that a queue of 'what ifs' arrived in her head.

What if Sam and Shaun hadn't got inside?
What if the ceiling had fallen on them?
What if Tina had been killed?
What if…?

It was too painful to think about.

As her sobs wracked her body, Shaun came to Thea's side, wrapping her in his arms as he took the place of the firewoman. Stroking her hair, he muttered reassurances that she only half heard, before turning to the firewoman and asking if he could take her home.

It was only after the bubble bath was being liberally squeezed beneath the running water into the vast Victorian bath that Thea realised she didn't know where Tina was.

'Don't worry. She's with Sam.'

'But Sam won't come inside. Tina needs to be warm.'

'They're in the kitchen.' Shaun tested the temperature of the water and then gently lifted Thea's arms and peeled her filthy jumper over her head.

Allowing herself to be undressed without thinking about what was happening, Thea considered the latest thing that didn't make sense. 'Sam's in the kitchen?'

'Yes.' Shaun tugged Thea's jeans down while trying to convince his body to ignore the sight of her naked body. 'Mabel and the gang are in the pub, and the police have gone. They've sealed off the mill and called Malcolm to tell him what happened.'

'Malcolm?' The sale. She'd forgotten about the sale. 'The mill was part of the sale. The manor might not sell now.'

'Which is why it's important that he knows it was an accident, not arson.'

Thea felt her legs sag as the implication of what Shaun said sank in. 'He wouldn't think I'd done it on purpose to stop the sale... would he?'

'Not by the time that police have explained the situation, he won't.'

Shaun lifted a naked Thea gently into the bath water. 'Try not to worry. The mill is more or less in one piece, Tina is fine and you're fine. Nothing else matters.'

Thirty-Eight

June 1st

Tina held onto Sam's hand. She wasn't sure if he was reassuring her, or she him. It didn't matter.

'But if I hadn't lit the candles…'

'You could have tripped over something and banged your head and bled out on the hard floor.'

'Unlikely. And not as destructive as a fire.'

'It was an accident. It wasn't your fault.'

Cradling the mug of honey and hot water Sam had made her, Tina timidly asked, 'When did you tell Shaun you'd been in the forces?'

'After John tricked Thea into going to the pub. Shaun wanted to know why I hadn't gone inside the manor with you to help check John wasn't hiding there. He was quite angry.' Sam paused. 'I had to explain why I wouldn't – couldn't – go inside to keep her safe.'

Not wanting to stop Sam now he'd started to explain, Tina remained quiet. She squeezed his palm tighter, warmed by his confession that he worried about her, just as Shaun worried about Thea.

'He'd more or less guessed anyway. Not the reason, but the background to the reason.'

'That you were in the services, you mean?'

Sam blinked in confirmation, but said no more, his mind busy trying to convince him that the kitchen ceiling was not about to fall onto his head.

'Is that how you knew to open the door of the mill with a knife?'

'A knife and brute force.' Sam scrubbed a hand over his face as he nodded. 'Not part of my official training, but a technique I picked up from an obliging local when we needed to get into a locked room somewhere far away from here.'

'I wish you'd told me.' She closed her eyes against the sting in her eyes. She felt as if they'd have grit and dust in them forever. 'Can you tell me?'

Sam sighed. 'I don't tell people. I don't tell myself.'

Tina moved her hand from his palm to his thigh and left it there. 'Claustrophobia?'

'Sort of.' Sam became very still, and Tina sensed he was working very hard to stay with her and not run outside.

'And despite that, you ran into a burning building and helped save Thea and me.'

'Anyone would have.'

'No, they wouldn't. Most would let their demons win.' Tina rested her head on his shoulder. 'I will listen whenever you like. When you're ready to tell me.'

Not wanting to move away from Tina, Sam ran a dirty yellow pigtail across his palm. 'I like you rather a lot.'

Tina burst out laughing. Tired, shaken and emotionally drained, suddenly she knew she was in danger of slipping into hysteria.

'That funny huh?'

She shook her head. 'Ironic, but not funny.' An image of Leon drifted into her head as she looked at Sam. Her laughter stilled as she kissed him on the lips. 'I was so sure I knew what I wanted, but I didn't have a clue. Thea kept saying I was wrong, but I wouldn't listen. I was so sure.'

Sam's reply was barely audible. 'I still may not be what you want when you've heard all I have to tell.'

'Or I might want you even more.' A waft of smoky sweat hit her nostrils as she moved her hand. 'And how you can be interested in me when I stink like a derailed barbeque, I don't know!'

Sam smiled. 'I'd run you a bath but...' He looked longingly at the door. 'I'm afraid my bravery is beginning to desert me. I have to go outside.'

As he stood, Tina saw how controlled his breathing had become. She laid a finger on his lips. 'When you're ready, you can run me as many baths as you like. They could be fun.'

Sam's face flushed with something that told Tina exactly how fun they would be. 'If that isn't an incentive to sort myself out then I don't know what is.'

Her limbs still wobbly, Tina accompanied Sam to the back door. 'Why don't you go back to your tent? I'll have a bath, borrow some of Thea's clothes and then drive home.'

'No way.' Sam was firm. 'You aren't driving tonight. Either you stay in the manor, or you come to my tent. But you are not getting behind the wheel of a car after all you've been through.'

'Absolutely right, young man!' Mabel strode into the kitchen; her face was a picture of determination and her lips were pursed. 'Tina, you're filthy and it's vital you relax those muscles. You've had a dreadful shock. I'll run you and Thea a bath each.'

Sam and Tina struggled not to look at each other in horror as Tina said, 'You're very kind, Mabel, but Thea's already in the bath and I can manage. Honestly.'

'Not a bit of it. I'll go and draw one while you get that drink down you.' Mabel gestured approvingly to the warm honey water Sam had made. 'I expect Shaun could do with a bath as well, and you can go with Bert, Sam. He's waiting for you in the car outside. Off you go.'

'Excuse me?'

Mabel lowered her tone. 'I'm sorry, I was being bossy again.' She gave a rueful smile. 'Bert always says I'm worse when I'm worried, and I've been so worried about you all and—'

Tina put out a comforting hand. 'You're amazing, Mabel, and I'd love you to run me a bath. Shaun and Thea have baths on the go upstairs anyway, but I'm sure you'd prefer a shower, Sam?'

'Well…'

Mabel clapped her hands as if her plan was all falling into place nicely. 'That's what Bert said. Reckon he's got the measure of you as an outdoor type, has my Bert. We've got one of those big walk-in wet room things. Horribly modern, but sensible at our age. You can even open the door onto the outside world if it helps.' Mabel paused, hoping Sam would understand what she was saying. 'Off you go. Sooner you're gone, the sooner you can get back here. It's a beautiful night. We'll have supper under the stars. Yes?'

Tina looked at Sam. Bert had guessed far more than she had.

'You're a very kind woman, Mabel.' Sam pulled his ponytail from where he'd stuffed it down the back of his jumper. 'May I ask, before I take you up on your clear-sighted offer, which armed service was Bert in during the war?'

Mabel puffed with pride. 'He was never allowed to say and I never pressed him.'

Tina watched as something unspoken passed between her companions. She'd never wanted to hug Mabel before. 'Mrs Hastings, you are wonderful.'

Mabel patted her hair unnecessarily. 'While you're soaking I'll get this warmed up.' Then, like a magician producing a rabbit from a hat, she pulled a giant lasagne from a shopping trolley she'd left by the door. 'Everyone needs to eat after a shock.'

'But Mabel...' Tina put a hand out to the old lady. 'We couldn't possibly ask you to—'

'Please.' Mabel suddenly looked shaken. 'I need to help.'

Tina gave her another brief hug and waved goodbye to Sam, running upstairs to shout a warning through the door of whichever bathroom Thea and Shaun happened to be sharing that Mabel was on her way.

'Are you alright with cars, young man, or would you prefer to walk? The cottage is only ten minutes away.'

Bert spoke easily, as if Sam's issue with confined spaces was the most natural thing in the world.

'It's just buildings.'

'Houses specifically?'

'Yes.' Sam's heart was racing fast in relief at escaping from the kitchen.

'Tina will be very proud of you for what you just did.' Bert slid the car into gear and drove them towards Upwich.

'She should be proud of Shaun too. Anyone who'd been passing would have tried to get them out.'

'I wasn't referring to the fire. You went inside with her. That's a big deal.'

'How did you know?'

Bert concentrated on taking the blind corner out of the driveway before saying, 'Why do you think I have a walk-in wet room that has a door to the garden built into it?'

Sam regarded the pensioner with increasing respect. 'I'm so sorry, Bert.'

'As am I. And yet here I am, with a crazy but incredible woman, a nice home, a lot of friends and a life that, eventually, began to feel worthwhile again. Mabel did that. She showed me life was worthwhile.'

'Tina.' Sam spoke the name wistfully as he watched the village pass by outside the car window.

'Be honest with her – as far as the Official Secrets Act will let you – and then let it go.'

'How?'

'By doing good things. Helping people.'

'Atonement.'

'Maybe, but while remembering you did nothing wrong.'

'How do you know I didn't do anything wrong?'

'I know.' Bert pulled the car onto his drive. 'Is that why you have a ponytail? Something the forces wouldn't allow you to have. A small personal rebellion perhaps?'

'Yes.' Sam gave a rueful smile. 'Although, as I'm always

tucking it out of sight so it doesn't get in my way, it's a fairly hollow victory. It can get as itchy as hell trapped between my shirt and my back to tell you the truth.'

Bert grunted a chuckle. 'Forwards is the way to look, young man. Always forwards. And right now,' Bert waved a key in Sam's direction, 'Forwards for you is around the back to the blue door. It'll take you straight into the wet room. Mabel has laid out a towel. The big grey one is yours.'

'Bert – I…'

'When my mother was alive, God rest her, she'd say "If there's nothing to say, say nothing." Wise woman, my mum.'

Shaun took the black bag full of Thea's smoke-ruined clothes and threw it out of the back door. It landed next to the one Tina had already deposited there.

'You okay, Tina?'

'All the better for having the smell of Mabel's cooking in my nostrils rather than smouldering fleece. Where's Thea?'

'Putting on every jumper she owns.' Shaun lowered his voice so as not to offend a happily bustling Mabel. 'She's still really cold despite the bath. Shock I suppose. I'm not sure she should go outside.'

'Thea's always cold. Her circulation is a law unto itself. I don't mind telling Mabel we can't eat outside if you're worried.'

'I think we should go outside though, because of Sam. He saved you both.'

'You both saved us.'

'I followed his lead. I was busy scrambling around for

something to help open the door while he actually got on with opening it.'

Turning so she was facing away from Mabel on the other side of the kitchen, Tina muttered, 'Sam told me about the forces.' Tina hugged her arms around herself. 'But no more than that.'

'He will when he's ready.' Shaun opened the nearest cupboard and pulled out six plates and pointed to the cutlery drawer. 'Can you grab some knives and forks?'

Bert's head popped around the door, waving to everyone in the kitchen, before addressing his wife. 'Hope that lasagne has magical properties, love.'

Unruffled, Mabel said, 'I assume you're referring to the number of people gathering outside. If so, there are three cakes in the bag. There's enough hot food for nine.'

'Derek's got a good blaze going on the bonfire.' Bert was anxious as he turned to Tina. 'Are you girls going to be alright with that? You've possibly had enough fire for one day.'

Tina hid her rapidly paling face as she went to the dresser to retrieve extra plates. 'This is a rather different sort of fire.' Her pulse rate increased as she added, 'I won't be sitting too close though.'

'Nor will I.' Thea came into the kitchen, looking as if she was wearing every garment she owned. 'But it will be good to be together.' She headed straight to Shaun, not caring if anyone saw them together, and tucked herself under his arm. 'We can have tomorrow's meeting early.'

Mabel's hands hesitated over the lasagne dish as she went to cut it into squares as she digested that her suspicions about Shaun and Thea being together in the house were right after all. Rather than comment, she said, 'I didn't ask how it went in Taunton.'

'Dinner first.' Thea came to Mabel's side and kissed her powdered cheek. 'Then work.'

Thirty-Nine

'It's funny how a bonfire smells comfortable, while a trapped fire smells terrifying.'

Thea stayed close to Shaun's side as they sat as far back from the flames as they could, while still benefiting from the warmth.

'If you want to get further away from the fire, all you have to do is say. No one will mind.'

Thea held him tighter. 'I won't pretend I'm exactly relaxed right now, but perhaps it's a good idea to do this. I don't want to become afraid of bonfires.'

Mabel's lasagne was being consumed at speed. As congratulations and thanks for her thoughtfulness for cooking for them combined with frequent checks that Thea and Tina were alright, the conversation drifted into speculating on the future of Mill Grange and its mill.

Thea knew the time had come. She had to tell them.

Shaun hugged her closer to his side as he felt her tense.

'Is it weird that no one's commented that we're together? Nor that Tina and Sam are sitting so close to each other you couldn't fit a teaspoon between them?'

'Bigger things to worry about, which is good, but I'd rather have had some scandal than...' Thea put down her plate of barely touched lemon cake. 'I'm not sure I'll be able to eat again until I've told them about the Trust's decision.'

Dropping her voice to a whisper, Thea added, 'I wish I knew who'd bought Mill Grange. At least then we'd know if it was a business intending to turn it into a corporate meeting place, or if it was a private individual who just hopes to live quietly.'

'Which is worse?'

'I have absolutely no idea.' Thea shifted uneasily. 'Shaun?'

'Yes?'

'It isn't you, is it?'

'The buyer, you mean?'

Thea suddenly felt shy about asking. 'I'm sorry, that was a foolish question. You'd have said.' Not giving him the chance to respond, Thea said, 'Unless it isn't sold anymore, of course.' She looked at Shaun. 'Do you think the buyer will still want it? Fire damage is expensive to put right. They might pull out.'

Shaun shrugged. 'It depends if the mill was included in the sale. Did Malcolm say?'

'No he didn't. I just assumed it would be.' She massaged her thudding forehead. Thea desperately wanted to go to sleep, but knew if she didn't share her news now, she'd never relax enough to manage more than a night of conscience troubling tossing and turning. 'Here goes nothing!'

Picking up a handy twig, Thea banged it on the side of her plate. Despite the crackles of the fire and the hum of her friend's voices, everyone turned in her direction.

They've been waiting for me to speak.

As Shaun whispered, 'You can do this' under his breath, Thea cleared her throat, apologising in advance for her husky throat. An apology that was brushed away under a series of dismissals and comments of 'of course you have a rough throat,' 'being trapped in a burning building does that,' 'we're just glad you're okay…'

Am I okay? Thea hadn't had a minute to think about that yet. She swallowed, taking a sip of water from the glass Shaun offered, concern deepening in his eyes.

I can do this. This is my new start. This moment. Now.

She raised her hands to bring the group back to order and gave a smile which she hoped didn't look as forced as it felt.

'I'm glad you're all here.' She nodded at Tina, who gave a secret thumbs up from the opposite side of the bonfire. 'Tina and I are fine. A bit shaken and in need of new clothes and some sleep, but thanks to Shaun and Sam we're in one piece and in far better shape than the mill.'

Derek raised his glass of beer in Thea's direction. 'Do I dare ask how bad it is inside the mill?'

'I don't know for sure.' Thea wiped her gritty eyes as she spoke. 'We aren't allowed back in until there's been a health and safety check. The impression I got was that the spinning-room is a write-off, especially the ceiling. The walls are smoke- and soot-stained, but it's the structural integrity of the building that needs checking. If that's compromised then it'll take more budget than we've got to put it right.'

'You mean the mill may have to come down?' Mabel pulled her coat tighter around her shoulders.

'Possibly, or it may just be a case of a massive clean-up and redecorate. We won't know for a few days. In fact—' Thea took another sip of water '—it may not be our problem at all.'

Every eye was focused on her as Mabel spoke for them all. 'What did the trustees say about Mill Grange's future?'

Not wanting to catch anyone's eye as she spoke, Thea stared at a small patch of earth just short of the bonfire. 'It's been sold.'

'What?!'

Suddenly everyone was talking at once. Gasps of 'but Mabel said it would never happen,' merged into 'sold, but weren't they supposed to tell us about selling it, not that it's a done deal already? How about Open Day?'

Through the cries of consternation, Thea spotted Mabel looking uncomfortable. Thankful that Bert was with her and had already grasped his wife's hand, Thea raised her voice as much as she could. The result was rather squeaky.

'I can answer some of your questions, but not all of them. First, Mabel's confidence at the manor's safety with the Trust came out of a conversation someone had with her – a conversation during which Mabel's good nature was cruelly taken advantage of.' She turned to Mabel. 'I'm sorry, Mabel. I should have told you how underhand John could be. I didn't want to burden you with my problems.'

'John?' The collective murmuring of his name as they

all bit back the desire to ask Thea about why John was a problem, sounded across the garden as loud as if they'd bellowed their queries skyward.

Deciding to clear the air in the hope the subject would then be closed for everyone, including herself, Thea cleared her throat. 'Some time ago, John was my boyfriend. The relationship was short and meant far more to him than me. He, to my never-ending bemusement, became obsessed with the idea of us getting back together. I hoped that, when I came here, he'd give up, but...'

Mabel went pale. 'But then you ended up doing the television broadcast and he found you! Oh my God, Thea, I'm so sorry, I had no idea!'

'Of course you didn't. You have nothing to be sorry for. And it turned out to be excellent for the manor, and it brought Shaun here. For which I'm more than grateful.'

Diane smiled, 'And now John's long gone, thanks to Mabel.'

Mabel blushed. 'With a little career advice ringing in his ears.'

Thea felt a surge of love for Mabel that she'd never have believed possible a few weeks ago. 'John aside, Mill Grange has been sold. Whether that sale will go ahead now that the mill has suffered a fire remains to be seen. According to the police and firefighters I spoke to, the fire report will state that it was an accident. If the Trust suspected arson in an attempt to stop the sale going ahead, then we could all have been facing some questioning from the police.

'However, that is not the case. It was an accident. The

wind banging the door closed caused a candle to fall and it hit the paper tablecloths under the fleeces.' Mutters whisked through the group again as Thea pressed on. 'We thought the flame had gone out. We were wrong.' Thea sighed. I'm blaming myself for dropping the candle, while Tina's blaming herself for having lit it in the first place.'

This time the mutters of protest were louder, each and every one telling the girls that it was nobody's fault. A fact underlined by Sam who, asking for silence stated, very firmly that if the firefighters, who were experts, could see it was an accident straight away, then that's exactly what it was.

Thea swallowed painfully as she moved the subject on. 'The Open Day will happen. The new owner wants us to hold it. A way of us thanking everyone for their support and giving the locals a chance to see the house.'

For a while all that could be heard was the crackle of the branches Derek and his students had piled into the blazing bonfire. Thea nervously shuffled as she awaited the outcry of protests and declarations that they wouldn't run the Open Day with her. She wouldn't blame them. Why should they put more effort into the manor when it had been taken away from them?

It was Sam who broke the contemplative mood. 'I think we should make the Open Day something special. It was going to be amazing anyway. Let's make it something no one will forget. We've sold how many tickets?' He turned to Tina.

'All fifty pre-sales. We were hoping for another fifty on the day.'

'And in the house, how many people could you comfortably have wandering around at one time?'

Thea leant forward, wondering where Sam was going with this. 'Fire regulations put the limit at seventy people at once, spread throughout the house.'

Sam thought for a moment. 'Let's work on the assumption that the mill is lost, for the time being at least, and certainly for the purposes of the Open Day. So, as the three crafts folk booked will need somewhere to work, or at least display their work if power issues stop them doing demonstrations, we need an alternative location. Marquees would seem a sensible answer. Anyone know someone local who supplies them?'

Bill raised a hand. 'There's a firm in Wiveliscombe. Does hire for events and stuff. I'll bring the phone number tomorrow.'

'Excellent.' Sam glanced at Thea, silently asking if she was alright with him making suggestions. As she nodded, he added, 'And perhaps we could go beyond the cups of tea and coffee, as well as Tina's excellent lemon cake, that we were going to provide in the kitchen.'

Sybil cut in from her spot by the fire. 'If we can rustle up an extra tent, then I'm happy to do an afternoon tea service. Cream teas and dainty Victorian style sandwiches.'

Thea felt bewildered. She'd expected them to be less than excited about Open Day now they'd lost the manor. It appeared the contrary was true. The restoration of Mill Grange was going to end on a high.

'A hog roast!' Derek announced. 'I know a bloke who does them. He'd come; I'm sure he would.'

Thea's head began to swim. She'd been so worried about them taking the sale of the house badly, yet here they were, happily pouring ideas into ways to let go of their project with a bang. She didn't have the heart to tell them that the budget was all but used up and that there was simply no money to hire marquees and hog roasts.

Forty

Thea leant against the trunk of a tree opposite the mill building.

The police tape barring the doors flickered half-heartedly in the breeze. No one had been allowed inside the building to see the extent of the damage since the fire two weeks ago.

Once the health and safety inspectors had been, Thea knew she'd have to go inside – assuming they said it was safe – and start to clean it up. Going into the mill again was not an appealing prospect. Just the notion made her feel nauseous. She thought of the three crafts folk waiting to use the space. They were all happy to use marquees instead, but if the mill was okay to use, Thea was going to have to make herself go inside.

She checked her watch. The inspector was due in ten minutes. Malcolm had told Thea she didn't have to be there, but she felt responsible, and despite telling Shaun she wasn't going to go, she'd found herself heading towards the mill anyway.

Now however, as she confronted the smoke-scarred structure, anxiety built in her and the taste of the smoke, which seemed to permanently live in her throat, started to cloy her senses. Ever since the fire she'd experienced a fatigue like she'd never known. *Perhaps it's not just reaction to the fire making me tired. Maybe it is relief that John is finally out of my life.* Thea breathed deeply as flashback images of being trapped inside the building somersaulted about her head.

Before she'd considered what she was doing, Thea strode away from the mill towards Sybil's place. She needed coffee to take away the sooty taste that her recent memories carried with them. Resolving to be back at the mill in time to see the inspector as they left, so she could get the verdict direct rather than waiting for Malcolm to report back to her, Thea pushed the bottom half of the par-open stable door. She wished Tina was with her. Her friend was visiting and assessing a long-abandoned church on the other side of the moor. Not having Tina's daily support was worse than not having her extra pair of hands to help out.

For the umpteenth time, she told herself it shouldn't matter. The sale was going ahead, with or without the mill. They were no longer fighting to restore the manor for the good of the village, but as an act of professional pride so that Mill Grange was in as good a state as possible when it was handed over.

Then there was Open Day.

Now likely to be confined to the manor itself, Thea was amazed at how much the volunteers were rallying around, even though their dream of having a house ready to open to the public permanently had been dashed. Even having to dig into their own pockets or ask for favours to acquire the required marquees hadn't dulled their spirits.

Waving at Sybil as she took a seat in the far corner of the café, Thea hoped no one would ask her questions about the house sale – questions she couldn't answer. She still didn't know who'd bought the house, or what use they had purchased it for.

Not waiting for Thea to place her order, Sybil walked over to her table with a black espresso in her hand. 'Scone, cake or crumpets this morning, love?'

'One of your gorgeous scones please. Cheese if you've got them. And a heart-attack-inducing amount of butter.'

Sybil laughed. 'Looks like you need it. You've lost weight since the fire.'

'I didn't mean to.'

Passing Thea's food order onto one of her waitresses, Sybil sat down. 'Are you sleeping?'

'Not as much as I'd like. At least I haven't had to move out of the manor yet. I've packed up the few bits I've got apart from my clothing. Tina's storing it at her place. There seems no point in me leaving Mill Grange until the night before the Open Day. That way I can be on hand to make sure it goes as smoothly as possible and last-minute disasters can be tackled.'

'Which is only a few weeks away.'

'Yes.' Thea downed her espresso in one.

Sensing Thea didn't want to talk about what was going to happen to her once the mill was sold, Sybil changed the subject. 'I thought I'd offer a choice of plain or fruit scones for the Open Day cream teas, along with a selection of jams and homemade clotted cream. Then maybe Bucks Fizz for those who want to splash out and tea and coffee for everyone else. How does that sound?'

Smiling, Thea could picture the sumptuous display Sybil was describing. 'Perfect. Just perfect.'

Shaun arrived in time to witness a drip of butter dribble down Thea's cheek as she took her last mouthful of scone.

'Lick that up before I'm tempted to do it for you.' Shaun winked as he sat down. 'As you weren't in your office or at the mill I assumed I'd find you in here.'

'I couldn't face seeing the inspector in the end. I'll intercept him as he leaves.'

'It was a she, and she's already gone.'

'What? I was told it would take an hour to do the initial assessment?'

Thea made to get to her feet, but Shaun put out a hand to restrain her. 'There's no point in haring off after her, she's gone to report to Malcolm.'

'Did you talk to her then?' Thea picked up the coffee jug that Sybil had delivered to her after the initial espresso had taken the edge off her desperate need for caffeine.

'She was throwing her hard hat into the back of her car as I arrived. Said the state of the mill was confidential information until she'd made her report to the Trust, but that we should not attempt to go inside. She also told me that she'd arranged for someone to come and put stronger padlocks on all the doors.'

Thea groaned. 'It's had it then.'

'Either that or it needs a great deal of work to make it safe to enter again. Clearly it wasn't safe enough for the inspector to do more than stick her head inside.' Shaun placed his palm over Thea's as Sybil drifted across the café with a second cup, so Shaun could partake of some coffee.

Quiet for a while, Thea murmured, 'We've got four and a bit weeks.'

'Yes.' Shaun reached across to steel some crumbs off Thea's plate. 'I should start work on my speech. Not sure what to say to be honest. I was going to rattle on about the benefits of the manor to the local population, but that's not really relevant now.'

'I wish I'd had the money to buy it.' Thea cradled her empty cup. 'Then I could have opened the place to everyone and I would only have to worry about finding a new job, not finding a home and a job.'

'If you could afford to buy Mill Grange, then you wouldn't need a job beyond running it, would you?'

'True.' Thea played a pair of silver tongs through the lumps of brown and white sugar in their Spode bowl. 'I keep wondering what will happen to the chickens. Gertrude and the gang are so settled together. What if the new owner cooks them or something?'

Shaun couldn't help but laugh. 'I'm sure the new owner will appreciate the need for fresh eggs every day. Just because they've got the house, doesn't mean they'll be barbarians with it. They might still open it to the public, even if it's just on bank holidays and stuff.'

'I suppose so.' She shifted uneasily in her seat. 'I'm not going to stay to find out.'

'What?' Shaun frowned. 'You're leaving before Open Day? But what about us?'

'Us is happening – at least I hope you still want us to as

much as I do.' Shaking her head fast to dispel his worries, Thea gripped Shaun's hand tighter. 'I'll do Open Day, but then I have to go. It's lovely here, but I couldn't stay and watch everything we've worked so hard to achieve go to waste. Logically I know that what's happened isn't my fault, but I still feel as if I've let Upwich down.'

'But Thea…'

'I know what you're going to say, Shaun, but I can't help it. I came here to save Mill Grange and get it open to the public. Now it's been sold off, the restoration is short of completion, although only just, and the mill is all but destroyed. I just thank Minerva that we didn't pull down the greenhouse. At least that isn't on my conscience.'

'Thea love, you can't take responsibility for everything that's beyond your control.'

'I know, but I do! What if the new owners don't care about the place? What if it's a status symbol purchase? What if they fill the place with hot-shot city people all complaining about the lack of Wi-Fi?'

'How about the possibility that they're good people, with a love of the countryside, but simply don't want people traipsing through their home all the time?'

Thea dabbed a fingertip over the crumbs on her plate. 'It makes no difference either way. I have no home and no job. I haven't even sorted out where to live during Open Day.'

Shaun was surprised. 'Surely you'll join me? That's what I was coming to tell you this morning. I've booked a room in a local hotel. I was going to invite you to come with me.'

Despite an immediate positive reaction from her body to this prospect, Thea was despondent. 'I'd love to, really I would…'

Shaun looked resigned, 'But?'

'But it's one thing our friends knowing that you and I are together, but do we really want Open Day overshadowed by newspaper reports of "celebrity archaeologist in romance with restorer of Mill Grange" type headlines?'

'Romance?' Shaun grinned. 'I like the sound of that.'

'You know what I mean. The radio and all the big regional papers are sending journalists thanks to Mabel and Tina's phoning round. I just want to slip into the background and let Mill Grange take centre stage. What if that awful Becky Gibson sees an article about us and does one of those "I slept with a celebrity" articles to *The Sun* or something?'

Shaun ran a hand over his short hair, making it spike at divergent angles. 'Then she'll have to get on with it. I always think articles like that make the exposer look rather pathetic. And I don't see how that has anything to do with you and me sharing a hotel room?'

'I know but...'

Shaun stopped her in her tracks. 'How about I book another room in the same hotel in your name?'

Thea smiled. 'Thank you.'

'Doing the right thing is one thing, love, but you can take self-sacrifice too far sometimes!' His expression made it perfectly clear he had no intention of them using both rooms even if they paid for two.

Grinning despite her fears for her future, Thea agreed. 'And then, once it's all over, you and I can get on with being us and I can get job hunting. I don't suppose you know where you're filming next? I would like to stay close, if that's okay with you.'

Shaun only just resisted the urge to give her a shake. 'I

told you, I need a new archaeologist on the team. I sort of assumed that would be you.'

'But we're together now and people might think—'

'I don't give a flying fig what people think. And before you say "shouldn't I have an official interview?" you've had one. Richard asked you lots of questions about your archaeological background when he finished up the table, didn't he?'

'Well yes, but we were just chatting.'

'No you weren't. He was asking lots of questions because I'd already mentioned I was going to ask if you'd fancy the job. So, you've done your interview. Therefore, Thea Thomas, I hereby offer you the position of onsite archaeologist for the duration of the filming of series twelve of *Landscape Treasures*. Do you accept?'

'I do.'

'Thank God for that. Now stop being daft and order some more scones.'

Forty-One

'Has Sam managed to go inside the house again?' Relieved to be having a day off work, Tina sank into the scullery's empty office chair.

'Not beyond the bathroom as far as I'm aware.' Thea, her hands on her hips, surveyed the freshly whitewashed room. Beyond her table and two chairs, the room was empty and ready to be turned back into a scullery for the Open Day in two days' time.

Tina sighed. 'Sam did so well to come into the kitchen with me after the fire. I'd hoped it would trigger something in him and he'd keep trying to come in.'

'Maybe he has. He could easily come in after everyone has gone home in the evenings. He has a key after all. It would be easier for him without the idea of Mabel watching to see how long it takes for him to bolt to the door.'

'Perhaps.'

Seeing Tina wasn't convinced, Thea asked, 'Have you

guys seen much of each other since you went back to your proper job?'

'Virtually nothing.' Tina slipped off her shoes. 'I've been working on the other side of the county for the most part and, as you well know, Somerset is huge.'

'Are you going to see him now?' Thea thought her friend was lacking her usual glow. 'Sam really cares for you.'

'Does he? I haven't heard from him since I left. I know he doesn't have a mobile, but there are plenty of phones and laptops he could ask to borrow.' Tina rubbed at the balls of her feet. 'I hate having to wear grown up shoes all day again.'

'That's weeks working in walking boots and then going back to wearing toe-crunchers.' Understanding Tina's desire not to talk about Sam, Thea asked, 'How about you, hun? You still happy with your job?'

'I suppose so. I used to love it.'

'But?'

'I got used to working with people, being part of something that wasn't just me on the road liaising between the trustees and landlords. And I got used to being more hands on. It's hard to give all the advice, but then not be part of implementing it now I've had a taste of how rewarding putting the ideas into practice can be.'

'Makes sense.' Thea pointed to her desk. 'Well, if you can face doing some implementing right now, I could do with a hand taking all that paperwork out to the boot of my car.'

'No problem – but let me slip my boots on first!'

★

Tina had almost told Thea she'd been wary about visiting Mill Grange that afternoon. She would have assumed it was because of being trapped in the mill fire, but it wasn't.

Her orders from Malcolm to get back to her old job had been so sudden, and she'd had so much to do, that she'd left Mill Grange with more haste than she'd have liked. The night after the fire, and the few wonderful hours she and Sam had spent cuddled together with their friends, already felt like a lifetime away.

As much as Tina would have liked to stay in Sam's tent with him that night, she'd been boringly sensible and slept in the manor. Her fear of freezing in his tent, combined with sheer exhaustion after the shocks of the day had taken over from any physical desires she may have had. Did have. Still had.

The day after the fire she'd raced around to get her files and laptop from the makeshift office, half-dead after a restless night disturbed by coughing and her imagination reminding her what could have happened if the boys hadn't found them. As she'd got ready to leave, Tina had found Sam sitting by her car. He'd held his arms out to her, and she'd flown into them without hesitating. After checking she'd had some sleep (very little) and that she'd eaten (a huge bacon sandwich with enough tomato sauce to drown in), Sam had told her he'd email her as soon as he could.

He hadn't. That had been a month ago.

At first she'd been so busy with work and so nervous about going back into the Taunton office after everything that had happened, that Tina explained away his lack of contact as him being as busy as she was. Then she'd wondered if Sam was waiting until he had time to ask her out... until she realised that dating Sam wouldn't be like dating other men. They could hardly go to a restaurant or the cinema if Sam couldn't bring himself to sit inside a building.

With each fresh day of no contact, Tina had been tempted to contact him – except she didn't have his email address and she didn't want to ask Thea for it. Especially as she knew Sam had all her contact details because he'd asked for them before she'd left.

On her drive to Mill Grange she'd considered the possibility that Sam may have left Upwich. That she hadn't heard from him because he'd regretted sharing his secret with her or that he'd found a new job or place to volunteer. After all, she and Thea weren't the only ones who needed to work beyond Mill Grange's restoration.

Now, as she followed Thea out to the driveway and her car, Tina felt herself avoiding looking either left or right. She knew she was being silly. She wanted to see Sam; she wanted to make sure he was alright. But the voice telling her he hadn't been in touch, despite his promise to do so, wouldn't leave her alone.

Tina's contrary thoughts were thwarted as soon as they hit the afternoon air. Two men Tina vaguely recognised were getting out of a van parked about one hundred metres down the driveway.

'Thea, aren't those blokes on Shaun's TV show?' As Tina asked the question, they saw Shaun stride across the garden, his hand outstretched towards the visitors in greeting.

'It certainly looks like it.'

'I take it from your tone that you didn't know Shaun had friends coming.'

'No I didn't.' Thea dropped her armful of files into the open car boot. 'It doesn't have the appearance of friends who just happen to be passing through, does it? In fact, the concept of "just passing" doesn't apply around here.'

Sam had joined Shaun now. He was looking far less surprised than the women had been to see two of the *Landscape Treasures* crew at Mill Grange.

'I've just remembered who those guys are.' Thea's eyes narrowed suspiciously. 'That's Andy and Ajay.'

'The geophysics team? The ones Shaun refers to as "the AA" when he's onscreen?'

'The very same.'

As Shaun saw Thea and Tina coming towards him, he flushed with pleasure. He appeared far too excited for someone who was greeting work colleagues he'd seen only a few weeks ago.

'Thea, Tina, let me introduce you to the show's geo-fizz team. Andy and Ajay, this is the unstoppable Thea Thomas, chief restorer here at Mill Grange and the equally amazing Tina Martin.'

'Pleased to meet you both.' Thea shook their outstretched hands. 'Forgive me, I'd have been here to meet you, but I didn't know you were coming.'

'Last-minute decision.' Shaun answered for them. 'The lads are going down to the place in Cornwall to do some more readings.'

Ajay's enthusiasm was contagious as he said, 'Shaun went on so much about how great this place is, we thought we'd come and take a peep before it's closed to visitors.'

Tina sensed Sam's gaze on her, but had yet to glimpse in his direction. She wasn't convinced. Her friend's expression told her Thea wasn't either, although she said nothing beyond inviting their guests into the manor for a tour.

'After all, I need to practise giving tours. I've pretty much worked out what I'm going to say when the guests come in, but a trial run would be a good idea; I'm a bit nervous. I wanted to go to the archivist's office in Taunton and get more information about the place, but somehow that never happened.'

'You'll be fantastic.' Shaun beamed proudly. 'I'm sure the AA won't mind being guinea pigs.'

'Although I'm sure Thea did want to have a practice run of her tour, I can't help thinking Shaun and Thea have steered his friends away so that we could be alone.' Sam spoke quietly as he regarded Tina.

'Probably.' She flicked her pigtails over her shoulders.

'After all, Thea knows I won't follow them, doesn't she?'

There wasn't a trace of self-pity in Sam's voice but Tina thought she detected something else. Annoyance? Anger?

'How have you been?' It wasn't a particularly dynamic sentence, but the silence that had fallen between them seemed to be filling up every inch of the summer air between them.

'I've been good.' Sam waved his words away as soon as they'd been spoken. 'Cancel that. What I should have said is I've been rather pathetic and I'm ashamed of myself.'

Tina wasn't sure what to say. She felt awkward and didn't know where to put her hands.

'You want to know why I didn't email.' It was spoken as a statement, not a question.

'Yes.' Not able to stay still any longer, Tina pointed towards the walled garden. 'Let's visit the chickens. I'd like to say goodbye to Gertrude and Tony and the gang. I can't imagine I'll have time again between now and Open Day.'

Falling in step with Tina, Sam said, 'The new owner is keeping them, so at least Thea doesn't have to worry about re-homing them as well.'

'That's good.' Not wanting to say anything else until Sam had explained himself, Tina lapsed back into silence.

Gertrude was sitting in the doorway of the coop. Her backside was spread out so much it blocked the door to all the others.

'Not the best parking, Gertrude old girl.' Sam rested his forearms on the fenced enclosure. 'She's got so much character, don't you think?'

'I miss her.' Tina kept her eyes on the hen, watching as she rearranged her feathers with a quick shake, before settling down again. 'I miss all of them.'

'I miss you.'

Resisting the temptation to turn around and forgive him instantly without waiting for an explanation, Tina said, 'You were going to tell me why you didn't send the promised email.'

'Cowardice.'

'I frighten you?'

'No.' Sam paused, gripping the fence so hard it looked as if he was physically holding it up. 'After the fire I took you inside the manor. It was a big deal for me as I explained.'

'But you did it.'

'Because you were frightened and no way was I going to let you go anywhere alone.'

'Someone else could have escorted me inside.'

Sam abruptly swung around and faced Tina properly for the first time since she'd arrived at the manor. 'I wanted it to be me. I wanted to be the one who helped you.'

Hoping that now Sam was talking, he'd keep going, Tina gave an encouraging dip of her head.

'After that evening I swore to myself that I would email you and that I would do it from *inside* the manor. I'd gone in beyond the bathroom once and nothing bad had happened, so I could do it again.'

'Go on.'

'I tried. Every day I thought I'd go in, but...' Sam threw his hands up in exasperation. 'You deserve more than a man who can't even walk into a large airy kitchen to tell you he wants to ask you out.'

'You don't need to be inside for that.' Tina wrapped her arms around him. 'I think I should tell you that I've always enjoyed camping and I love picnics.'

'If this was my house I'd have a bench just here.' Tina stretched her legs out in front of her as she sat next to Sam on the grass, their backs resting on the garden wall.

'It's a perfect suntrap.' Sam waved a hand at the dilapidated greenhouse. 'If I was the owner, I'd save that. I can't stop picturing it full of oranges, lemons and grapevines.'

Tina paused before she asked, 'Do you think you'd be alright in a greenhouse? The glass is so open and light.'

'Less enclosed you mean?' Sam shrugged. 'I suspect so, especially if there was a door each end which could be left open.'

He was so still and quiet that Tina held her breath.

'I got help at first. Lots of help. Everyone was so kind. It wasn't a case of another soldier being ignored in the grips of PTSD. I was looked after, but it felt so pointless. There were so many others that deserved help more than I did.'

'You deserved help too.'

'I did not.' Sam suddenly reached out to take her hand, and then pulled it back again. 'Sorry. I didn't mean to snap. My friends lost limbs and their minds. They need help. I have no worries by comparison.

'I left the counselling centre and started my own self-treatment plan. Staying outside and working hard for worthwhile causes.'

'Hence coming here.'

'Yes.' Sam risked placing a palm on Tina's leg. When she didn't object he added, 'I hadn't expected to stay here this long. Usually, after a few days, people start asking questions about why I won't go inside or label me a weirdo. I'm always moving on.'

Hardly daring to ask, Tina whispered, 'And this time? Where will you go next?'

'That's just it. I don't want to go this time. Somehow, against the odds, everyone has accepted that I don't go indoors and not asked questions.'

'You fit in here.'

'Yes.' Sam blinked. 'And I'm having trouble getting used to that too, although I'm not complaining about it.'

After a few seconds of sitting in silence, Tina said, 'If I asked you what had happened, could you tell me?'

Sam held her hand tighter as he cleared his throat. 'There's much I can't tell you, because the nature of my work then remains confidential.'

'Understood.'

'You'll have guessed I was trapped in a building in frightening circumstances.'

Sam's free hand scratched at his thigh up and down so fast Tina thought he might make a hole in his jeans, so she reached over and took it firmly in her hand. 'If you aren't ready to tell me, I can wait.'

'I'm okay. Especially now you're here.' Sam held her gaze. 'You are here, aren't you?'

'I'm not going anywhere.' Tina knew she meant it, but until she heard her words out loud, she hadn't realised how fervently.

'There was a fire in a house. I can't say where I was, but there's a lot of sand there.'

Tina understood, and fear for what might have happened to the gentle man beside her clutched at her heart. *He was peacekeeping.*

'Four of my mates were inside trying to get locals out. I saw the fire go up. I'm not sure how the blaze started, but there was a strong smell of petrol. I went in to help and we got all the locals out, but then the ceiling of one of the rooms collapsed. One of my friends...' His voice cracked. 'Dale. He was trapped under rubble and the others ran back to get him out. I was pulling a local woman to safety. By the time I ran back in to help the others it was too late. I couldn't battle through the flames.

'The next thing I knew, the building was falling in. I was yanked free as I was nearest the door, but the others... I never saw them again.'

Forty-Two

'That was wonderful. You're a natural.'

Thea smiled at Andy's kind words.

'I fluffed loads of it. I'm sure I was going to say more than I did.'

Shaun slipped an arm around her shoulders. 'You were great. And there's no need to worry about what you're going to say. You're clearly knowledgeable and the anecdotes about doing up the house were fun. If people have any questions they'll ask you.'

Ajay agreed. 'You're obviously passionate about the place.'

'You're very kind. I know this was never my home, but I've spent nearly every waking hour here for weeks. I'm going to miss this place.' Thea ran a hand along the banister with affection. 'I hope the new owner loves it as much as I do.'

'I'm sure he will.' Andy stared up at the moulded ceiling.

'He?' Thea pounced on the pronoun, her eyes landing on Shaun. 'Do you all know who has bought Mill Grange?'

Andy backtracked fast. 'I meant... well, I suppose I just said "he" automatically. Sorry. It could just as easily be a woman.'

'Umm.' Thea was not convinced. The idea that Shaun might have purchased it after all was fast re-forming in her mind. After all, now she thought about it, her attempts to ask him about the possibility had never been answered properly.

Ajay turned to Shaun. 'We'd better get on if we're going to finish up before we go.'

Gesturing towards the back doors, Shaun said, 'If you guys get set up, I'll be there to show you where to survey in a minute.'

Biting her tongue until their guests had disappeared outside, Thea dipped her head to one side. 'Are you going to tell me what's going on, or do I have to set Gertrude on you?'

Taking her hand, he winked. 'Follow me.'

'I repeat, what are you up to, Shaun Cowlson?'

'Isn't it obvious? I'm taking a beautiful historian for a walk around the grounds that she has been so much a part of restoring.'

Thea poked him playfully in the side. 'That is not what I meant and you know it.'

'Patience, woman.' Shaun cradled Thea's small palm as he walked her around the back of the house where the perambulation path Sam and the students had cleared. 'Just imagine you are the lady of the house, being taken for a stroll by your suitor before lunch.'

'That makes me sound like I should be a dog on a lead.'

'I believe there are people who like that, but I was thinking more of a walk and a sneaky snog in the shrubbery.'

'That can be arranged.' Thea was about to kiss Shaun's cheek as a deposit to what was to come, when she suddenly said, 'Hang on, where is everyone?'

'By everyone, I assume you mean Mabel and crew? I saw Sam heading into the woods earlier and I spotted Tina looking at the chickens out of an upstairs window.'

'Did she look happy?'

'I saw the top of her head. Hard to tell.'

'Sorry, silly question.' Thea moved closer to Shaun's side. She began to relax, enjoying their rare moment of privacy during daylight hours. 'And the others?'

'Day off.'

Thea stopped dead. 'What?'

Shaun, who had been expecting an avalanche of panic, wrapped his arm around her shoulders, and pointed up at the manor. 'I know you're about to tell me that Open Day is in two days' time and there is a heap of stuff to do.'

'Well, it is and there is!'

'Yes, but most of it can't be done until tomorrow as it's last-minute stuff. The marquee man isn't coming until five o'clock this afternoon, and he brings his own team to put them up. Sybil is baking at her place and the manor is so clean you could eat off the floor. I think everyone deserves the day off before tomorrow, don't you?'

'Of course they do, but…'

'I know I've been high-handed and all that, telling the volunteers to take the day off without consulting you, but I have good reason, I promise.'

'Which is?'

'Look up there.' From their position at the back of the garden, Shaun gestured up the slope to where Mill Grange sat. The sun bounced off the grey slate tiles, making the specks of granite in the stonework twinkle in the morning light. The grass was mown, the flower beds blooming and the benches placed around the grounds were clean, varnished and lined in smart regimented rows. Any Victorian that happened to be passing would have most certainly approved. 'You did that.'

'I didn't. I mostly sat in my office while other people did that.'

'Don't split hairs. You got it to work. You took all the volunteers and moved them on from doing a bit of painting here and a bit of weeding there, to the restoration of a manor house, inside and out, on a stupid budget in a tiny amount of time.'

'It isn't finished.'

'It would have been if the Trust hadn't kept moving the goalposts.'

'I suppose so.' Thea allowed herself to admire the view. There was no denying it looked fantastic. 'I don't suppose you know someone who will guarantee sunshine on Saturday?'

'I don't, but Mabel is bound to.'

Thea couldn't help but laugh. 'That's true.'

'It's time to stop beating yourself up about what you haven't done, and think about what you have achieved.'

'I tell you what.' Thea swivelled round to face him. 'I will stop giving myself a hard time, if you will tell me the truth. What are you up to, Mr Cowlson? And this time, don't sidestep the answer with guff about the volunteers earning a day off.'

'But they did.'

'I know they did. Now, tell me, or I'll—'

'You'll what?' Shaun picked her up, so her feet hung a foot off the ground and he could give her a kiss.

'I have no idea, but I'll think of something.'

Delaying his response with a kiss that felt as if it could stop time, Shaun reluctantly pulled away and lowered Thea to the floor. 'I have something to show you. Then we'll go and see how the AA are getting on.'

'They weren't just passing then?'

Shaun chuckled. 'No one "just passes" here.'

Sam stroked Tina's hair out of its right plait. The action of unknotting and teasing out the kinks in the blonde tresses was blissfully relaxing.

Tina's head was on his shoulder, her eyes were closed. As they sat in comfortable silence, she thought her heart would break for the man next to her. He'd saved lives, lots of them, and yet he was crippled with the knowledge that he hadn't saved three of his friends. Tina was used to solving problems; it formed the largest part of her job after finance balancing. This however, was one problem she couldn't solve.

'It's okay.' As if reading her mind, Sam said, 'I'm not expecting you to find a solution to this. There isn't a solution, there's just finding a way to live.'

Staying where she was, not wanting the spell to break, Tina whispered, 'I'd like to help you though. Find a way I mean.'

'I'd like that. I have to tell you though, I have nightmares. There's a long way to go before I reach where I want to be.'

Tina shifted her legs, so they hooked themselves around his, bringing them as close as they could get on the walled garden floor. 'Where do you want to be?'

'In a house, with the woman I love and a family.' Sam swallowed. 'Does that sound corny?'

'No. It sounds perfect.'

'And to be working in a worthwhile way. Doing something good for other people.'

'Like this?' Tina nodded towards the chicken coop they'd built together.

'Or something similar. I'll need to earn some money again soon. My forces pension can only stretch so far.'

'I'm working. We'd be okay until you're ready, especially if we are only paying camping fees, not rent. The ultimate savings plan.'

Sam stopped stroking her hair and turned to look at Tina properly, his eyes searching her face for any sign that she could be joking. 'You would live in a tent with me?'

'Yes.'

'But you have possessions and you need to be smart for work and...'

'And there are a million problems, but you forget, I'm a problem solver. I'll think of something.' She kissed him slowly. And don't forget, I have a room in a rented house, so I can leave my stuff there until the lease ends in three months, and we'll have worked something else out by then.'

Sam was in shock. 'You really want to?'

Tina started to laugh. 'You can't be that surprised surely?'

'I'm hardly a rich older dude with a BMW.'

'You're better than that. You're real.'

Thea hesitated as she peered through the gap in the wooden gate into the walled gardens. 'I'm not sure we should disturb them.'

Shaun smiled as he followed Thea's line of sight. 'At last! I was beginning to think Sam wouldn't tell her how he felt.'

'I could say the same about Tina. Sam is so far from her usual type. Thank goodness.'

'Sam did ask me to find him before we went back to the AA though.'

'Oh, so Sam knows what's going on, does he?' Thea's eyebrows rose. 'Well! So much for me being in charge.'

Shaun stuck his tongue out at her as he pushed open the door as noisily as he could so that the human occupants of the garden were warned of their approaching presence.

Deliberately keeping a few paces behind the men as they left the walled garden and headed towards the part of the garden where the woods merge into the grass, Thea whispered, 'Are you two properly together now?'

'Yes.' Tina couldn't stop the beam that spread across her face. 'It's not going to be easy, but it is going to be worth it.'

'Did he tell you why he can't go inside?'

'He did.'

'Good.' Not wanting to put Tina in a position where she might have to break a confidence, she didn't ask more questions, but covertly pointed towards the men in front of them. 'Have you any idea what they are up to, beyond the fact that they've organised for a geophysics scan of the grounds?'

'Well, there's only one reason they'd want one of those, isn't there?'

Thea agreed, 'Because they think there's something to find under the ground archaeology wise and...'

Both women came to the same conclusion at the same time.

'The Trust!' Thea spoke before Tina, who was nodding manically. 'That's why they sold! If there's even a sniff of an expensive excavation to pay for, it would eat up all their funds.'

'Especially after that financial cock-up ate into the funds all that time back. I wondered why Mill Grange was the house that the Trust chose to sell when there are other houses less accessible for public visits that they could sell. This is finally starting to make sense.' Tina scooped her loose hair up into a loose bun, in a manner that showed she meant business. 'But they'd need a reason to scan. Geophysics is expensive; you can't just do it on a whim, even if you're friends with a TV archaeologist.'

'Which means Shaun found something on one of his walks.'

The girls ran towards the van.

The pot shard was small. Even with Thea's practised eye, she was sure she'd have missed it in the undergrowth. Shaun however, with his more recent experience – and, as it turned out, his suspicion there was something here to find in the first place – hadn't missed it.

'And you've just found one?' Thea held it in the middle of her open palm and traced the shape with a fingertip.

'So far.' He watched as Tina and Sam stared at what looked like a square-ish stone. 'It was here. Exactly here.'

Thea crouched to where Shaun had stuck a tent peg he'd borrowed from Sam, at the very edge of the hinterland between the sloping lawn and the path between the woods and garden. 'How much can Andy and Ajay do before someone at *Landscape Treasures* starts asking questions about budgets?'

'Only four square metres.'

Thea traced a rough shape in the air with a finger. 'Then, if you agree, I think they should use this as the right edge and run north and east.'

Shaun pulled out his phone and showed Thea a text he'd sent Ajay a few days earlier. It said "North and East from find. As much as budget will allow."

'You know what it is, don't you?' Shaun asked.

'Oh yes.' Thea stroked it reverently. 'And so do you.'

'Well, we don't.' Tina and Sam had linked hands as they stared at the recently washed shard.

'It's Roman. Part of a mortarium to be precise.'

Forty-Three

'We'll have the results in about three hours. Ajay promised television time turnaround.'

The four friends sat around one of the three picnic tables Derek and Bill had made for the garden. They were making serious headway into one of Tina's lemon cakes. The girls both had clipboards in front of them. Tina was making a note of everything left to do for the Open Day in thirty-six hours' time. Thea was drawing the pot shard which sat in the middle of the table, while Shaun took out his tape measure and calculated how big it would have been when it was intact.

Sam stroked the top of the pot fragment. 'What is a mortarium anyway?'

'The bowl part of a Roman pestle and mortar.' Thea picked it up so Sam could see the underside. 'If you feel here, it's got a rough, gritty texture. That was part of the lower bowl. It had a deliberately pitted surface to help grind herbs, or whatever else needed pounding into a paste or powder.'

'And you can tell that from one tiny piece of pot?'

'Sure.' Thea turned to Shaun, who had finished calculating the measurements of the shard, looking at him expectantly.

'It had a diameter of twenty centimetres I'd say.'

'That would be in line with the style and size of such pots at the middle to the end of the Romano-British period.' Thea was trying not to get excited. 'And unless I'm very much mistaken – which I might be of course – this is from Gloucester.'

Shaun's head snapped up. 'You think so?'

'A hunch, no more.'

'Rubbish, this is your speciality. Gloucester?'

'I think so. That makes it from about AD 55-90. It's rare to find it so far to the south west, but to be honest it's unusual to find Roman stuff in this region anyway.' Thea glanced towards where Shaun had found it. 'And there was no sign of any other pieces?'

'No. I'd love to have found a piece of flange or rim or something, just to confirm its origins.'

'As I said, I can't be certain, but the material is the right sort of pale red-brown, and has—' Thea lifted the shard up to the sunlight '—fine inclusions of quartz sand and limestone. The underside also has a hint of the traditional thin cream or white slip used to finish such pots in the Gloucester area.'

Tina smiled across the table. 'Look at you two all historied up!'

'I hadn't realised how much I missed this bit.' Thea blushed happily as she picked the four-centimetre-wide piece of pottery up. 'The chance to investigate something that would have formed an everyday part of a normal human beings life thousands of years ago is so special.'

Not wanting to spoil Thea's mood, but knowing he had no choice, Shaun asked, 'Will you tell Malcolm about finding this?'

'I suspect he knows, or at least suspects.'

Tina nodded. 'It's only a theory, but we think he must have got wind of a possible site under the grounds. And with Exmoor being on the very outer edge of Roman success in Britain, there is little chance of any such site not being investigated.'

Sam was confused. 'Why is that a bad thing? They're a historical trust, aren't they?'

'They are.' Tina laid down her pen. 'But excavations cost money.'

'Would the trust have to pay? Surely the people doing the dig pay for it?'

'Each case is different. In this instance I imagine it isn't so much the costs involved in the excavation itself, but the fact that it would have held up the opening of Mill Grange. Think about it in terms of a farmer and his field. If a Roman villa is found in a farmer's field and is declared of special interest and should be excavated, the farmer isn't paying for the dig, but he does lose that field's yield and profits for the length of the excavation, potentially forever.'

'So Malcolm and his team would lose the income from the visitors they predicted?' Sam frowned. 'But if I was them, I'd be thrilled. A rare Roman site on the grounds of a beautiful Victorian manor. Surely that's two attractions in one to draw the crowds?'

'If red tape, health and safety and all the other legal requirements that go with that sort of historical site weren't an issue, I'd agree with you. But it isn't that simple, sadly. It ought to be, but it's not.'

'That's daft.'

'Modern life often is.' Tina added, 'In this case it's academic anyway. As the Trust was in financial difficulties anyway, they had to dispose of a property to keep afloat. Far better, in their eyes, to lose one that will cost more than expected to open to the public now, even though it would eventually earn them more income, than to lose one of the less accessible properties that's already up and running.'

'It seems dishonest that they've sold the house and grounds, and not told the owner what might be lurking beneath.' Thea sighed.

'I suppose they might have told them, but I doubt it.' Tina considered her employers. 'Since the extent of the money worries has become apparent, Malcolm and Grant have become less history lovers and more bank managers.'

'Fear of losing your job can do that to you.' Thea gave the pot shard one last stroke. 'Talking of which, I'm going to lose this one with dignity and style.' Accompanied by approving nods from her friends, Thea stood up. 'As much as I've enjoyed my trip into the more distant past, I ought to pull myself together and focus on all things Victorian by finishing emptying the scullery and my attic room.'

'Don't you want to wait for the results from geofizz?'

'Of course, but I don't have time to wait doing nothing.' Thea passed her drawing to Shaun. 'You go and check on them. Oh, and not a word to any of the others. Especially Mabel. She'd be so delighted that, whether we find anything or not, it would be all around Upwich in less than half an hour.'

Shaun smiled. 'Agreed. I think we'll find something though.'

'Me too.' Thea gazed across the gardens. 'Now I've studied the ground with an eye to the possibility, I'm inclined to agree.'

'A villa?' Sam asked.

'Unlikely. More likely a temporary camp or even…' Thea paused. 'No, let's not tempt fate.'

'You think you know what it is, don't you?' Shaun's eyes shone. 'I really need you on my team if you can work out what's beneath the earth from the lumps and bumps alone. It'll save us a fortune in geofizz scanning.'

'I'm wishful thinking.' Thea picked up Tina's list. 'All we have is one pot shard, some lumps and bumps in the ground and a suspicion that we've worked out why the Trust chose Mill Grange as their sacrificial lamb. We could be whistling in the wind.'

Shaun unhooked his long legs from the confines of beneath the picnic table. 'I'll go and check how the lads are getting on. I've got them tucked away in Moira's backroom. Only place with a good enough signal around here for them to work.'

'Was she okay with you hiding more people there?'

'She's a wonderful woman, that Moira. Thinks she's hiding more celebrities.'

'Which she sort of is.' Tina smiled.

Shaun kissed Thea's cheek. 'I'll be back as soon as I have news.'

Since the smoke damage from the fire had dented her already meagre clothing collection, it didn't take long for Thea to stuff her few garments into the large rucksack that stood, propped in the corner of her attic room. A few of her things still littered Shaun's borrowed bedroom, but otherwise, it had taken a depressingly short amount of time to tidy and pack away the evidence of her life for the past few months.

Standing at the window, Thea studied the view, enjoying the vista of the garden merging into the woods while she could. One more night in Mill Grange.

Shaun would want her to spend it in his room with him. She'd like that too, but Thea had an almost childlike urge to spend her last night where she'd spent her first one. Where she'd crouched frightened while the nightjar had woken her in alarm, where she'd lain worrying and wondering about what John would do next, where she'd spent so many hours planning how to make Mill Grange the best visitor attraction she possibly could. Where she'd wondered if Shaun really liked her or if he was just after a fling; at least the latter was something she was certain of.

She'd come to Mill Grange single, a little lonely, and with a man who refused to leave their brief moment of shared past alone. Now she had the chance of a future with an amazing person who seemed to like her as much as she liked him.

It was too early to think beyond like. Yet the other four-letter word beginning with 'l' and ending in 'e' had almost formed on her lips when they'd been together a few times.

But what about Mill Grange?

'Coming here wasn't pointless.' She spoke the words boldly, trying to edge away the lingering doubts that crowded her head. 'The house looks great and the day after tomorrow we can show off what Mabel and the others have achieved.'

The pheasant she'd been addressing as it crossed the lawn far below did not appear impressed by her claim.

'We've sold fifty tickets, and with the promise of one of Sybil's cream teas, Moira's cider tent and Bill's mate's hog roast, even old Alf from the café can't fail to approve of our efforts on Upwich's behalf.'

But you burnt down the mill.

The thought arrived from where it had been lurking at the back of her head and refused to leave. *It isn't going to matter how well tomorrow goes, I'll always be the girl who dropped the candle.*

Determined to move her mind forward, Thea looked across to where Shaun had found the pot shard. Despite the trees and flowerbeds, her aerial view reinforced her view that there probably was something under the soil. But whether it was what she hoped it was, or whether it was a disused Victorian rabbit warren, would have to wait to be seen.

'Someone could have dropped the pot shard. They could have had it in their pocket, after picking it up somewhere else.'

She knew this was unlikely too. But not impossible.

'Concentrate on the here and now. Think Open Day. Then think what comes next.' Thea piled her small tower of novels up on the desk. 'And if they do find a Roman site, so what? I'm nothing to do with this place after 21st July. It'll be the new owner's problem.' Thea froze. 'We could leak the information. If the new owner finds out they have a possible ancient monument in their garden, especially one of significance, they might pull out of the sale.'

The pheasant tilted its head in Thea's direction, as if she had finally said something of interest.

'Anyone who has purchased Mill Grange to get away from it all is hardly going to want a load of archaeologists and sightseers traipsing around their garden.'

Forty-Four

'Did you know that bit of pot was from a mortarium?' Tina passed Sam another handful of grain for the chickens. 'Once I held it, I knew it was Roman, and I could have guessed it was a bit of mortaria because they are the most distinctive pieces of Roman pot beyond the bright orange Samian ware, but beyond that my knowledge ends.'

'If I'd seen it, I'd have assumed it was a bit of masonry from the house or just some random stone.'

'Which is just as well. All that extra training Thea and Shaun did would have been wasted if any Tom, Dick or Sam could spot the difference.' Tina smiled. 'Thea did archaeology because she'd been burning to do it all her life. It was her passion from a young age. I did it because I wanted a degree, but I didn't know which one to choose. Archaeology is a good one to pick in those circumstances. You get to learn computing, surveying, excavating, history, geology, architecture, construction techniques, how to excavate and field walk and how to develop patience. Lots of patience.'

Sam tucked his ponytail into the back of his jumper. 'Can I ask a rookie question?'

'Go for it.'

'What does geophysics actually do?'

'Sorry, I thought you knew from watching the show.'

'Television doesn't play a big part in my life.'

'Of course, I didn't think.' Tina continued awkwardly, 'It's a special underground survey using radio waves, so you can see anything that's buried without actually having to dig. The boys will put all the data into a computer to create a plan of what's underneath the garden.'

'And from that, Thea and Shaun will work out what the shapes revealed could once have been?'

'Yep. Sometimes it's obvious, especially if it's a rectangular villa or something. Other times, it's very much harder. Just random marks in the soil. This will be tricky I suspect, as only a tiny fraction of ground has been surveyed and the ground has been reworked in different ways in the past.'

'But we could see something amazing.' Sam was suddenly serious. 'You get to be outside a lot, don't you? As an archaeologist I mean.'

'Yes, although the lion's share of time is spent writing and analysing data.'

'Could you do that outside?'

Tina tilted her head to one side in a gesture not unlike Gertrude's when she was sizing up the competition for Tony Stark's affections. 'You're serious, aren't you? You're thinking about training to be an archaeologist?'

'It's always fascinated me, although I'm not sure I'd be any good at it.'

'I could help.' Tina slipped an arm through his as they

left the chickens to their own devices and headed towards Sam's tent. 'I'm not as skilled as the others, but I know the ropes. And it's not hard to get a job on a dig. Learning via experience is the best way.'

Sam pulled her closer as they walked along. 'I think I'd like that.'

'I should tell you that the pay varies from lousy to non-existent. Most new diggers are volunteers.'

'Work experience is always badly paid, or not paid at all, whatever you do.'

'That's true.' Tina felt a tug at her heart. 'Will you ask Shaun for a place on his team?'

'I don't think he'd want a complete rookie, not when the telly cameras are all over the place. I'd be too afraid of messing up. Anyway—' he lifted up Tina's chin and stared into her eyes '—I don't want to leave Exmoor now I've found you.'

The level of relief Tina felt took her by surprise. 'I'm so glad you said that,' she said, kissing him before pulling away, 'but no way am I going to stop you if you need to go away to train. This could be the perfect job for your rehabilitation.'

Hugging her close, Sam felt tears prickle in his eyes that he badly didn't want to shed. 'I contemplated being a gardener. I know a lot about plants and stuff because my grandfather was a gardener, but although it's outside whatever the weather, there's no real challenge to it. No surprises.'

'Is that why you didn't want the greenhouse to come down? You could picture it as if your granddad might have got it.'

'That and the fact it's stunning. All those tiny panes of glass.'

'Well, let's hope the new owner feels the same.'

Thea's room was as tidy as it could be. She went into Shaun's bedroom and retrieved her toothbrush and the few other bits she'd left there. Hoping he wouldn't be offended that she wanted to spend the last night alone, she found herself making his bed and tidying up his pile of jumpers. They smelt of wool, deodorant and Shaun.

Inhaling his scent, she stroked the pillows on the bed and pulled up the linen. She was almost at the door again, when Thea doubled back. Taking a piece of paper from her pad, she sat down and started to write.

'Any word from Shaun?'

Sam called into the manor from the back doorstep as he saw Thea walking in his direction.

'Not yet,' said Thea, who was carrying a fold-up chair under each arm. 'Just let me dump these in the laundry so Diane has something to sit on when she's giving tours downstairs. Then we'll go to Moira's. Tina around?'

'In the scullery, disconnecting the computers.'

Thea failed to keep defeat from her voice. 'It feels like we're stripping ourselves from the place, doesn't it?'

'A bit.' Sam hovered at the threshold, his feet butting up to the point that could take him inside, but not crossing it. 'What will you do next?'

'Shaun has offered me a place on his team. Off camera. I hope.'

'That's fantastic, but why off camera? I imagined he'd want you on camera. You're very photogenic and highly knowledgeable.'

Thea felt her habitual pinking starting in the face of a compliment. 'I don't really want to be on screen. Look what happened last time.'

'John's gone. I don't think he'll be back.'

Thea pushed back her shoulders. 'I'm sure you're right. I'll round up Tina and we'll see you outside the pub.'

'The idea keeps going around and round in my head, but I can't bring myself to do it.'

Thea had explained her thought that, if the new owner discovered about the possible Roman remains, they might pull out of the sale, and then Mill Grange wouldn't be sold.

'Of course you couldn't. You're a nice person.' Tina hesitated. 'It's a good idea though. Isn't having scruples a pain?'

'John wouldn't have hesitated. He'd have seen leaking the news as heroic and a way to prove he loved me.'

'Which is another reason for us not to do it.' Tina hooked her bag higher up her shoulder as they walked towards the village. 'Anything John Sommers might do, I don't want any part of.'

Thea sped up her footsteps. 'I can't wait to find out what Ajay and Andy have discovered. If they've discovered anything, that is.'

Shaun, Ajay, Andy and Sam were in Moira's back garden, huddled around a laptop perched on a patio table. Just one glance at Shaun's face told Thea they'd found something.

'Tell me?' She sat next to Shaun as Ajay swivelled the laptop into the best position for everyone to see.

'This here—' he pointed to a grainy picture that appeared to be a lot of different grey dots '—is the area we surveyed. As you can see it is out of focus at this range. We can only get it all on the screen at this distance, even though it was only a tiny area. Once we've had a bit more time, we can compress it and—'

Tina interrupted, 'Can you just tell us what we're looking at?'

Relieved that her friend had got straight to the point, Thea leant forward, as if being closer to the evidence would speed up the results.

Ajay grinned. 'No problem.'

Pressing a few buttons, he started a mini film show which slowly increased the resolution of the picture on the page. Shaun gripped Thea's hand as they watched. No one dared speak as they watched the dots forming into a defined and unmistakable right angle.

'A wall? The corner of a wall?' Sam looked hopefully at the archaeologists.

Thea's gaze remained on the screen. 'Okay, if we go on the assumption that this particular group of Roman builders stuck to roughly the same design as others in the area, then I think we can guess at the corner of the structure being about here.' Thea pointed to a spot on the screen. 'Can you focus in on this area please?'

Ajay obliged as Shaun spoke to Thea. 'Your hunch wasn't wishful thinking, was it?'

She didn't answer. Her heart was thudding hard in her chest. Eventually, after staring at the semi-blurred image for a long time, Thea said, 'We need more surveys. Very soon. Tomorrow, in fact.'

Shaun and Andy were talking logistics in seconds, but Sam raised a cautionary hand. 'I hate to rain on your parade, but we can't. The marquees are going up soon. Open Day, remember?' When no one answered, he added, 'What do you guys think we're staring at anyway?'

Andy got up. 'Whatever chat you guys are about to have, I think it's going to require beer. I'll get them in.'

Ajay joined his friend. 'I'll help. I also think we'd better see if Moira has room for us to stay over. But I've got to tell you, Shaun mate, the land out there has been churned over and dug into different styled gardens for generations. The chances of us finding anything as clear as this image, beyond the patch surveyed, is next to non-existent.'

Andy agreed, 'Not only that, but we have to be on the road by ten tomorrow morning. If you do want a few extra patches doing, we need to plan the markers out tonight and survey at six in the morning.'

Thea was thoughtful. 'Do you think it could be all done and hidden away before the volunteers arrive? I'd put money on Mabel at least being here by seven.'

'Not a hope.'

'Then I think we should leave it.'

'But Thea…'

'I know what you're going to say, Shaun. This is important. Really important, but so is the Open Day. Mabel, Derek and the others have worked so hard. The people of Upwich are looking forward to it and I've let them down enough already. These remains have been hidden for long enough to survive two more days.'

Wishing her friend wasn't right, but knowing she was, Tina agreed. 'And if we did have more results, what would it matter? The house is sold. Unless they employ a surveyor who advises against the sale, the remains aren't the Trust's to make a decision over after the 21st. And they certainly aren't ours.'

Feeling as if someone had burst his bubble, Shaun said, 'I suppose so. Thanks though, boys. Let's get that beer and some of Moira's finest pub grub.'

After the men had gone in search of sustenance, Tina noticed Thea's downcast face. 'Come on, there's still lots to celebrate. Your new job and the fact that the house is so well restored despite everything, not to mention our lovely new relationships.'

Biting back her frustration over the future of the house, Thea asked, 'You and Sam okay?'

'We are. I wish I'd listened to you sooner.'

'That's what I keep telling everyone.'

Shaun unfolded the speech he'd been working on and sat on the edge of his bed. He hadn't expected to find it made for him, and he smiled at the thought of Thea using time she didn't have to make sure they were comfortable. She'd be up soon. He tried not to think about that or he'd never rehearse his speech.

The meal in the pub had been perfect. Thea got on well with the AA boys and was going to fit into the *Landscape Treasures* team perfectly. Despite their disappointment about finding a new treasure but not being able to do anything about exploring it, they still had lots to look forward to. He intended for him and Thea to start celebrating as soon as she joined him.

He was about to start reading his speech again when his eyes fell on a piece of paper tucked between the sheets and his pillow.

I'm writing this in case life takes over and I don't have the chance to tell you in person that I'm glad I found you – or that you found me.

I hope you will forgive me for not sleeping in here with you tonight. This is our last night at Mill Grange and I want to spend it in my little attic room. I can't really explain why because I'm not sure I know the reason… but it isn't because I don't want to be with you. It's just something I need to do. Hope you can understand that. Thea xxx

Shaun sighed. 'I thought we had something to celebrate. Maybe not.'

Forty-Five

Thea stared up at the ceiling. Now she was in bed, alone, she wasn't sure why she'd needed to be in her attic room so badly.

After an hour of tossing and turning, she pulled a jumper on over her pyjamas and got out of bed. Padding along the corridor and down the stairs, she hoped Shaun was still awake. She needed to talk to him about what she suspected they'd found in the garden.

Knocking lightly, hoping he wouldn't mind her contrary arrival, Thea poked her head around the door.

Shaun wasn't in bed, but was seated at the little desk, the printed-out plans from Ajay spread in front of him.

'What do you want?'

Shaken by his less than friendly greeting, Thea backed away. 'I'm sorry, I… I couldn't sleep. Suddenly I wondered why the hell I'd needed to be in that room on my own so badly and… I'm sorry.'

Shaun's expression remained unreadable. 'We walked

home together and you zipped off to your room so fast I thought you were desperate for the loo or wanted to get a warmer jumper or something. You never said a word about wanting to be on your own, even though you had the chance. Then I found that bloody note.'

'I didn't mean to offend you, I just thought—'

'No, you didn't. You didn't think at all, Thea. Did it cross your mind that this is our last night here? In this place, where we got together for the first time?'

'I—'

'No, it didn't. You just wanted to go back to a time before us. A time when you could stay safe in the knowledge of being all sorry for yourself over John, and worried about Mill Grange and nothing else. Have you any idea how that made me feel?'

Forcing herself to stand her ground, and not be the Thea of old, who would have either apologised or run away or both, she said, 'Actually I do. I made a mistake with that note and with not talking to you about it first. I was about to apologise to you, and I still will if you'll let me.'

'Go on.'

She could see Shaun was mellowing already, and it suddenly dawned on her that this was a man as insecure as she was when it came to relationships.

'When I was in the attic packing away all my stuff earlier today, it felt right to end my journey at Mill Grange where it began. It wasn't a case of ignoring all that's happened, but of coming full circle in an attempt to let go. But once I was in bed, I couldn't settle. Not just because of everything that happened today, but because I realised I didn't want to work it out or think about it on my own. I wanted to share it with you. Is that okay, or should I go back upstairs?'

Shaun got up from his desk. 'I was trying to learn my speech for the opening ceremony.'

'Right.' Thea wasn't sure what else to say.

They stood, three metres apart, neither moving, but neither wanting to leave or order the other to go.

Eventually, Thea said. 'I think we found a Roman fortlet today. Maybe even a fort.'

The light that she'd seen shine in Shaun's eyes earlier came back. 'That's what I thought. Fortlet, rather than full-blown fort.'

'If it is, then it's situated in the perfect place to keep control of where the two rivers join and the terrain surrounding it. Take away the trees that are here now, then from the vantage point of the hill, you could see for miles.'

Their discomfort and hurt pride was forgotten in the face of the possibilities offered by the past. Thea sat at the desk, pulling Shaun's printed geophysics plans towards her. 'So the Romans established a legionary fortress at Exeter around AD 55. That base had a support network of smaller forts manned by a garrison of around 10,000 men spread across the surrounding geography.'

'We're a long way from Exeter here.'

'We are yes, but Exmoor did have some outlying posts. To date we know that there are the remains of two fortlets at Old Burrow and Martinhoe. The second of those overtook the first after it fell out of use. Neither was very big; each held about sixty men.'

Shaun pulled a map out of his rucksack and opened it

out, finding where Old Burrow was marked with his thumb. 'Weren't Old Burrow, and then Martinhoe built to keep the Bristol Channel under surveillance between about AD 55 and 75? Presumably they'd have been used to keep up communication with the Roman fleet which waited in the Silures of unconquered South Wales at the time.'

'That would make sense.' Thea added her own thumb to the map. 'And then there's a larger fort here, at Rainsbury.' She tapped an area of Exmoor only a few miles away. 'That's why I'm sure this is a fortlet, not a fort. We're too close to Rainsbury. There's no need for anything other than a holding fort or territory marker here.'

'Like a tomcat peeing on his land.' Picking Thea up and tucking her onto his lap so they could study the map together, Shaun confessed, 'I'm not going to be able to let this go. New owner or not, this is important.'

'I know. Exmoor is one of the few places with Roman occupation this far south west. They usually stuck to earthworks and used little in the way of brick and wood like they did with the more permanent structures; they are so hard to find.'

'But there were definitely bricks or stonework coming through in the geofizz.'

'Exactly.' Thea beamed up at Shaun, her excitement for their potential find helping kill off her stupidity in hurting his feelings by staying away from him on their final night at the manor. 'Loads of such places could be hidden under buildings like Mill Grange. After all, the location is sought after for obvious reasons. The pleasure of the view for a start. Why would we imagine that just one generation wanted to use it for strategic or visual advantages?'

Shaun, who'd managed to concentrate on the map alone until he'd pulled Thea onto his lap, gave a ragged grunt of agreement, before abandoning his struggle with desire and allowing his eyes to fall on Thea's cleavage. 'At the risk of being told off, I think I prefer my current view.'

'Over the discovery of the archaeological find of the year?' Thea lifted his chin so that his eyes met hers.

'Oh yes.' Shaun's voice became husky. 'I think it only fair to tell you that, if you don't intend to stay the night you should leave now. I won't follow you, and I'll understand you're leaving as we have a big day tomorrow and the next day. We'll need our sleep so…'

Thea silenced him with a kiss. 'Who needs sleep?'

Forty-Six

A jay and Andy shamelessly flirted with Mabel and Diane as they washed, dried and buffed up a vast supply of cups and saucers and glasses. They were lining them up on the kitchen table as Thea and Shaun came into the kitchen rather later than they'd planned the following morning.

'Thea, my dear!' Mabel beamed as Shaun made a beeline for some cups of coffee. 'Why didn't you say we had more television personalities on the way?'

'Because I didn't know. It was a surprise for all of us.'

'We were just passing.' Andy winked at Diane.

Ajay flapped his drying up cloth playfully in Mabel's direction. 'And we're hardly personalities, lovely Mabel. More geeks with techno toys.'

'Rubbish.' Mabel patted her hair in a girlish way. 'You two find everything. Anyone who watches *Landscape Treasures* knows that.'

Andy polished a glass so hard with his cloth it squeaked.

'Did you hear that, boss? We should have our own spin-off show I reckon.'

'Is that right?' Shaun grinned at the rows of empty vessels his colleagues had got ready to be taken out to Sybil's marquee. 'I didn't expect to see these two so early in the morning.' He turned to Mabel and Diane. 'Normally the AA only surface once the digging has been done.'

'Cheek!' Ajay stuck his tongue out.

'Are you lot always this childish?' Thea rolled her eyes at Mabel, but her smile was wide.

'Yep. Growing up is optional. We opted out.' Shaun lifted the kettle in a gesture to the others to see if anyone else wanted a drink. 'How's it going outside? I saw from the bedroom window that the marquees have already arrived.'

'Been non-stop since seven.' Mabel spoke making it very clear she had been wondering why Thea hadn't been there to supervise their arrival.

'That's excellent.' Thea, not rising to Mabel's bait, and certainly not wanting to share the fact that it had taken a great deal of effort on her and Shaun's behalf to leave the comfort of their blanket cocoon, said, 'I'm going out to them now. I think a few large slices of Tina's lemon cake would go some way to keep their strength up, don't you?'

Thea couldn't wipe the joy from her face. She felt as if her skin was glowing and that it must be plain to everyone who saw her how happy she was, and exactly why she hadn't had much sleep last night.

Crossing the gardens to where Bill and his friends were

discussing the number of poles and guide ropes required for the task in hand, Thea called out to Tina and Sam who were looking equally content as they emerged from the walled garden, a bag of chicken feed in hand.

'Morning you two. Gertrude and Mr Stark behaving this morning?'

'So far.' Tina grinned. 'Although I think that Gertrude has a rival for his affections. Betty had definitely got her eye on Tony this morning.'

'Which one is Betty?' Thea felt a sudden rush of sadness. She'd been so excited about getting the chickens to Mill Grange, and now she couldn't even remember all their names.

'The tiny one with the extra fluffy feathers.' Sam was watching the men across the gardens. 'I ought to go and see if they need a hand. Shall I deliver the cake, Thea? I'm guessing it's for them?'

'Thank you. Yes, it is.'

Taking the plates of sliced cake, Sam asked, 'Did you and Shaun come up with any ideas as to what our hidden treasure might be?'

'We did.' Thea lowered her voice for fear of the sound carrying across the garden. 'I need to do some more research before I'm sure. It's so sad to think it might remain covered and officially undiscovered.'

Sam nodded. 'Shaun could use his influence on the new owners perhaps? Approach them once they are settled in with a mind to suggesting a *Landscape Treasures* episode to uncover the site?'

'It crossed his mind, but there are so many factors to consider, not least that the schedule for the next series to be filmed is already sorted, so it would be another twelve months before he could even consider approaching them with questions in that direction.'

'Until then it's a secret between us four, yes?' Sam gave Tina a quick kiss on the cheek and strode off across the lawns.

Tina watched Sam tuck his ponytail out of harm's way as he walked away. 'I am going to have to get him to cut that thing off. God knows why he has it when he spends his whole time shoving it down the back of his T-shirt so it doesn't get in the way.'

'Maybe you should lop it off in the night?' Thea regarded her friend with an expression that plainly asked if she'd slept with Sam last night.

Tina poked her in the ribs, 'No I didn't. I spent a pleasant evening with him in his tent and then I went to bed in the manor like a good girl. You and Shaun did though, didn't you, you saucy minx!'

'That obvious?' Thea flushed, looking around her in case anyone else was in earshot.

'Only because I've known you a long time.' Tina smiled. 'You do look a bit tired though, hun, although no one is going to question that in the circumstances. Extra strong coffee for you today, I think.'

'When Sybil is ready for her coffee-making equipment to be tested later, I'll be first in the queue.'

Fresh air, the activity around her and lack of sleep seemed to be catching up on Thea all in one go, and it still wasn't even half past eight in the morning. Looking up at the manor, watching the early sun catching the flecks of granite in the stonework, Thea saw Mabel gathering the volunteers by the main doors, her arms waving all over the place.

Tina frowned. 'Whatever is Mabel doing? It looks like she's giving them all a telling off.'

Thea shook her head as she approached the small group. 'I suspect that she is explaining the route of the guided tour.'

'I thought you were doing the tours?'

'So did I.' Thea started to walk faster. 'I think it's time to be a grown up. Could you be a star and go and fetch me a clipboard and some paper?'

'Which one?'

'It doesn't matter. They all have lists on a mile long, and every single thing on them needs doing before tomorrow.'

July 20th

'How many cups and saucers did you say we had?'

Shaun gently took hold of Thea's hands and prised the clipboard out of her grip. 'We have done everything that it is humanly possible to do today. Time to stop worrying about cups and saucers.'

'Do you think Mabel minded not being the one who's going to do the guided tours?'

'Not now you've appointed her chief guest greeter.'

'Right.' Thea sat down with a thump on the sofa under the drawing room's bay window, before leaping up again with a jolt as the tiny part of her brain that was still awake reminded her that Diane had spent ages brushing and straightening all the furniture and she wasn't supposed to ruin it.

'Come on.' Shaun took her hand and led her outside.

'Where are we going?' Thea pointed to the manor. 'We're not done yet.'

'Thea, everyone else went home hours ago. It's ten o'clock at night. You have barely eaten or stopped moving since we got up this morning after, need I remind you, a fantastic night - but one that held little in the way of rest. You are going to bed now.'

'But I haven't checked to make sure that the attics are tidy.'

'Tina did that.'

'What about the scullery? Are the old iron pots and pans arranged as if they're drying after a wash?'

'Diane did that.'

'Oh.' Thea's stomach gave a rumble worthy of a hungry elephant.

'Should we just—'

'No.' Placing a firm arm around her shoulders, Shaun steered Thea towards the passenger seat of his car and buckled her in place before climbing into the driver's seat. 'Thea, you are exhausted. There is nothing else you can do tonight. And if you tried, it would go wrong.'

'But—'

Shaun leant over and kissed Thea's cheek. 'But nothing. We're going to the hotel now and then we're going to order a light supper and sleep. And before you ask, no I didn't order two rooms even though I promised I would. I guessed you'd be beyond knackered tonight and need cuddling to sleep.'

Thea opened her mouth to object, but closed it again very quickly, thanking him as she relaxed back against the seat.

She hadn't intended to fall asleep on the journey to Taunton.

Shaken gently awake by Shaun, Thea blinked into the closing night.

'Come on, love, I've booked us in and room service is rustling up a couple of toasted sandwiches. I'm afraid we're too late to use the restaurant.'

Surprisingly refreshed after her nap, Thea climbed out of the car and grabbed her bag from the boot. 'It looks lovely. Where are we?'

'Outskirts of Taunton. The Blackdown Hotel. In the morning, when it's light, you'll be able to see the Blackdown Hills out of the bedroom window.'

As Shaun let out a lion's roar of a yawn, Thea took his arm. 'Come on, I'm not the only one who had no sleep and worked like stink all day.'

Forty-Seven

Dreams of Roman forts, cream teas and Mabel getting cross with people for sitting on the beds merged with visions of the anonymous new owner bulldozing the house down to build a multi-storey car park.

As a nightmare image of six feet of concrete being poured over the area where she suspected a Roman fortlet to be hidden, Thea sat bolt upright in bed.

'You okay?' Shaun rolled over, pulling Thea to his side.

'The gardens are listed along with the house, aren't they?'

'You know they are.' He stroked her hair from her face. 'What's up?'

'What if the new owner destroys the garden or redesigns it in such a way that the fort is destroyed before we know if it really is a fort?'

'They won't. Not straight away anyway. They'll have enough to do once they move in just getting the house how they want it.'

'But the house is perfect. We've made it lovely.'

'We have, but we've made it into the perfect place to view life in the past, not as a comfortable place to live in the here and now.' Shaun gave Thea a smile. 'What if we get up and grab a hearty breakfast and go and make today the best Open Day of all time?'

'What time is it?'

'Six.'

'Six!' Thea jumped out of bed and ran for the shower. 'I wanted to be *there* by six. If we aren't there before Mabel then goodness knows what trouble her good intentions will have caused.'

Sybil gave Thea a hug; her face was alight with pleasure as she gestured to the bustling tent.

Every one of the foldable tables and chairs was occupied with people tucking into cream teas and sipping Bucks Fizz, tea or coffee. The atmosphere was calm and cheerful, with a happy hum of conversation. As Thea listened she could hear nothing but praise of the manor, the day, and the brilliant sunshine which had blessed them with its presence.

'The marquees were such a great idea,' Sybil said effusively as she forced a cup of coffee into Thea's hands, despite her protests that she didn't have time to drink it. 'It was a crying shame about the mill, but I can't help thinking this is better, having all the crafts and so forth on site in the gardens. More chance of everyone visiting them. After all, it takes effort to walk to the mill, and why would anyone want to do that when the gardens are so lush?'

Thea agreed as she saw old Alf talking in animated fashion to Bill. Sybil's most regular customer was clearly enjoying his rare change of tea-supping scenery. 'I'm about to do the rounds to make sure everyone is okay in the craft tents.'

'Well, I've taken them all top-ups of tea and cake because they've all been too busy to come and collect their own. So that's got to be good.'

Thea checked her watch. 'Thanks, Sybil. Forgive me, I must dash, I want to see everyone before I go back to the next round of guided tours this afternoon.'

'No problem.' Sybil returned to her tea delivery duties, calling, 'Don't forget to eat,' over her shoulder.

Having failed to convince Sybil that she should have a marquee to sell her felt ware from, Sybil had instead put them in contact with a fabulous enameller. Hannah had turned up bright and early with a portable kiln, a positive attitude and a huge trolley containing a vast collection of copper shapes, crushed glass and all sorts of other bits and bobs that Thea was dying to play with.

There was no chance of that, even if Thea hadn't been due back in the house. All four of Hannah's workshop seats, where visitors were having their first go at enamelling, were taken. A small queue had formed of people waiting for a go at making pendants, while Hannah's husband was doing a brisk trade in selling necklaces, key fobs and brooches that his wife had made earlier.

Exchanging a brief thumbs up with Hannah, Thea moved on to the spinner, who was deep in animated discussion with a group that Thea recognised as WI friends of Mabel's. Leaving them to it, she went into the knitter's tent. As soon as she ducked under the canvas door, Thea's nostrils were assailed with a waft of sheep wool and lanolin. Taking a minute to inhale the heady scent and enjoy the bustle around her, Thea meandered back outside and strode through the sunshine, muttering her thanks to Minerva as she went.

According to Sam, as he worked with Mabel on the door, they had already sold three times the original fifty presold tickets, and even though it was gone three o'clock, they were still admitting visitors.

Moving between the guests, Thea speculated who the new owner might be. Suddenly everyone was a potential candidate as the new owner of Mill Grange.

I hope they love this place as much as I do.

Her eyes drifted over to where the geophysics team had done their secret survey. A man in a suit was standing there on his own, most definitely apart from everyone else. Thea shivered as she forced her feet to move on towards the house and her duties there, rather than going to find out what he was doing.

As she reached the back door to pick up her notes for the tour due to start in five minutes, she saw the furniture expert Richard chatting to Shaun and Ajay.

'Hi Richard, I'm glad you could make it.' Thea gave him a brave smile as she asked Shaun if she could have a quick word before she did the tour.

Coming to one side, Shaun beamed, 'It's going so well. I'm so proud of you!'

'There's a man in a suit sniffing around the you-know-what.'

'Really?' Shaun's sunny complexion darkened. 'Do you want to go and ask him what he's doing?'

'I can't, I've got to do the last tour now.'

'Okay love, I'll go. You do what needs doing. I'll see you

in the kitchen afterwards.' He gave her hands a squeeze. 'I wanted to speak to you before I do my talk anyway.'

Seeing he was nervous, Thea kissed his cheek. 'You'll be fabulous. Just pretend there's a TV camera watching you rather than people.'

'I hear you're joining the team.' Richard came up behind Thea as Shaun walked onto the grounds. 'That's great news.'

'Oh yes, thanks, Richard. I'm not one for the limelight, so as long as I can stay behind the cameras that'll be great.'

'That's a shame,' Richard looked at her appraisingly. 'You'd be an excellent partner on camera with Shaun. A bit of female intelligence to counteract his male charm.'

'You're kind, but I don't think so.' Thea blushed. 'I have to admit I'd rather stay at Mill Grange. Such a shame it's going to be closed to the public.'

'It is indeed.' Richard checked his watch, 'I'm on the next tour. Should we get going?'

Tina found Sam counting the entrance fee money at a table by the drive.

'How many through the doors?'

'You aren't going to believe this.'

'Go on?'

'Two hundred and fifty-eight.'

'Seriously?'

'Yep! If my maths is correct, that's £1290.'

'Wow!'

Sam took a safe tin from beneath the table and folded a roll of five-pound notes inside it. 'Could you be a star and take this inside? I don't like to keep it here all in one place.'

'Of course.' Tina took the proffered blue tin from him. 'Although I'm not sure where to hide it. There's no safe as such.'

'Anywhere out of the way until we can do a proper count up later.' Sam's face glowed. Tina had never seen him so relaxed. 'Just look at everyone, they're so happy.'

Tina took the weight off her feet by sitting on the chair Sam had abandoned. 'So sad they won't get to enjoy it all the time.'

Sam was thoughtful. 'We don't actually know they won't, though, do we? I mean, we've all assumed the new owner won't want to open up, but they'll have to keep the place, and houses like this always need working on. They'll have to make it earn its keep.'

'True.' Tina smiled at his contagious optimism just as Shaun arrived.

'You got a minute, Sam? I could do with a hand over by the far marquee, one of the guide ropes needs tightening and it's a two-person job.'

'No problem.' Sam turned to Tina. 'Will you hold the fort for a minute? I'll be back soon so you can take the money inside.'

'It'll be good to sit down.' Tina slipped off her shoes. 'I've been helping Sybil as a waitress and carrying dirty dishes up and down to the kitchen. I reckon I've walked a marathon today.'

Shaun checked over his shoulder. No one else was in earshot. 'Sam mate, the guide ropes are fine. Don't tell the girls, but there's someone I want you to meet.'

★

Mabel and Bert found Thea in the attic.

'There you are, lass.' Bert shot his wife a warning glance. 'Everyone is having a fabulous day, but it's time to do the speeches now. We've been hunting all over for you.'

'Is it five already?' Thea spun round from the window, where she'd been enjoying the attic view for the final time. 'I'm so sorry. I was taking a last look from up here. I lost track of time.'

Mabel gave Thea a brief hug. 'You've been fabulous. It's quite right you should take a moment to yourself, but Shaun and everyone who's left have gathered on the main lawn ready to do the announcements and official opening – or whatever it is now we aren't opening.'

'Thanks for everything, Mabel. I'm so glad you were here. I'd never have got all this done without you.'

'Yes you would, dear, but I'm glad I was here too.'

Tina grabbed Thea to one side as soon as she hit the fresh air. 'Something is going on. I think the new owner must be here.'

'Why do you say that?'

'Look.' Tina pointed across to where Shaun and Sam stood by the microphone the AA had set up. The man in the black suit was with them.

Thea felt her stomach do a somersault as she moved forward. She passed Ajay, Andy and Richard signing autographs for *Landscape Treasures* fans. Sybil was handing out the last of the cake among the crowd of visitors. The familiar and reassuring faces of Derek, Bill, Diane and many of their student helpers there, and she could hear Mabel and Bert bickering quietly behind her.

The man in the black suit didn't look like the sort of man who'd want an archaeological excavation in his back garden. Perspiration dotted the back of her neck as Shaun caught sight of her. Her pulse calmed a fraction as his smile widened. Thea could see he was nervous, but was doing his best not to show it.

This was it. Time to find out who the new owner of Mill Grange was.

Forty-Eight

Shaun had begun his speech by thanking so many people for coming, and then launched into a vote of thanks for the volunteers in general and Mabel, Diane, Bill and Derek in particular, before moving onto Tina and Sam. Thea listened with one eye on the man in black. She was so intent on her study of the stranger that she almost missed Shaun's request for her to join him at the microphone.

Inwardly cursing him for drawing attention to her when she'd rather hide at the back of the crowd, Thea hoped no one would notice how melancholy she felt. This really was the end of her time at Mill Grange. So much had happened, and she felt she hadn't had time to process any of it.

'Ladies and gentlemen, let me introduce you to Miss Thea Thomas. Thea came to Mill Grange a few months ago to help oversee the final stages of the manor's restoration. I think those of you who have taken the tour, or just explored the house and grounds alone, will join me in thanking Thea for doing such a wonderful job.'

As a rousing round of applause echoed around her, Thea felt herself turn a deep scarlet. She turned to Mabel, who was clapping as hard as everyone else as she sent a nod of approval her way. Hoping like hell that Shaun wasn't about to pass her the microphone, Thea muttered her thanks as, mercifully, Shaun carried on with the speech he'd rehearsed so often she knew it as well as he did.

Five minutes later, having officially introduced everyone to the team from *Landscape Treasures*, and saying that autographs were available should anyone want one, he wrapped up with another thank you to everyone for coming and to tell them that the grounds would be closing in half an hour.

Then, just as Thea began to relax, he cleared his throat again.

'Just one more thing, ladies and gentlemen. I have a message for you from the new owner of Mill Grange.'

Thea's head snapped up and she found herself looking straight at Tina, who was equally bewildered. A silent tug at her arm revealed that Mabel had spotted two more faces in the crowd that she hadn't noticed.

'Malcolm and Grant are here. Did you invite them, Tina? Thea?' Mabel scowled. She still hadn't forgiven Malcolm for what she saw as his spinelessness in letting the manor go.

The girls shook their heads as they watched the trustees move to the front of the room and approach the man in the black suit.

'That's it, isn't it? All over.' Thea sighed, 'I thought it must be him.'

Mabel had taken a firm hold of both girls' arms and was manoeuvring them to the front of the crowd before Thea could protest, with Bert coming up behind them, mumbling something about resistance being futile.

Shaun caught Thea's eye, but rather than pull a sympathetic grimace, he winked.

'What?' Thea whispered out of the corner of her mouth, 'Tina, did you see Shaun wink or am I imagining things?'

'If you're imagining it, then so am I.' Tina put her hand out to Thea as she watched Sam. He was talking to the suited chap, his brow furrowed.

'Come on Shaun, spit it out, man.' Thea could have hugged Bert as he called across the crowd. 'Don't keep us in suspenders.'

Mabel poked him in the ribs. 'Bert, really, you mean suspense.'

'I know what I mean, Mabel love.'

Shaun turned to Malcolm and Grant, who signalled agreement before the speech continued. 'I have been asked to tell you, the good people of Upwich, Exmoor, Somerset, Devon and beyond, what the future of Mill Grange holds.

'Mill Grange will be opened to the public on special occasions, but mostly it will be used as a creative retreat for those recovering from the trauma of accident or incident suffered while in the forces. A place of readjustment for those who have suffered a life-changing injury.'

Tina and Thea stared at each other, their mouths open.

While the village applauded approvingly, Bert broke the stunned silence that had spread over the women. 'That young Sam's the buyer then. Good for him. Good chap, that one.'

★

The air was still. Everyone had gone.

Mabel and her team had made short work of the washing up and the marquees were empty and ready to be taken down the next day. The entrance money had been safely delivered to Bert, who was detailed to guard it with his life. Everything else, Sam had declared, could wait.

'How?' Tina's delighted expression was openly puzzled.

'I have a full forces pension doing nothing and an inheritance from my parents that I haven't touched. I didn't feel I deserved it.'

Tina laid her head on his shoulder as Thea sat opposite them at the nearest picnic table. 'Why didn't you tell us?'

'Because I might not have got it. The surveyor came today. If he hadn't, the sale wouldn't have been official yet. I didn't want to get your hopes up and then dash them again.'

'The surveyor?' Thea frowned. 'The man in the black suit?'

'Yes. He did a survey on the quiet on and off while you were asleep, out of the manor and, well, here and there really. It's all been a bit awkward, but worth it.'

Tina was having trouble keeping up with events. 'You have an inheritance that means you can afford a manor house?'

'Yes. I just needed something worthwhile to do with it.'

'But…?'

Sam was suddenly awkward. 'I'm the son of an old school earl. An earl who isn't exactly chuffed with how I live my life, but an honourable man anyway. I asked for my inheritance early as I'm a third son. I'm very much the spare. Better to have me out of the family picture somewhere doing something suitably charitable and useful.'

As Tina sat there getting over the shock of dating an earl's son, Thea said, 'Can I ask a question?'

'Of course.'

'You've just purchased a large house and a burnt-out mill that you've never been inside beyond a glimpse of the kitchen and the lower bathroom.'

'True.'

'How are you going to run the house as a retreat if you can't go inside it?'

'I'm not. Not yet. I will once I can, but until then I'll live as I am, in my tent in the garden.' Sam looked at Thea while reaching for Tina's hands. 'I was rather hoping you and Tina would like the job. Part-time, of course, to start with.'

Tina's mouth was opening and closing like a goldfish as Thea asked, 'Part-time because?'

'Because I need you to run the excavation at the same time. What do you think, Thea? Fancy managing the opening of the house to the public in the summer and leading the excavation of the Mill Grange Roman Fortlet the rest of the year?

'And Tina, do you fancy being co-manager with Thea and teaching me the finer points of excavation when I'm not busy being the retreat manager?'

'But?' The women spoke in unison as they looked at each other and then Sam and Shaun.

'Oh, I should probably add, that it would be part of the job description to live at Mill Grange.' Sam gave a cheeky smile. 'After all, I can't go inside and we'll still need coffee and lemon cake, won't we?'

Epilogue

The hotel in the Cotswolds was perfect. Small enough to be exclusive but not so small as to feel they were on display.

As Shaun opened the door to their bedroom, Thea let out an exhalation of breath that she felt she'd been holding in ever since Shaun had bundled her in the car once Sam's bombshell had sunk in.

'Did that really just happen?'

'You mean did Sam buy the manor and offer you a job? Yes.' Shaun led Thea by the hand and sat her on the edge of the four-poster bed. 'You didn't give him an answer though. Will you take it?'

'I can't do it. I've already taken a job with you on *Landscape Treasures*.'

'True, but as I'm well in with the lead bloke, then I think I can swing it that he'll release you from all obligations to the post, if that's what you want? If you'd rather work at Mill Grange.'

'And live there. I wondered if I could have the room you were using.' Thea climbed astride Shaun's lap and grinned. 'So, how would the lead bloke on *Landscape Treasures* feel if he had to travel around Britain without me for part of the year?'

'He would pine naturally, but he rather hopes that, once Sam has the retreat up and running, and it isn't the holiday season, you'd come and help him out anyway.'

'I think that could be arranged.'

'There I was thinking I'd finished work for a while.' Thea pushed Shaun back against the bedcovers. 'It appears that the restoration of Mill Grange has only just begun.'

Acknowledgements

Writing *Midsummer Dreams at Mill Grange* has been a joy, and I'd like to thank a few of the people who've helped me along the way.

First, the team at Aria (Head of Zeus), especially Rhea, for being so passionate about this novel, and the Mill Grange stories to follow.

Also, to my lovely agent Kiran; many thanks for your patience and your wisdom.

To the Nicholson family, in particular Tammy, who welcome me and my colleague, Alison Knight (along with many of our Imagine students), to Northmoor House in Exmoor each October, for an annual writing retreat. Northmoor House is a place of unending inspiration, which forms the backdrop for Mill Grange.

Finally, to my family and friends, who support my constant need to write with regular deliveries of coffee, chocolate, and kind encouragement.

About the Author

From the comfort of her cafe corner in Mid Devon, award winning author JENNY KANE wrote the contemporary women's fiction and romance novels *Midsummer at Mill Grange* (Aria, 2020), *A Cornish Escape* (2nd edition, HeadlineAccent, 2020), *A Cornish Wedding* (2nd edition, HeadlineAccent, 2020), *Romancing Robin Hood* (2nd edition, Littwitz Press, 2018), *Another Glass of Champagne* (Accent Press, 2016), *Jenny Kane's Christmas Collection* (Accent, 2016), and *Another Cup of Coffee* (Accent Press, 2013).

Under the pen name Jennifer Ash, Jenny has also written The Folville Chronicles (*The Outlaw's Ransom, The Winter Outlaw, Edward's Outlaw* – published by Littwitz Press), *The Power of Three* (Spiteful Puppet, 2020) and *The Meeting Place* (Spiteful Puppet, 2019). She also created four audio scripts for ITV's popular 1980s television show, *Robin of Sherwood. The Waterford Boy, Mathilda's Legacy, The Baron's Daughter* and *The Meeting Place* were released by Spiteful Puppet.

Jenny Kane is the writer in residence for Tiverton Costa in Devon. She also co-runs the creative writing business *Imagine.*

All of Jenny Kane's and Jennifer Ash's news can be found at www.jennykane.co.uk

@JenAshHistory

@JennyKaneAuthor

@Imagine_Writing

Jennifer Ash https://www.facebook.com/jenniferash historical/

Jenny Kane https://www.facebook.com/profile.php?id= 100011235488766

Imagine www.imaginecreativewriting.co.uk

Hello from Aria

We hope you enjoyed this book! If you did let us know, we'd love to hear from you.

We are Aria, a dynamic digital-first fiction imprint from award-winning independent publishers Head of Zeus. At heart, we're committed to publishing fantastic commercial fiction – from romance and sagas to crime, thrillers and historical fiction. Visit us online and discover a community of like-minded fiction fans!

We're also on the look out for tomorrow's superstar authors. So, if you're a budding writer looking for a publisher, we'd love to hear from you. You can submit your book online at ariafiction.com/we-want-read-your-book

You can find us at:
Email: aria@headofzeus.com
Website: www.ariafiction.com
Submissions: www.ariafiction.com/we-want-read-your-book

🅵 @ariafiction
🅥 @Aria_Fiction
🅞 @ariafiction

Printed in Great Britain
by Amazon